AFTER POMP AND CIRCUMSTANCE

After Pomp and Circumstance

High School
Reunion as an
Autobiographical
Occasion

VERED VINITZKY-SEROUSSI

THE UNIVERSITY OF CHICAGO PRESS
Chicago and London

VERED VINITZKY-SEROUSSI is a lecturer in the Department
of Sociology and Anthropology and the Institute of
Criminology at the Hebrew University of Jerusalem.

The University of Chicago Press, Chicago 60637
The University of Chicago Press, Ltd., London
© 1998 by The University of Chicago
All rights reserved. Published 1998
Printed in the United States of America
07 06 05 04 03 02 01 00 99 98   5 4 3 2 1

ISBN: (cloth): 0-226-85668-2
ISBN (paper): 0-226-85669-0

Library of Congress Cataloging-in-Publication Data

Vinitzky-Seroussi, Vered.
    After pomp and circumstance : high school reunion as
an autobiographical occasion / Vered Vinitzky-Seroussi.
        p.   cm.
    Includes bibliographical references (p.   ) and index.
    ISBN 0-226-85668-2. — ISBN 0-226-85669-0 (pbk.)
    1. Class reunions—United States.
    2. Autobiography.   3. High school graduates—United
States—Interviews.   4. Social control—United
States.   5. Identity (Psychology)—United States.
I. Title.
LB3618.V56   1998
371.8—dc21   97-35174
                                              CIP

For Netta

Contents

Acknowledgments

My first thanks must go to the women and men who opened their homes and their hearts by letting me interview them. The canons of confidentiality prevent me from naming them, but without them I could not have completed this project. Their stories made my own come to life. Thanks, too, to Edward Aegerter and Donna DeFillipis for providing me with access to relevant material.

During the years I have been engaged in this study, many colleagues and friends have read different versions of this work. I am particularly indebted to Dianne Barthel, Eyal Ben-Ari, Erich Goode, Michael S. Kimmel, Frank Romo, Judith Tanur, Barry Schwartz, and David Weisburd. Jeanne Kidd, Catherine Marrone, and Ann Rotchford of the Department of Sociology at the State University of New York at Stony Brook created a wonderful support group through their genuine caring, generosity, and love. I would like to thank Pamela Chase for a conversation she has probably forgotten but which I certainly remember. Ruth Rossing has been wonderful in helping me cope with the fact that I am not a native English speaker while editing an earlier version of this book. Kennie Lyman edited the final version of the manuscript patiently and with much care and criticism. Last but not least, at the University of Chicago Press, Doug Mitchell, Claudia Rex, and Sara Leopold handled the publication process with care and patience.

Stanley Cohen and Eviatar Zerubavel deserve special appreciation for believing in me years before I believed in myself, and for their valuable comments and continuing support. Special thanks also to Nachman Ben-Yehuda, for getting me started, for being there when I needed him, and for all his assistance, advice, comments, and support throughout the last twelve years. My deepest gratitude goes to Robert Zussman, who has been the best advisor anyone could dream of. His comments, support, criticism, friendship, and understanding have been invaluable. Moreover, he is the one who made me rethink and rewrite this manuscript when I thought I was done, and I thank him for not letting me quit when I was ready to do so.

Grants from the Lady Davis Foundation, a VATAT postdoctoral fellowship, and the hospitality of the Department of Sociology and Anthropology and the Institute of Criminology at the Hebrew University of Jerusalem all made the writing of this book much easier than it would have been otherwise.

I would like to thank Elisa and Rafael Seroussi, Shula Vinitzky and Shmuel Shiber for providing me with child care, thus helping me to combine my different roles. I am thankful and grateful to Yair Seroussi for standing by me for the last decade. His love, confidence, and patience continue to be invaluable.

I came to the United States as a foreign student. It was a place where I had no past, a place where I could start building my reputation from scratch. No one remembered how I cried on my first day of kindergarten, no one knew anything about my years in high school, no one knew my ex-boyfriends. No one knew my biography. In a place where I had no past, I found myself writing about autobiographical occasions. Then, five years after I had arrived at the State University of New York at Stony Brook, I graduated and went back home to Israel. In a place where I did have a past, I had to create and narrate the autobiography of my last five years. I had to go through the same process my informants had gone through as they prepared for and went to their high school reunions. The research and the theory became an everyday practice. It has not been easy but it has shown me once again that behind every researcher who stands outside and watches hides a person who wishes to solve the same difficult puzzles.

Jerusalem, 1997

Introduction

Joanne, a twenty-eight-year-old law student, was caught in emotional turmoil when an invitation to her tenth high school class reunion intruded into the midst of her busy everyday life. I met Joanne during her lunch break. She works part-time at a law firm, waiting impatiently for her schooling to end and her career as an attorney to begin. She is blond, blue-eyed, well spoken, and well dressed. Along with many of her friends, she anticipated her reunion with both fear and hope. On the one hand, she wanted to attend in order to finally shake off the image she had projected in high school: "People thought I was sweet," she said sadly, "and I was tired of that. I'd like them to think that I'm successful and looking good." On the other hand she was not sure who she really was: "I don't know if I was popular. I don't really know who I was. That was one of the reasons I wanted to go back to my reunion," she said later, and attending her reunion carried the promise of finally resolving this personal puzzle. While reassured that her best girlfriend from school would join her at their reunion, she still could not overcome the fear she felt as that night approached: "I was shaking. I felt that if I got there, and no one would even look at me, so maybe I was nothing."

Not being recognized and not being sure what her past consisted of—let alone what her present would look like to her former classmates—were not the only issues Joanne pondered. A letter attached to the invitation, asking her to write a short description of her life since high school, made her quite anxious. It had taken Joanne a few years, during which she had held several jobs (none of which she liked), to discover what she really wanted was to be a lawyer. Trying to respond to the request in the letter, not knowing exactly how to explain the fact that, at twenty-eight, she was still in school, she said to herself, "Gee, I spent a lot of time in school; people will think I'm lazy or not doing well."

The preparation process did not stop at the cognitive level. She made sure that her very handsome husband would escort her. "I wanted my friends from school to know that I never ended up with my boyfriend from high school," she laughed. Very conscious of her appearance in general, and how she wanted to look at her reunion in particular, Joanne and her husband spent hours searching for the perfect dress. She knew exactly what she wanted: "a dress that was sexy, figure-flattering but classy." In fact, she admitted, "I cared as much about how I looked as I did on my wedding day, probably even more."

Her reunion experience left her pleased but still puzzled. To her great surprise, she discovered that she seemed to have had many friends in high school. "The highlight of my night," she recalled with a big smile, "was a guy who was very, very popular in school. He was standing there with three other very popular guys, who I had thought wanted nothing to do with me. He called me over, and they wanted to take a picture with me. I felt I'd made it that night." But the question of whether she had overcome her past was not resolved; it pleased her to learn that "people made it sound like I was a flower that blossomed," but it also raised some questions regarding her past. Had she been popular or not?

While watching herself, she watched others' struggles as well. With a certain degree of satisfaction, she smugly observed that "some of the very, very good-looking jocks" were there, still single, and "crying in their beer because they'd wasted time."

Summing up her experience at the reunion, Joanne concluded the interview by saying glowingly: "I don't need to go to another reunion in my life. The reunion was the best medicine for me, for my insecurities, for not believing in myself."

Perhaps.

Like Joanne, insecure about still attending school at the age of twenty-eight, we often ask ourselves what we have done with our lives. The question compels us to take account of ourselves. It calls for us to "write" our autobiographies. In asking who we were and what we have done and become, we also ask who we are now—in effect, what are our identities. People carry their identities with them, but become conscious of identity only as a consequence of differentiation, both individual (among roles and over the life course) and social (among different people). Moreover, people most frequently become conscious of their identities at moments of transition, which are often also moments of crisis. In this sense, a preoccupation with identity is perhaps distinctively modern, a consequence of the high levels of differentiation characteristic of urbanism and a highly developed division of labor.[1] One of those reflective moments takes place when our social and personal past encounters our social and personal present, as it does at a high school reunion.

Throughout our lives we are engaged in identity-work, in managing the past, the present, and the relationship between them. On the psychiatrist's couch at a time of crisis or in the privacy of our own homes in moments of more or less spontaneous self-reflection we write and rewrite our own autobiographies. Although autobiography is defined in the dictionary as "an account of a person's life written by himself,"[2] writing biographies and constructing identities is not solely a personal matter. As Ralph Turner observed, the individual identity is "a selective working compromise between [a person's] ideas and the images forced upon him by his imperfect behavior in actual situations."[3] Regular, socially constructed situations existing in our lives demand much the same process as the one that takes place privately, and from these settings, too, autobiographies emerge. Furthermore, the autobiographies emerging from social interaction and the social drama surrounding it contain a dimension missing when we are alone. To be concrete, it is not enough that I decide that I was popular in the past; I need the people who shared that past with me to acknowledge it, to affirm my perceptions of the past. We need a social context not only to evoke the past, but also to inform and confirm that past.

In a recent article, Robert Zussman coined the term "autobiographical occasion" and complained that while "many of the recent studies of autobiographies display a refined sensibility about the relationship between accounts and identity and about the internal structure of narratives . . . they have attended less to the social structures that dictate the occasions for and character of those narratives."[4] One such autobiographical occasion, the high school class reunion, is the subject of this book. Thus, this book examines the cultural resources and structural limits—as generated by autobiographical occasions—with which and in which people construct and reconstruct their own identities in contemporary American society; it also examines the outcome of this enterprise.

The public character of social settings enables us to look into the ways in which people construct their identities. More important, since major parts of our lives take place within social settings, those settings are not only research sites but critical tools in the everyday construction of identities. Those occasions affect the agenda, the limits, the potential, and the content of the narratives told.

This book is about the social construction of identities within an autobiographical occasion. It is about the resources brought to the social setting from both the past and the present, the inevitable tensions inherent in such resources and settings, the hierarchy and norms by which we are evaluated, the community from which part of our identity derives and to which we relate. It is about the audience through which and in relation to one writes the autobiography. Just as Joanne wanted her former classmates to know that she had not married her former boyfriend and to see their reactions, so other returnees look to reunions as an opportunity to learn about themselves and to inform others about themselves. Reunions generate both hopes and risks. They involve negotiations and selection, the choices and the constraints out of which our identities are built.

People attend reunions in search of a community to which they can anchor their identities. They wish to know who they were and who they are, they look for coherency and consistency between their past and present and between their inner feelings and outer appearances: they are looking for themselves. What they find is a fragile community that is invented in front of their own eyes, a community that turns into an informal form of social control. They find that the past is hard to reach and the attempt to transfer and construct knowledge about themselves is limited. And they find that the very social setting that provides resources for the construction of identity, and may even enlighten it, can also threaten it.

High School Reunions as Autobiographical Occasions

High school reunions, although episodic and unevenly attended, are a critical vantage point from which to make sense of identity in contemporary America. What is perhaps most remarkable about reunions is the thoroughness with which they telescope the life course as they bring the present into contact with the past, conflating roles as they legitimate curiosity about all aspects of the attendee's life. Reunions, then, become significant junctures at which men and women are asked to recount stories of their own lives.

At the same time, however, reunions are only one of a broad class of events that may be thought of as autobiographical occasions. First dates, job interviews, retirement dinners, professional conventions, birthdays and anniversaries, homecomings, and different therapies all require us to reflect on our lives and to provide accounts of them.

I should stress that the stories told at autobiographical occasions are narratives, not mere lists, assemblages of dates or facts, put together without logic or motivation. Rather, they are selective accounts with beginnings, middles, and ends, constructed to tell stories of success or failure, triumph or defeat. Autobiographies are not necessarily fixed entities; they include—and are often organized around—excuses, justifications, explanations.[5] In this sense, the autobiography is not only the story of a life, but may become a fundamentally moral account in the broadest sense of that term.[6]

Not all autobiographical occasions are the same. While there are many dimensions to autobiographical occasions, some are especially significant for an understanding of class reunions as such occasions.

1. *The scope of the autobiography presented.* With the possible exception of first dates, psychotherapy, or the growth of intimate relationships, reunions are likely to be the occasions at which we are asked to construct our autobiographies in their fullest form. Unlike a job interview, annual conference, or retirement dinner, in which the autobiography is limited to career-oriented material, the reunion demands an autobiography that covers most if not all aspects of one's life.

2. *The time factor.* The frequency and length of autobiographical occasions affect to a significant degree the narrative that can be and is told. Unlike birthdays or anniversaries, which are annual events, and therapy, which is typically a weekly event, the reunion—coming most frequently at intervals of ten or twenty years—requires an account that goes beyond the episode or the update to a synthetic account of a major part of the life span.

Moreover, similar to a first date or job interview, a reunion is a "one-shot event." Since reunions are usually held every ten years (and many people attend only one reunion in the course of a lifetime), returnees may have only one opportunity to construct their autobiographies in that specific social context. One is unlikely to get a second chance, an opportunity to rewrite the autobiographies if the first draft was not convincing or satisfying enough.

While the interval between reunions determines the scope of the autobiography demanded and limits the number of chances of presenting it, the length of the occasion limits the time one has to narrate it. Reunions are short events—most often lasting only a few hours. The narrative that can be told in such a time frame is more often than not a very short one.

3. *Pressure to attend.* Autobiographical occasions vary also as to how mandatory one's participation is. The pressure to attend a family reunion or anniversary may be intense, but attendance at a high school reunion is almost entirely voluntary. This has a profound impact on the narrative that can be told. There is always a chance that the most significant people from one's past might choose not to attend, and thus the opportunity to construct specific knowledge—whether about the past or about the present—may very well be lost. On a more abstract level, the voluntary character of reunions testifies to the limits of the present to commemorate the past. The entire class—as it used to be—is never there. Not only are our attempts as individuals to construct identities problematic, but so, too, are our attempts to relive a collective past.

4. *The audience.* The size of the audience limits the length of the story that can be told. Unlike other brief autobiographical occasions, such as first dates and job interviews, where only a few people are involved, reunions attract many participants. Reunion-goers who try to carry on conversations with a number of former classmates (and most do) find the autobiography they can narrate must be short.

More importantly, when people recount their autobiographies before an active audience which shares their past, the stories become negotiable. While the authors of written biographies usually exercise sole control of their stories—perhaps with some imaginary reader in mind—the storytellers at class reunions not only tell about themselves, but hear about themselves in the stories of others. Thus, the nature of the audience at reunions has a significant impact on the narratives that can be and are recounted, at least those that involve the past. The audience, which becomes one's co-authors, may confirm one's claims about who one used to be, or it may contradict them. Only the present, which is not shared with former classmates, carries the potential of being represented as one will. Moreover, the makeup of the audience is also important to the story that is told and to the satisfaction felt by the narrator. The acceptance of one's story by some people is more important than its acceptance by others. Unlike family reunions and therapies, the power to confirm autobiographies at class reunions is vested less in our intimate friends and family and more in former classmates whom we have not seen in years. The presence or absence of these key people and the degree to which they are willing to confirm one's story, or even enhance it, is important to the success of the narrative. The active role of the audience in the composition of the stories told testifies to the fact that the construction of autobiographies is often a social act.

Ultimately, however, the audience at reunions is not other people, but oneself; Joanne's reunion was "medicine" for her own insecurities. Because the accounts that are generated are autobiographies, or biographies of oneself, they have a special relevance to private, internal matters. Those texts of identity are an effort to say not only what one has done, but also who one is. They are an attempt to persuade others to accept a self-conception, an identity, and, in so doing, to persuade oneself of its accuracy.

5. *The focus of the occasion.* Autobiographical occasions serve a wide variety of purposes. Job interviews are focused on getting a job or finding the best future employee, depending on your point of view; the agenda on a first date may be finding out whether the person in front of you is the "one and only"; family reunions celebrate the existence of the family and attempt to preserve its unity. Class reunions mark the existence of a class, celebrating a community that existed in the past and to which one can return in the present.

And yet, despite the American tradition of reunions organized by classes, the concept of a high school "class" is not a particularly solid one. The class, the cohort as a collective, is a formal delineation of age and academic placement rather than a substantial social unit. Nonetheless, in the process of exploiting the past and creating a collective memory— even the mere gathering—high school reunions create a community for the returnees. More than a reminder of a collective past, high school reunions invent a community for its returnees.

The community that is formed at reunions is fragile, selective, voluntary, and limited; in many ways, a "one-night community." Nevertheless, such a community provides reunion-goers with a sense of belonging otherwise only episodically experienced by adults in modern American culture. By looking into the type of community that reunions provide, we derive greater understanding of identities that result from resources offered by reunions. No less important, this book witnesses a touching search for a community among contemporary Americans. Although the community found is perhaps a telling comment on American culture, it aptly suits one of the dilemmas of this culture, the one which confronts community and individualism.

Autobiographical Occasions and the Construction of Identities

The high school reunion as an autobiographical occasion generates four major issues for the social construction of identities: controlling the identity one presents, encountering the past, managing threats from the vagaries of the life course to our assumptions of continuity, and managing the almost inevitable tension between different facets of our identity. More specifically, as occasions that demand the narration of one's life in the presence of participants who have grown up together and who are all the same age, reunions turn into an informal process of social control. Thus, high school reunions provide former classmates with a normative hierarchy against which they can judge and be judged. As occasions that encompass one's social past, reunions carry the promise of providing a locus from which questions about who one was stand the chance of being answered, thus offering the possibility of touching one's past. As highly episodic events that reach back in memories they evoke to adolescence or beyond, reunions force participants to deal with whatever discontinuities they may find over the course of their lives to date. And as bounded events, rarely lasting more than two days and often limited to a few hours in a single site, reunions confront those who attend with the temptation to sacrifice a story they themselves think coherent to the dramaturgical exigencies of the moment.

IDENTITIES AND SOCIAL CONTROL: THE WAY WE ARE

Unlike other autobiographical occasions such as retirement dinners, family reunions, and even first dates where the participants vary in age, the participants at reunions come from the same area and were all born in the same year. This is not simply a technical point; it implies an equality of life opportunities and a shared journey (with some variations) across the life course. Thus, excuses that people may use in other occasions and areas of their lives ("he is much older than me"; "she grew up in a well-to-do family that could send her to private schools") will not work here. Reunions grant us an audience which is a living witness to the past and a benchmark of the present. We account for ourselves while regarding a mirror composed of people who shared their past with us. Such a mirror can be quite harsh.

The promise of a class reunion might be of returning home. We were even granted a community. The twist, however, is that once we have invented this community, we are doomed to find out where we are placed within it throughout an informal process of social control that characterizes autobiographical occasions in general and class reunions in particular. The process of social control at reunions is about who we are. This process gives the social construction of identities its agenda and context. It creates the questions we ask as well as the answers we hear. Furthermore, it underscores the limits constraining what can be done with the past by reinforcing the privileged status of the present, the culture within which we live as adults.

The notion of social control in current sociology tends to be linked to dark visions: prisons, mental hospitals, and the like.[7] Social control, we imagine, is for those who deviate from the norm. However, this does not mean that nondeviant populations go through life without being controlled, regulated, rewarded, or punished. By overlooking the ways in which nondeviant populations are controlled, we are missing important dimensions of both social control and social life more generally.

High school reunions are an example of an informal, noncoercive form of social control aimed at nondeviant populations. The requirement to account for one's life and cope with its limits is a mechanism of social control and a force through which the social order is confirmed and one's identity within that order defined and assigned. Reunions as social control allow and force returnees to reflect on their lives and to account for them publicly. As a result, reunion-goers might gain knowledge of a sort hard to find elsewhere in modern life: explicit statements about the normative order and their own place within a socially constructed hierarchy.

The fascination of high school reunions as social control lies in the condensed evaluation of every significant sphere of a person's life: family, career, place of residence, financial situation, and physical appearance. Since high school reunions are voluntary, escape from their control might be possible. However, I will argue that such escapes are limited. Throughout our lives, there are many private and public reminders of the passage of time that force us to reflect on our lives and judge ourselves according to terms set by others (e.g., fortieth birthday parties, the twentieth anniversary of the Woodstock festival, the thirtieth anniversary of John F. Kennedy's assassination). Indeed, modern forms of social control lurk in wait for us in many different corners of our lives.

IDENTITIES AND MEMORY: THE WAY WE WERE

Of course, the past is the primary source for autobiography and for our sense of identity.[8] Past incidents, and the way we recall them, are the ingredients from which autobiographies are constructed. Though we tend to think about autobiographies in terms of the past, they are told in the present. Who we are now affects how we perceive the past, how we shape, reshape, or even invent it. In most cases, we encounter the past from the present point of view and with present needs in mind.[9] Nevertheless, the past is never completely mute and does inform the present.[10]

Relationships with the past exist through memories which within autobiographical occasions involve more than one individual. In that sense, the collective memory operating at reunions plays a major role in the construction of autobiography. Although the notion of "collective memory" may imply detached relations with the past, it may also involve more personal memory. It is very much part of us. In that sense, Schuman and Scott's definition of collective memory as "memories of a shared past that are retained by members of the group, large or small, that experience it" is the closest to what I mean.[11] The way the collective remembers itself, common events, and specific individuals who are (or were) part of the collective, as well as the way individuals remember a shared past—all are resources on which we draw when we construct our identities.

Collective memory has recently gained attention within sociology. However, most discussions of collective memory take place on the level of the nation. In contrast, this book stresses the microsocial level of constructing collective memory and how collective memory penetrates our everyday life. What is effected by history books, museums, and national iconography for our macrosocial past is effected by class reunions for our personal past.[12] This study will explore the ways in which a collective past (or what is perceived as such) is exploited in the present, primarily by its organizers. I will discuss the construction and the organization of collective memory, arguing that the collective memory is selective with regard to who remembers and what is remembered. The memory that is created is not a literal or photographic memory of the past. It is a memory that is exploited by the present. It is a memory in which and through which we are to find ourselves. Moreover, whether or not class reunions alter personal memories, the public enactment of the past provides a new dimension, a memory of a collective. And this new dimension facilitates the notion that there was a class in the past, and that there is a community to which we can relate in the present.

This study addresses both the public and formal enactment of the past as well as the informal encounters that reunion-goers have with one another. Although one can distinguish between public enactments of the past and personal reminiscence, they affect each other. Both discourses are based on the notion of memory and thus share many of the same problems inherent in that notion. Furthermore, public enactment of the past in many ways affects the conditions under which casual reminiscence takes place. By understanding how high school reunions are structured and organized, one may gain a better insight into the framework in which reunion-goers perform. Moreover, the disproportionate power of reunion organizers over the "official story" of the past impinges on the ability of returnees to share past knowledge with others. But even beyond the constraints of the event, the past is more elusive than tangible, the audience—sometimes absent altogether—does not necessarily cooperate, people are more concerned with their former friends' lives since graduation than they are in discussing the past, and the reminiscence that actually takes place appears to be less a resource for the construction of one's identity than an assault on it. The promise of high school reunions to provide an encounter with the past seems a hard one to deliver.

IDENTITIES: BETWEEN PAST AND PRESENT

Identity is always bound up with the past, "because," as Hewitt tells us, "people have memories and because they use them to take stock of and keep track of the self. . . . The self is never merely an object in the particular situation, but also an object linked to past and future."[13] In addition, some social settings and situations dictate the management of identity. These situations are the ones that force us to remember what we were and who we are;[14] high school reunions are such social settings.

At first glance, it seems almost archaic to speak of continuity of identity in the age of postmodernism. The self, we learn, is "saturated," "fragmented," and sometimes hard to find at all.[15] We are confronted with claims that a single life story integrated across situations and over time is fast disappearing from American society. I am skeptical of these claims and argue that contemporary Americans not only feel the need to create coherent biographies of themselves but do so with some success. The notion of continuity in our understanding of processes of identity formation is confirmed in this study. Continuity thus remains an integral and fundamental component of identity[16] "because"—to borrow again from Hewitt—"human beings are meaning-driven creatures, [who] look for connections between things and events over time."[17] Moreover, chaos and discontinuity in one's biography generate fear, feelings of meaninglessness, even a sense of madness.[18] Having a "reasonably stable sense of self-identity," states Giddens, calls for "a feeling of biographical continuity."[19] Whether this cry for a coherent narrative of one's biography comes from within or from without is beyond my concern. What is clear, however, is that within a social context that couples the past and the present, the participants insist on such accounting.

Although a sense of continuity is crucial to identity, the intersection between the way we were and the way we are poses a threat to that sense. We might encounter promises we have never kept, changes we have difficulty explaining, or new and different interpretations of our past and present. Thus, a major concern of the present study is to demonstrate how people manage these threats to their sense of continuity, and how successful they are in attempting to align their past and present. Contemporary Americans may look for changes in themselves, but at the same time they try to explain change away and tend to ignore it, more often than not by invoking the notion of a "true self"—some form of an inner essence of oneself that has not changed—which is independent of both appearance and behavior. They strive to create a world where almost everything makes sense, is consistent, and coheres.

IDENTITIES: BETWEEN SITUATIONS AND BEYOND THEM

Discontinuities are not the only challenge posed by the intersection between the way we were and the way we are. There may also be discontinuities between who we believe ourselves to be and who others believe us to be, between situated identity and personal identity. Hewitt describes situated identity as "an organized set of impulse responses within a defined situation, responses that are more or less shared with others."[20] Situated identity is an aspect of identity that is public, socially enacted and negotiated, bounded in time and place. It involves an "effort made by ordinary people to make sense of themselves in relation to community and culture."[21] In contrast, by personal identity I mean those understandings of the self that are both internal and that transcend particular times and places. Personal identity, as Hewitt has observed, involves "a sense of continuity, integration, identification, and differentiation constructed by the person not in relation to a community and its culture but in relation to the self and its projects."[22] To be more concrete, personal identity is what Turner calls "self conception . . . I-myself as I really am."[23] It is a felt idea of who we are. In this sense, personal identity is more internal than situated identity.

Although they may be analytically distinct, situated identity and personal identity are not independent. Situated identity affects personal identity; personal identity is brought into social situations. If we are fortunate—if who we would like to think of ourselves as corresponds with who we seem to be—there is no conflict between situated identity and personal identity. But we are rarely so fortunate. And reunions exemplify the almost inevitable tension between personal identity—the one we bring to situations and with which we leave them—and our situated identity—the one we enact while meeting others. In this work, I examine the ways in which those who attend reunions cope with this tension.

The challenge at reunions is to provide a biography which is not only convincing to others at the reunion (situated identity), but which one can believe oneself (personal identity). Whereas situated identity is limited to the reunion itself, the personal identity is what one carries away from the reunion. Even if returnees succeed at their reunions, their victory may be compromised: they might survive the night, but will they survive as themselves? Thus, this book goes beyond the different techniques of impression management by emphasizing not only the limits of such techniques, but also the implications they bear for the construction of both situated and personal identities.

Moreover, although we are confronted with claims that identities, which are internally felt and integrated across situations and beyond, cannot easily be found within American society, I will argue that although class reunions tempt returnees to sacrifice their personal identity to the dramaturgical exigencies of the moment, the techniques used also reveal the efforts ordinary Americans exert to maintain a level of personal integrity. We return here to the claims—already raised in the previous section—regarding maintaining identity over time. Only now, the argument revolves around identity that is beyond situations and across them.

Although I use the term "biographical identity" to describe the issue of continuity and the term "personal identity" when discussing the tension between the different facets of identity, the concepts are roughly equivalent. At reunions the two dimensions come together so that sometimes it is difficult to distinguish between them and the challenges they pose. For example, consider the former cheerleader who is now divorced and overweight, or the boy once voted most likely to succeed whose career is now foundering—both situations raise an obvious problem. This problem, however, is not simply one of the present and its presentation; it might also suggest that the former cheerleader and the boy once most likely to succeed were not what they seemed in the past. At the very least they must give explanations for the dramatic twists their lives have taken. The past as a context and its interconnectedness with the present makes surviving this specific social setting a problem for the construction of both biographical and personal identities.

High School Reunions and American Culture

Reunions in general and high school reunions in particular are well embedded in American culture. Such events are held throughout the United States. Over 200 companies thrive on planning and organizing reunions. Reunions are either the focal point or the background for scores of movies (*Beautiful Girls, Peter's Friends, The Big Chill, Peggy Sue Got Married, Something Wild, The Return of the Secaucus Seven*). Many television series have devoted at least one episode to a class reunion (*All in the*

Family, Civil Wars, The Trials of Rosie O'Neill, Married with Children, Cheers, Designing Women, Sisters, China Beach). Both Geraldo Rivera and Phil Donahue, the popular talk show hosts, have spent at least one hour on high school reunions. Popular books discuss reunions (*Class Reunion, How To Prepare for Your High School Reunion*) and various television commercials use reunions as an incentive to buy or use certain products (a jeep in one, diet yogurt in another). The plethora of material concerning reunions reflects their cultural power. The reunion is not something that is "out there," but something very much "in here." Reunions generate their own myths and ethos which are crucial to their success or failure in becoming resources in the construction of identities in contemporary America. In this book I will take a behind-the-scenes look at class reunions, and explore their myth and their ethos.

Structure of the Book

The past and the present are integral ingredients in the construction of autobiographies and identities. Hovering over this process is the occasion—the high school reunion itself—which provides returnees with the promise while at the same time setting the limits, the agenda, and the structure within which and through which returnees attempt to narrate their life stories. The structure of this book parallels these confluences; it moves backward and forward between past and present as well as between the macrosocial dimensions and the microsocial encounters and accounts, between the structure and the dimensions of autobiographical occasions and their outcomes.

Although past and present are intertwined and the macro/micro dimensions are obviously linked, the internal logic by which this book is organized reflects an attempt to separate—as much as possible—the past and present as well as the different spheres in which autobiographical occasions take place.

This book is divided into two major parts. Generally speaking, it moves from macrosocial processes to microsocial interactions, and from the past to the present. Thus the first part (chapters 2, 3, 4, and 5) emphasizes macrosocial processes as well as the different dimensions of autobiographical occasions, while the second part of the book (chapters 6, 7, and 8) focuses more on microsocial interactions and the outcomes affecting the construction of identity. Each of these two parts encompasses a linear movement from the past to the present. Although the issues regarding one's identity are more salient in the second part of the book, they are by no means absent from the first part. Thus the dimensions of the occasion and its structure—the macrosocial processes as well as the micro-social interactions—are intertwined, very much as they are in real life.

Behind the issues I raise and the arguments I make lies the social scene. Thus, before I turn to the substance of the study, I describe the research site (chapter 1). Integral parts of the social scene are the people who attend reunions, as well as those who do not. The differences between these two groups touch on most of the main themes of this book and are thus also part of chapter 1.

Chapter 2 is centered around the notion of community, a major theme within American culture. I claim that class reunions create their past class, and hence invent a present community for the returnees. The past validates and provides the legitimation and the context for present encounters and for the sense of community and belonging contemporary American life often lacks. Chapter 2 begins with the past and moves to the present; chapter 3 carries this process further by focusing on the present, claiming that the community invented at class reunions becomes a point of reference from which individual returnees get a broader perspective on their own identity. In effect, this chapter argues that class reunions become a modern and informal form of social control.

Chapter 4 introduces the audience and its meaning for the construction of identities. Chapters 5 and 6 focus on the encounters—both collective and personal—with the past. Chapter 5 addresses the notion of collective memory, arguing that class reunions construct a memory of a collective which is determined primarily by the organizers and the structure of the event. Chapter 6 discusses personal encounters with the past, contending that the attempt to touch the past is at best only partially successful and, at worst, doomed to fail. In this light, class reunions as a social context for such encounters are less a resource for the construction of identity than an assault on it.

Chapters 7 and 8 discuss the present in the past. Chapter 7 discusses continuity of identity, the premise being that contemporary Americans' search for changes is actually a struggle to ignore them, to view the world as rational and consistent. Chapter 8 discusses the tension and connectedness between situated identities and personal identities. Although the different facets of identity have a life of their own, they are not altogether separate. Moreover, contemporary Americans are loath to confront tension between outer appearance and inner beliefs. Chapter 9 is the conclusion, summing up and reflecting on the findings presented in the rest of the book. The Appendix describes the method employed for this study.

One

The Research Site and the Attendees

$\mathcal{W}$hen the sun goes down, usually in the summer and always on a weekend, one can find restaurants, catering halls, and hotel lounges all over the United States turning into a stage on which past and present play their complementary parts in a play called "high school reunion." This chapter sets the scene for what follows by describing the research site as well as the differences between those who attend their class reunions and those who choose to stay home.

Somehow, I expected high school reunions to take place at the old school gym where the former classmates once held parties; the reality in most cases, however, is different. High school reunions rarely take place at the actual schools because of the prohibition on serving alcohol on school premises, lack of proper air-conditioning systems, liability costs, etc., as well as the prevalent attitude of organizers who imagine their class reunions to be more like weddings than any other kind of event. There do exist less formal reunions where former classmates and their families may gather for a picnic in a park, usually not far from the school, and some reunions offer their participants several activities.[1] The majority, however, center around a dinner-dance in a banquet hall. It is this kind of reunion that I have chosen to study.

The entry point to the hall in which a reunion takes place is the parking lot in front of the hall. The cars that people drive to their reunion or the chauffeured stretch limousines hired to wait for them are part of the show.

Reunions never begin at the time stated on the invitation. Usually the only ones present at the stated time are the organizers, who want to make sure that everything runs smoothly. Being "on time" for a reunion means arriving half an hour to a full hour after the official time. All in all, the formal event takes about five hours (roughly from 8 P.M. to 1 A.M.).

A greeting table stands at the entrance to the hall and is operated by the reunion organizers—either professionals or former classmates—who collect tickets. Though invitations to reunions are sent long before the event, there are always people who buy their tickets at the door. In rare cases, people attempt to enter the reunion without a ticket; the security staff of the hall take care of such incidents and remove the gate-crashers.

The reunion actually starts around the ticket table, which—after the parking lot—is the first place people see each other. It is a noisy gathering place: the excitement, the thrill, the delight at seeing "old buddies" all evoke a cacophony of exclamation—"Hi, how are you doing?" "Oh, my god, it's Linda!" "Oh, my gosh, I can't believe this!" "Look who's here!" Everyone hugs, kisses, laughs, and smiles.

The often raucous scene at the greeting table makes it difficult for the reunion organizers to get people registered and into the hall. They usually hand the former classmates name tags, either ready-made or made-to-order, sometimes with the returnees' yearbook pictures. Some tags are blank stickers on which attendees must write their own names, a seemingly simple and straightforward action. Some reunion-goers, however, refuse to because they want to see how many people still recognize them. For many of the women there is a minor crisis as they decide whether to write their maiden names, their married names, or both. In the most extreme case I came across, a thirty-eight-year-old woman literally forgot what her name had been in high school. In another instance a woman asked me, "What do you mean 'my name?' My real one or my maiden name?" as if we were discussing two different worlds, one of which was make-believe. Even a reunion, apparently, cannot make life before marriage "real."

Some returnees vehemently oppose wearing their yearbook pictures throughout the reunion. Some dislike the way they looked in high school; others resent walking around displaying living proof of how they have aged. Nevertheless, most people end up wearing the name tags and thanking the organizers for saving them from having to guess who they are talking to. One of my informants called her reunion "a Halloween party" because it was so hard to recognize the people.

The catering hall usually has one, two, or even three bars in different corners. In most cases, the price of the ticket includes drinks. Only rarely are reunion-goers asked to pay extra, although at some reunions the free bar becomes a cash bar from 11 P.M. onwards. Because the organizers want people to mingle, sit-down dinners are not popular at reunions. A formal dinner around tables tends to generate island-like clusters of people who do not get a chance to move around freely. Buffet dinners, on the other hand, force people to get up from their seats in order to get the food and hence to see other people.

The center of most halls is arranged as a dance floor with a DJ or a band on one side. For most of the evening, the music is somewhere in the background. Only during the last hours do people dance. DJs are preferable as they cost less and are less dominant than bands. Even with background music, people have a hard time hearing each other. In some cases they have to scream their life story over the volume of the music. In fact, one of the most common complaints reported about reunions was that the music was too loud. The music is almost invariably a combination of songs popular during the reunion-goers' high school days and current pop music.

Like much else at reunions, the quality and quantity of decorations depend on the budget. Basic and almost obligatory are balloons and banners in the school colors. Sometimes banners proclaim the name of the high school and the interval of years since graduation—"Central High School 1970–1990." Napkins, candles, or tablecloths are also often in the school colors.

Some of the tables hold a few copies of the class yearbook, brought to the reunion by members of the class. In all likelihood, reunion-goers have already looked through their own yearbooks before the party, and probably will do so again afterwards. At the reunion itself, however, there is precious little time to spend going through the books.

Also common at reunions is a memorabilia corner with old high school souvenirs, including invitations to the junior and senior proms, the class trophy cup, old school newspapers, pictures taken on the school trip to Washington, football shirts, and more. The memorabilia corner is often the personal collection of one of the organizers. A board on which class members put current pictures, business cards, and newspaper clippings is "a corner of the present." The pictures are usually wedding pictures or family photos of holiday celebrations (often with a Christmas tree in the background and all the family members dressed up). Also popular are shots of vacations to exotic places (with Hawaii at the top of the list). When former classmates cannot attend the reunion but want to be represented, they may attach a brief note to the picture describing what they do, where they live, and how much they wanted to be part of the reunion.

The appended newspaper clippings usually recount personal successes or interesting bits of information (for example, about a former classmate who had triplets). The business cards generally come from those who have "made it": vice president of a well-known investment bank, a brain surgeon, psychiatrist, architect, lawyer, financial consultant, and so forth, or those who own their own businesses.

The dance floor at the center of the hall is surrounded by round tables seating ten to twelve. The tables usually have flower arrangements, and are with or without candles, balloons in the school colors, and ashtrays.

Although a dress code is seldom explicit, an informal dress code is evident. With minor variations, men wear suits and ties, with a tuxedo or two at every reunion. Among those who attended high school during the sixties, a few still come in jeans and flannel shirts. The overwhelming majority of women treat their reunions like weddings or grown-up versions of the prom. Few wear casual dresses, and even fewer wear pants. Most come in evening dresses, with small purses and high-heeled shoes. Dresses with sequins and elaborate embroidery are common, and black is the color of choice. Heavy makeup is common, as are expensive hairdos. Diamond rings, earrings, and necklaces as well as different sorts of gold and silver jewelry are much in evidence. Some women prefer classic business suits while others wear very tight and provocative, short dresses.

From the sidelines, without hearing the conversations, one sees small groups of people standing and talking, holding drinks and sometimes cigarettes. Reunion-goers tend to cluster in groups of three or four, although couples chatting together are not uncommon. Some sit at tables to talk. Few, however, get into long, in-depth conversations. Groups form and disintegrate within a few minutes; then new groups form and dissolve, a process that is repeated all evening long.

Among the crowd are a few considerably older guests, high-school teachers, and staff members. In most cases they stand or sit apart from the crowd.

At all times people move between the hall and the busy restrooms. The restroom (at least the ladies' room) is an integral part of the reunion. While taking care of makeup, dresses, stockings, and other needs, conversations are held and notes compared.

It has recently become fashionable to videotape reunions, with classmates asked to spend a few minutes with the videographer to provide him or her with a brief synopsis of their lives since graduation. At the very least, a professional photographer is hired, and a favorite subject is the class picture. The photographer arranges rows of chairs and tries to get all the class members (and only the class members) to sit. Grouping the class is not easy, and the DJ usually has to beg the classmates over and over again to take their seats for the picture. Common, too, is a picture composed of close-ups of the class members at the reunion. Those pictures are sent later to the class members who paid for them. Also popular are pictures of the classmates, their old friends, and their current spouses, shots taken either by a professional photographer or by members of the class themselves.

About two hours into the night, after the food is served, many reunions hold a fifteen-minute program, usually comprising a toast to the class made by the main organizing committee members. Often, awards are made—a T-shirt, a plaque, or a bottle of champagne—to the classmate with the most children, the couple from the class married the longest, the one who came the greatest distance, and so forth. Sometimes a slide show of high-school shots takes place, or a few members of the old school band play and sing some songs. Many reunion committees send questionnaires to the classmates well in advance and read the results aloud at the reunion: the average number of pounds gained since high school, the number of marriages, the types of cars owned and jobs held, the houses bought, and statistics on sexual activity since high school. At some reunions the current principal of the school congratulates the class, praising its achievements and taking pride in the school's present situation.

Four hours into the night the dancing usually begins. Married classmates most often find themselves dancing with their current spouses. Sometimes old girlfriends dance with each other. By this time people are beginning to leave, but the majority stay and keep talking in groups until the party is over. Some continue the reunion at a nearby diner.

When reunion committees have money left over, they may give the classmates a souvenir: a commemorative T-shirt, a mug, or a little flag. Almost every reunion provides its returnees with a class directory listing class members (mainly those who attended) and their addresses, professions, and marital status. In some cases the list also includes reflections written by members of the class especially for that volume, lists of memories from high school days, and current information about the class.

Who Attends

Somewhere between 30 and 40 percent of each high school class attends its reunions. My findings suggest that gender plays no role in who returns and who does not. Attendance, however, is far from random. Graduates are more likely to attend if they were successful in high school, if they are successful as adults, and if they maintain friendships that, in effect, bridge the past and the present.

Attendance at class reunions is voluntary. Unlike family reunions, where relatives can often exercise significant control and more or less force attendance, former classmates only rarely coerce their former friends to come. As a result, the difference between those who attend and those who do not attend their class reunions becomes more interesting and, as we will see, the voluntary character of these reunions has a major impact on both collective constructions of the past and the personal encounters returnees have with their own pasts.

Like other autobiographical occasions in one's life, class reunions bring the past into the present, or at least carry the promise of doing so. Reunions are, in part, about who one was in high school, about reminiscing, and about using the past as a resource in the construction of one's identity. Thus, one should not be surprised that those who attend reunions had more success of various sorts in high school than those who do not attend. In particular, people who choose to attend their high school reunions are more likely to have been people who were heavily involved with extracurricular high school activities.[2] As table 1 shows, the more activities in which a student participated while attending high school, the more likely he or she is to attend a reunion.

Another indication of the prominence of the past at high school reunions has to do with memories from a specific era and social setting. At class reunions, one would expect to find more people who remember high school happily than those who do not. And in fact, in a study of reunions by Lamb and Reeder it is stated that "the returnees consistently rated themselves as having been happier and more popular than did the nonreturnees."[3] My findings are ambivalent on this point. On the one hand, they provide additional support for Lamb and Reeder's view: a higher percentage of reunion-goers had good memories of high school than did nonattendees (77 percent versus 67 percent). But on the other hand, these findings should be read cautiously; too many people (at least in my study) claim to have good memories of high school. In fact, hardly any-

Table 1. Attendance at Reunions by Activities in High School

Activities	Attendees (%)	N
0–2	23.4	907
3–5	34.6	411
6 or more	40.2	97

Data on school activities was collected from yearbooks of the class of 1970 and 1980, Central High School.

one acknowledged having had growing pains. However, many who attended their reunions spoke about having mixed feelings or bad memories of high school while only one of my informants who did not attend complained about high school. Though I cannot easily generalize (because there were not enough interviews with people who did not attend their reunions), the combination of returnees with bad memories, nonreturnees who hardly complain about high school, and a finding that so many people claim good memories of high school makes me suspicious about the link between good memories and attending reunions.

Memory is not a fixed entity. Memories in general, and changes in memories in particular, although oriented to the past, have a great deal to do with present needs and circumstances.[4] Recollections of the past are as closely connected to the present as to the old days of high school themselves. This might explain why one is more likely to find people with good memories of high school at reunions: their present may be what shapes the way they view their past and what enables them to engage with that past.

Thus, the present is at least as powerful as the past in explaining attendance. At reunions, former classmates are called on to tell who they are in the present. This informal requirement involves an informal process of social control in which returnees compare themselves to how everyone else is doing. Using the present to engage and re-engage with the past, in the context of a process of social control, may make attendance uncomfortable for those whose present lives are somewhat flawed.

Two small-scale studies found that the "two groups [the returnees and the nonreturnees] were almost identical with regard to . . . marital status and level of education."[5] My findings, however, contradict those studies and in that sense confirm the notion that there are certain resources in one's present that make the engagement with the past more appealing. In the most critical aspects of one's life—family status and career—there are differences among those who attend as opposed to those who choose to stay home.

Family status consists of two central elements—marriage[6] and children—and both affect attendance. The returnees showed a larger proportion of married people (79 percent) than did the nonreturnees (59 percent). Similarly, 68.5 percent of the returnees had children, compared to only 51 percent among the nonreturnees.

Being married and having children are still important and much-appreciated values in American society. Having a family may be perceived as an achievement, while not being married is often perceived as

Table 2. Attendance by Type of Job (percent)

	Came	Did not come
High contact and control	69.0	60
Medium contact and control	19.5	26
Low contact and control	12.0	14
(N)	(195)	(112)

Note: Jobs were coded according to degrees of power and control over people and contact with people, with the assumption that the more contact and control one has on the job, the more prestigious it is. To illustrate how occupations were scored: garbage collector = low contact and control; secretary = medium contact and control; lawyer = high contact and control. Homemakers were coded following their spouse's occupation.

a failure. As resources in the construction of identity, marriage and parenthood are likely to make people feel that their lives are "in order" and ready for inspection.

One's life at work is a somewhat more complicated issue to measure. And yet, as table 2 shows, the returnees included more professionals, more people who are in charge of people and businesses (coded in table 2 as having high contact and control at work), more people whose jobs are perceived as more prestigious, and fewer whose jobs are less prestigious or rewarding (coded as having medium or low contact and control at work). It is safe to say, then, that people who are considered successful in their careers are more likely to attend reunions.

My interviews reinforce this finding. Current problems of all sorts discouraged people from attending their reunion. For example, ten years after graduation, Janice, who had wanted to become a jewelry designer, found herself working as a secretary. Barry lost the business he had opened and, twenty-five years after graduation, realized that many of his dreams would never come true. At the age of forty-three, Lucy was a housewife with no children and a disabled husband; Nancy worked in a fast food restaurant to support her two children after being abandoned by her husband. All four cases exemplify a much wider phenomenon. It is hard enough to cope with one's own personal failures; it might be even harder to face an audience that knows one's past and, at least in one's own mind, consists of people who have put their lives in order. Moreover, by attending a class reunion, people run the risk of spoiling past identities. They might face people who are their own age and share a similar background, yet who seem to be not only in a different but also a better station in life.

Many of the returnees attend their reunions knowing that they have the "right load" with them. They have something that they think other people (as well as they themselves) are looking for—a story they are proud to tell.

It is not only the past or the present that accounts for attendance, but also the ties between past and present. In many cases, these ties take the form of friends with whom one has kept in touch. While 85 percent of returnees keep in touch with friends from high school, only 64 percent of the nonreturnees do. Those friendships retain and maintain something from high school days, and may even create a sense of continuity between the past and the present.

Although returnees do not attend their class reunions in order to meet their close friends, those friends are often the ones who urge, and on rare occasions even coerce, former graduates to attend the reunion. Without such friends the chances of attending diminish. Losing touch with people from high school might indicate (and create) a greater psychic and social distance from that specific past than characterizes those who still maintain close ties with people from that era. Those without friends from high school may have already bypassed that moment in the construction of their identities.

None of this would matter a great deal if reunions were events graduates attended casually and without great emotional investment. But they are not. Reunions carry deep and powerful meanings both for those who choose to attend as well as for those who choose not to. One does not attend a class reunion because there was nothing else to do that night or because of an affinity for parties in general or because the location is convenient.[7] Originally, I thought that distance would make a difference in attendance. My expectation was that people who still lived in the area would be more likely to attend the reunion (which always takes place somewhere in the vicinity of the high school) than those who lived far away and would have to fly in or drive for hours. However, my expectations were not met (see table 3).

In all but one case (Central High School, twenty-fifth reunion) the findings are straightforward. Having to make an extra effort to attend a reunion does not discourage people from attending. On the contrary, it seems that people who live far away are more likely to attend than those who live nearby. This finding might suggest that people who live in the area are less motivated to go to their reunions since they can see former classmates whenever they want. That, however, is not the case: no one mentioned this as a reason for not attending. Furthermore, people were surprised to learn at their reunions that so many of their former classmates actually still lived in the area. In any event, distance is not a factor in the decision to attend reunions and does not deter people from coming, even if it makes the trip more expensive and complicated.

The notion that a class reunion is not a matter of convenience is re-

Table 3. Attendance at Reunions by Distance (percent)

High School	Reunion	Less than 120 Miles		More than 120 Miles	
Main	10th	24.7	(620)	30.2	(63)[a]
Garden	20th[b]	27.9	(470)	41.1	(124)
Central	10th	35.9	(513)	35.8	(53)
	20th	26.7	(592)	35.5	(172)
	25th	17.7	(450)	12.7	(126)
Total		26.6	(2,645)	31.0	(530)

Note: Data for this table came from lists of class members and the names of the states where they live.

a. The cells of those who live at some distance are much smaller than of those who live near by in general, and those who graduated in 1980 (i.e., the tenth reunions) in particular. The disproportion represents two different things. First, many more people remained in the vicinity of where they grew up than moved away. Second, at the tenth reunion, many people are still unsettled in their lives. Hence, their addresses are temporary and in many cases correspondence with them is through their parents, who still live at the original address.

b. Due to lack of data about the place of residence for Garden High School's former classmates, I matched another school for which I could get the data. The school I matched to Garden High School (class of 1970) is Main High School (class of 1970). The similarities between the schools and the neighborhoods are substantial.

inforced by my findings that less than a quarter of the nonreturnees reported that they did not come because of prior or more important obligations for that specific night. There is something about high school reunions that makes people come even though they live far away, and makes people stay away even when they live in the area. If a few put off their decision to the last moment, they do not do so casually or out of indifference but out of a deeply charged ambivalence. Class reunions are not—at least to those invited—trivial events.

Choosing an Autobiographical Occasion

The differences between those who attend and those who do not attend reunions are worth considering because they tell us something about the players in this event and their concerns—concerns that surround reunions as an autobiographical occasion. High school reunions are an intersection of past and present. Returnees have to deal with how they were and who they were in the past, with how they are and who they are in the present, and with how everybody else was then and is now. We should not be surprised that there are differences between the returnees and the nonreturnees both in terms of who they were and who they are.

Resources of the past are brought into the reunion experience. For example, participation in sports or drama clubs makes a difference many years after the club meetings, football games, and shows are over. Those whose pasts were filled with activities about which they can be proud are the ones who chose to include that past in the construction of their current identities. Different people select different vantage points from which to make sense of their lives. Resources from a specific past might provide the comfort necessary to engage with an intersection between that past and the present.

Reunions, however, also address the present. The differences between those who attend and those who stay home also suggest that certain present resources—mainly marriage, parenthood, and a prestigious job or successful career—allow people to engage in a reunion and make the reunion itself easier. If the present informs the past, and if reunions create a ground on which an informal process of social control takes place, the returnees seem to have more of the "right" resources than the nonreturnees.

In between the past and the present are memories and friends with whom one has kept in touch. People who attend have more positive memories of high school than those who do not attend. It makes sense that people would not want to return to places they hated or where they suffered. However, given the ever changing character of memories, it is hard to overlook the role of the present in the creation of those memories, both good and bad. That the returnees are more likely to report good memories from high school than the nonreturnees may have as much to do with present circumstances as with the past.

More attendees than nonattendees kept in touch with people from their class. Those close friends make returnees more comfortable when entering the hall in which the reunion takes place while facing a curiously unfamiliar past and present. Those close friends bridge the two different times and relieve somewhat an important source of pre-reunion anxiety—that of not being recognized.

Yet, there remains a great deal that cannot be explained away. Statistical probabilities are not always predictive in individual cases. Moreover, individuals are individuals in the sense that they have some degree of freedom to choose to do or not do certain things, in a form hard to explain in traditional sociological terms.[8] Modernity, as Hewitt observes, "has encouraged the release of impulses toward freedom and autonomy that are every bit as much part of human nature as are impulses toward authority and community."[9] At class reunions we do find people no one would have expected to see—people no one remembers—while at the same time there are others everyone was sure would attend who are missing—class officers, star athletes, class celebrities in general.

The differences between those who attend and those who do not tell the reader something about the people who choose this specific autobiographical occasion in order to inform the past and the present. These differences also reveal something about the people who are subjected to the process of social control, and they tell us something about the nature of the collective that is created by the reunion. They tell us about the people who are using high school reunions to reconstruct their identities.

However, understanding the differences between those who attend high school reunions and those who do not does not take us very far towards understanding what actually takes place at reunions. Both the dynamics of the reunion and the preparation for it force returnees to connect past memories and expectations with present reality as they try to construct a coherent life story. Even those who do not return are not exempt from this process. They may not have to tell their stories to former classmates, but they cannot escape asking themselves the questions inherent in such narratives. Reunions involve issues of community, social control, memory, managing the threats to one's sense of continuity, and the tension between outer appearance and inner beliefs. They showcase the ways in which autobiographical occasions affect the narratives people tell as well as the ways in which they deal with autobiographical occasions. In this sense, a high school reunion is a case study in American culture, and it is in this spirit that I shall be considering them in the coming chapters.

Community, Continuity, and
the One-Night Stand

$\mathcal{T}$he celebration of reunions implies that there has been a union in the first place, a community that existed in the past to which one can return in the present. The problem is that there was no real union in the past and hence no community. Thus, what actually takes place at reunions is that a class is constructed, and what generates this construction is the search for some form of community.

The search, however, derives its strength from yet another source. "Well-socialized American adults in the 1980s are supposed to desire community,"[1] as they "move around and therefore often find themselves living in communities of strangers."[2] If communities are important to Americans—as a great deal of literature suggests they are[3]—why not look for them in the past? Much as does symbolic ethnicity, American class reunions might fulfill the "American need to be 'from somewhere.'"[4] Thus, if former graduates succeed in constructing their past class, they may convince themselves that they also have a present community to which they can relate.

In the process of exploiting the past and creating a memory of a collective, simply by virtue of the act of bringing former classmates together, reunions create a community for the returnees. Though limited, such community provides reunion-goers with a sense of belonging rarely found in modern American society. By witnessing the community created by reunions, returnees may learn about themselves. Moreover, returnees attempt to claim that the present community is a continuation of past experiences, and thus we can observe, at the macrosocial level, the same uneasiness which individuals experience—albeit much less intensely—when confronted with a threat to their personal sense of continuity. Somewhat more generally, community membership is a resource in the construction of identities. Thus, a look at the type of community that reunions provide might offer a better understanding of the character of identities resulting from resources available at reunions, as well as another perspective on contemporary American culture.

The Creation of a Community

Unlike schools in most European nations and many other countries where the class is a "central structural unit,"[5] most American high schools are "shopping mall high schools."[6] They are structured more like universities than elementary schools. Children entering large public high schools are assigned to a homeroom based on alphabetical order. They spend only a few minutes a day in this "class"—time enough for attendance to be taken and announcements made. They are then assigned to subject classes based on specific requirements, their abilities, their schedules, and sometimes their preferences. Thus they may share class time with a large number of members of their chronological class, but they do not have continuous longterm contact. Therefore, students hardly experience high school as part of the same group of people, within the same social context. The class, the cohort as a collective, is a formal delineation of age and academic placement rather than a substantive social unit. It is not the major framework in school, where both social subunits (cliques) and units that transcend the cohort (e.g., the football team) constitute more palpable social entities. A glance at various high school yearbooks confirms this. The pictures of the graduates are arranged alphabetically, while most of the group photos are shots of the different school clubs and teams (e.g., photo club, band, football team). Other collective student activities pictured in the yearbook—such as plays and other performances—bring students together only briefly.

Moreover, the class is not a unit that existed in the minds of its members to begin with. It should be noted that the returnees indeed have no doubt that they graduated from a specific class and that they will remain members of that class for the rest of their lives. But how do they recall this unit?

From the interviews I conducted it seems that in most cases the memory of the class is remarkably vague—"we used to have fun." Only very seldom could former classmates be as specific as Barbara was:

Our school year wanted to be really wild. We always had trips, and, whenever we went, we would ruin it. We went to Washington and the guys ripped the street signs down and we got into trouble for that. (Housewife, tenth reunion, Main High School)

In most cases, detailed memories of high school have very little to do with the class as a unit; rather, they are memories either of oneself or of specific encounters with others.[7] For instance, Rob, a CPA attending his tenth reunion at Central High School, said that his good memories of high school were of how "I worked for the school paper," while his bad memories had to do with the fact that he "wasn't that social." Annie (social worker, twentieth reunion, Garden High School) recalls "coming home crying because I hadn't made cheerleading." Greg's reminiscences of his high school days illustrate the type of recollection of most of my respondents, memories of encounters with others in high school:

Well, there was this girl that used to sit next to me in homeroom . . . she had always gone out with this guy who was like two years older than us . . . so it was like, "don't look at this girl cause this guy is gonna kill you" . . . but I got to her and we kind of passed it around the school that we were cousins, even though we weren't. . . . I don't think I really had the desire to go out with her but being that she had this big boy friend . . . so we stayed friends." (Owner of a plumbing company, twentieth reunion, Garden High School)

Even when respondents talked about the existence of a unit transcending immediate interpersonal encounters during high school, they seldom meant the class but rather the cliques:[8]

We [the cheerleaders] thought we were cool. There would be about six of us who would go to the Spanish deli behind the school [though] none of us spoke Spanish. We'd buy a big jar of beer or something, and would each take sips before the game, and we thought that that was so cool. You can't get drunk on one beer but we would act silly and then go out and cheerlead and giggle and laugh. (Leslie, teacher, tenth reunion, Main High School)

In high school you could always identify people, what group they belonged to, what clique, whether they were Jewish or Catholic or Protestant or one of the jocks or the hoods. The men [hoods] greased back their hair, wore black leather jackets, boots. (Keith, artist, twenty-fifth reunion, Central High School)

In my high school . . . there was a middle hallway. You knew who was who by where they hung out in that center hall. There was a board, and in front of that there was always a group of five to

twenty-five people. Those were the popular people. They could be
the cheerleaders, the president, usually well-liked people. . . . On
the other end of the hall you had your honor society, and you knew
it was just that way . . . and then you had the jock-jocks, the girls
who were masculine. I don't remember being part of that small
group of very, very popular [kids], but I had friends who were and
so I could stand there. (Joanne, student, tenth reunion)[9]

For some returnees, what reminded them of their high school days
was their observation that the cliques still existed:

I felt there was a big separation at the reunion. I felt the Jewish
people in one place and the non-Jewish people in the other place,
like it was in high school; I felt that very, very strongly. They didn't
mix. . . . I was sad to see that, but that's how it was in high school.
(Beth, optician, twentieth reunion, Central High School)

[At the reunion] there was segregation between the Jews and the
non-Jews, like it was in high school. (Rob)

Others felt that high school days were long gone since the cliques could
hardly be discerned and everybody mingled, creating a feeling of one
group, one class, *in contrast* to high school days, when sharp distinctions
existed between groups and individuals.

At the reunion, nobody was in their own little clique, everybody
was together; the people who were in their own cliques that never
bother with people below them were going to each other [saying],
"Hi, how are you?" It felt good, you know, that everybody was able
to talk to everybody. (Barbara)

In general, most returnees saw the same cliques at the reunion that
they had seen in high school. Nonetheless, as Donna—a student attending her tenth reunion at Central High School—put it, "there was no
longer a barrier between us." Another reunion-goer expressed a similar
sentiment:

I saw that [the cliques], but you know, I saw a lot of mingling again.
I saw a lot of people [together] and it wasn't like that at school.
(Leo, manager, tenth reunion, Main High School)

"A lot of people," as Judith (lawyer, tenth reunion, Central High School)
put it, "crossed over." The same impression—maintaining the clique but
also stepping out of it—was echoed by those people who had belonged
to the cliques. Thus Dana (executive, tenth reunion, Main High School)

said that she "talked to everybody in my clique but I also talked to a lot of people outside my clique."

If anything reminded the returnees of their high school days, it was the cliques. And cliques are not synonymous to a class. If indeed there is a unit that may be called a class, it is one that is invented and reified at the reunion and not before. Through the gathering, through the program organized by the reunion committee, through the group picture, and through the "reunion yearbooks" provided when they left the hall, the returnees' impression of a transcending class "out there" (and "in here") is created. People who can hardly recall any detailed memory of their class as a unit nevertheless have no problem talking about their class in "we" terms. "It was exciting," says Eve (beauty consultant, twentieth reunion, Central High School), "to see that *our* class did so well. *We* produced a lot of doctors. . . . You look and you see that the majority of *our* students all have careers, and that is definitely an achievement in today's society." "I think they turned out okay," adds Tom (chiropractor, twentieth reunion, Garden High School). "I think that, overall, the class turned out pretty good. It feels good to know that my class is contributing to society." Former classmates who can scarcely remember who was voted "best looking" can easily identify the current success story of *their class*. People who did not belong to any of the cliques gain a sense of community at their reunion. Returnees leave their reunion feeling that they belong to a certain class, to a certain cohort.

A Search for a Community

Why invent and reify a class when it meant so very little in the past? The answer to this question lies in the search for community in the context of which autobiographies are told, and for a source of belonging in current American culture, in which the notion of community is important to individuals who rarely experience it. Whatever their age or their socio-economic background, most of my informants complained about lost friendships and the absence of community in their current lives. This feeling of present alienation as opposed to past association is well echoed in Eve's portrait of her past and present way of life:

> I think that what I miss the most today is what I had then, when we knew everybody on the block, and you knew everybody's kids. It was a community. And now I know the neighbors, and it is like they want to say, "Hi, how are you?" but they put up a wall: "I don't want to know you." And that is the case in many places. If I got a flat tire and I knew my daughter was coming home and I

wasn't gonna be there, I would never call my neighbors and say, "Could you let her in?" I'd let her sit outside first, because that's how I feel they would want it to be. That is the message I get from them. As a kid I could have knocked at any door at any house and said, "I got lost" or "I'm hungry" and there would have been no question. It was "come in." And I miss it. Today you lock the door and that is the end of it.

Whether some form of community ever really existed in Eve's or anyone's past is a question I cannot answer. Nonetheless, the returnees do feel that they have lost a group, a community, a collective—something to which they once belonged. Even when their memories of the past are not good, they express longing. Thus, though Vincent (technician, tenth reunion, Main High School) complained to me during the interview about the "peer pressure" in high school, he sadly reflected—in the presence of his wife—that former friends "just go their own ways and you hang out by yourself."

Jeffrey's account is also revealing of the need people have for community:

> The sense of community is important to me. I think it's missing from life in general, and I guess that's also why people have families. I'm forty-something years old and I'm beginning to wonder about the choices that I've made. . . . If you don't have a family it seems to me [that] the sense of community could be even more important. (Social worker, twenty-fifth reunion, Central High School)

At the age of forty-three, Jeffrey is married with no children. He has worked in many places and has never felt satisfied; life is too complicated and too emotional for him. Detached from the "real world" in general, and from himself in particular, he was surprised even to find himself still alive for his twenty-fifth reunion. Yet, with all the alienation he feels he seeks a community. What makes Jeffrey's account an even stronger testimony to that desire and the way in which a reunion can fulfill it, is his answer to my question as to whether his former classmates "as a group" are important to him. Jeffrey answered clearly: "No, but the sense of community is important to me, and [the reunion] was a possibility for that."

The desire for some form of community is there, but the options for finding an adult community seem limited in contemporary American society, and the past appears to afford a reasonable albeit partial source. "Where else," asks Michael, a lawyer recalling his twentieth reunion, "can I enter a hall in which five hundred people are happy to see me?" Where else in a culture where "home is no longer where the heart is"[10] and shopping malls have replaced the "neighborhood stores," can individuals be with so many people they know? Where else can they feel such "belonging?" Even if not all of Michael's former classmates are actually happy to see him, he does not have to be introduced to them, as is the case in other spheres of life.

Barbara had a great time at her tenth reunion: "there were so many people to be with: every time you turned around, you were bumping into somebody. It was good." Nicholas (owner of business, twentieth reunion, Central High School) felt "a class, a body, the camaraderie, the feeling of a group" on the night of his twentieth reunion, and he could not believe "how strong it was." Leslie, who describes herself as a shy person suffering from a "fear of crowds," could not get over how "great" she felt at her tenth reunion. "I got over that shyness of a group because I felt comfortable there." Susan (student, twenty-fifth reunion) also used the word "comfort" when referring to her reunion. "You get such a good feeling," she said quietly, having difficulty putting her emotions into words. "You feel a sense of belonging. We were all sitting in that room [the catering hall] and we felt we belonged there. I don't know why." "It's good to have reunions," Jesse (municipal employee, tenth reunion, Main High School) sums up his experience—"like it's good to have a family, it's unity." Jesse's comparison of a school class, which has only tenuous reality as a social unit, to a family is a measure of the hunger he has for a sense of belonging to a community. These examples show that the need Americans feel to belong to a unit transcending themselves is such that they are willing to accept even a flimsy invention of such an entity.

Another aspect of the desire to feel belonging is revealed in the returnees' search for commonality between themselves and their former classmates. Twenty-five years after graduation, Ernie (art director, twenty-fifth reunion, Central High School) "wanted to know how many other classmates have gone through life experiences like I did, the divorce and that sort of thing." At the time of his twenty-fifth reunion, David (lawyer, twenty-fifth reunion, Central High School) found himself comparing experiences with people his age who, like him, had children applying for college. Though we can understand such encounters as an attempt to reaffirm one's own decisions and choices, David's articulation makes it clear that the concept of community is the one he means: "anytime you have a shared life experience, there is a certain bonding that occurred."

The desire for a present community and for a sense of belonging does not stop at the level of emotional satisfaction within the group, nor at the search for common life experiences. While the class may not have been an important part of their actual past, at their reunions returnees want and expect a public and formal enactment of their cohort. Where a program was held (as at Garden High School's and Central High School's twentieth reunions and Main High School's tenth reunion), most returnees wished it had been longer. Where there was no formal program— where in essence returnees were left to fend for themselves and interact in much the same way they did in school—they complained that the reunion "was lousy" (Carol, occupational therapist, tenth reunion, Central High School) and that it "was lacking something" (Chuck, policeman, twenty-fifth reunion, Central High School). That "something" could have been "a formal announcement to the class" (Donna), "mention of the people who had died" (Matthew, teacher, tenth reunion, Central High School), "something more organized [than] . . . just people going into the room" (Ron, lawyer, tenth reunion, Central High School), or "an open mike for people to get up and reminisce or tell anecdotes about high school. There was no attempt whatsoever to bring up the past" (Jeffrey). That past is not Jeffrey's personal past (which he could recall and reminisce about without benefit of a formal program), but rather the public embodiment of a collective. "It's not enough to have a bunch of old suburban weirdos now get together in a hotel somewhere and dance to some bad music," Jeffrey summed up his reunion experience. For people who wish to claim some form of present community when the past is basically its sole legitimation, it is definitely "not enough" to see others like oneself running around, trying to find some recognizable faces in a crowd. In order to claim a past-based present community, the existence of some kind of a shared past must be validated and confirmed formally, some kind of a collective in the past must be legitimized, in this case, a class.

As noted, this process is a dialectic one and thus also applies to the present. While former classmates discuss their present lives in private conversations, they still seek some kind of a public enactment of their existence as a collective. "The reunion was very cold," criticized Marcia (business owner, twenty-fifth reunion, Central High School); "once you got there and found the right people, there was no nurturing, there was no, 'Hi everybody, I'm so glad you came.'" The absence of some kind of communal agenda bothered the returnees, who were anxious to experience something transcending the personal domain, something that would present a shared past and present. A collective demonstration of a present grouping might validate the existence of a past class and thus in return might testify to the existence of a present community which contemporary Americans so wish to experience.

Continuity and Community

To a certain extent, class reunions fulfill the need to feel that we came from somewhere, that there is more than the "here and now," that there is also a "there and then," and that we were part of it. Moreover, both the "here and now" and the "there and then" transcend the private sphere and reach well into some communal experience. The dialectical and reciprocal interdependence of relations between the current sense of community and the construction of a former class recurs in the return-ees' attempt to establish a sense of continuity between their social past and their social present. Reunion-goers not only invent a community at the reunion; they also allege that it is a continuation of past experiences. A detailed discussion of the notion of continuity can be found in chapter 7 of this book; at this point, suffice it to say that while a sense of continu-ity is a major component of one's identity,[11] it seems that people wish to maintain it not only within their very own personal lives, but also within their more public existence.

The notions of continuity and community were one of the main mo-tives that drove Maryellen to organize both her twentieth and her twenty-fifth reunions, and to promise that she would organize future reunions as well. When asked why, she replied, "It is just a continuation of school . . . just to keep the class together as a unit, for them to come back to Central . . . and be a group again. . . . It was important to see everybody as a group" (school employee, twenty-fifth reunion, Central High School).

We can also see the search for continuity in returnees' desire to have their class officers in general and the class president in particular—the closest to what might symbolize the class as a whole—attend the reunion and address the participants, as well as initiate and get involved in or-ganizing it. Hope (housewife, Central High School), who organized her twentieth reunion, could not believe that "only one of the four class offi-cers came," while Donna expected "an announcement from people who were some kind of leaders." The absence of former leaders, or their failure to play a leadership role when they do attend, jeopardizes the sense of continuity that reunion-goers crave. The sense of continuity is so impor-tant that, even when one's memories of former class leaders are not par-ticularly favorable, returnees still wish to see them at the center of the event. Thus, though Barbara (as well as many other of my informants from that class) was happy that the people who put together the class prom did not organize the reunion, she was bothered because she had expected some kind of continuity and assumed that the people who had been active in high school would similarly take a leading role in the re-union ten years later: "Everybody was saying that it was weird that the people who ran the prom weren't involved in the reunion."

The importance of class continuity is expressed also in the way in which people created it for themselves. Many of my informants ordered the "class picture" taken at the reunion by a professional photographer, as they wanted to preserve a memory "of the class." Many of those who did not frame it chose to put the "reunion picture" together with their high school yearbook, making it in effect not part of whatever happened to them in the year of the reunion, but part of what happened to them in the course of the year of graduation, thereby creating for themselves a sense of group continuity. Similarly, Hope's huge envelope of newspaper clippings about different people from her class—carefully collected over the years—was attached to her yearbook.

The sense of continuity is built not only between high school and the current reunion but from one reunion to the next. Thus, Donald (executive, twenty-fifth reunion, Central High School) regretted not attending former class reunions because "there was a bond between people who came to the twentieth [reunion], they formed a group." In many ways Donald felt that he joined the class "too late," that some attachment had been built in the course of the twentieth class reunion that left him an outsider. At Garden High's tenth reunion, Jimmy and Patricia—the orga-nizers—gave a bottle of champagne to one of their classmates (for being the oldest graduate). When Jimmy called that woman to invite her to the twentieth reunion he was astonished to learn that she "still had that bottle of champagne at home. 'I hadn't opened it in ten years,' she told me, "I think something is written on it 'the class of 1970.' She does not want to open it up. I wish she would bring it to the twenty-year reunion" (fireman, twentieth reunion, Garden High School).

A bottle of champagne that is not opened for ten years is no longer a bottle of champagne but an item of memorabilia connecting a person to her past. It symbolizes not only that past but also the continuity evolving from that past. The desire to establish a sense of continuity is so great that even a memento from a past reunion not from school itself can be-come a treasured keepsake.

In an era where belonging is more likely to be something one reads about in novels but does not feel, a sense of belonging to some commu-nity—even one that no longer exists or never existed—might be one of the only ways to feel part of something larger than the individual and the family. Whatever the content of one's encounters with the past, of ultimate significance is the fact that one has a past to relate to, one that transcends the individual experience. It is important to know that past images and old friends are there waiting for us to get "in touch" with them, maybe for the first time.

One-Night Community

Listen to Frances:

> Being [at the reunion] is offering your support for the whole reason behind the reunion. Just being there even if you have nothing to say for the night, at least you are there and you made it a crowd. . . . It's a piece of continuity. Not only is it something from the past but it is a piece of continuity. I can depend on having this group together again in five years. It is not just a function that you attend and then it's over. It keeps you related to the past, it ties you in with a group of people in the future. I liked having had the experience in past reunions. It binds me to these people because, whether I run into them or not within the next five years, we all have something in common five years from now. Though we all have our different lives, we will get together in five years. I have something in common with those people, even though they are like strangers to me. I share a standing invitation in five years and I like that." (Housewife, twentieth reunion, Garden High School)

In a few very emotional sentences, Frances has encapsulated the essence of this chapter. The first thing that comes to Frances' mind is the "crowd" that reunions offer. The foundation of community, for Frances as well as for many others, lies first and foremost in the crowd it creates. Such perception sheds some light on an enigma that prevails at class reunions. While returnees attend reunions hoping to talk to specific people, they will not settle for a small-scale event; they want to see "a crowd," the more people there the better. There is something special about a hall filled with people who all graduated from the same school at the same time, even though the reunion-goers barely knew many of them in the past and seldom recognize them in the present. Reunions present the possibility of realizing a hope, of having a group to which one can belong and relate. Jeffrey, whom we met earlier, expresses this ambivalence well: he viewed his class reunion as one of the only options available to him to feel a sense of community, yet when referring to his former classmates he asked, "Who are these people anyway?" Frances goes even farther when she attributes value to "just being there, even if you have nothing to say for the night." People scattered around the hall have created a crowd, making it look and even feel like a community.

Contemporary Americans do search for continuity and community in their lives, perhaps in vain. Moss and Moss, who discuss reunions between parents and children, state, "Reunion is the enactment of the wish to maintain the continuity of the tie. It carries the illusion that separation has not occurred and will not recur."[12] If relationships between parents and children, which are certainly much more complicated and profound than those between former classmates, bear what may very well be an illusory sense of continuity, what can be said about relationships between people who see each other once every ten years? In the case of class reunions, the concept of community and continuity are questionable ones at best. The class—a social unit of dubious significance in the past—is constructed and created as a community with some kind of shared past that is expected to provide its returnees with a sense of belonging. But it is a belonging based more on a notion that there is some kind of continuity—which might not be found elsewhere—than on membership in an active community. Maurice Halbwachs states that "the permanence and interior appearance of a home impose on the group a comforting image of its own continuity."[13] What is interesting about reunions and the notion of continuity is that "home" need not even be there. In the reunions I studied, continuity was not achieved through holding the parties on the grounds of the school. In some cases, the schools had been torn down altogether. Yet simply by seeing the people again—and it is never the entire class as it used to be—people manage to get a sense of continuity. They seem willing to settle for half a loaf, able to cobble together from the limited material at hand a past with which they feel an ongoing connection, perhaps implying that they cannot derive a feeling of continuity, let alone community, almost anywhere else. In modern American society, where so little is held in common and there are so few places where people are known for years, looking backwards may be one of the very few ways to experience the feeling of community as adults, and a class reunion might be one of the few places where one feels belonging.

The community that is formed at reunions is fragile and limited. It is in many ways a one-night community. Interestingly, the overwhelming majority of the returnees would not like to turn their class reunions into annual events. Returnees search for community, and they may even discover it at their reunions, but they are not willing to invest more than one visit every few years. Still, they would not give it up. Similar to ethnic groups which make "no claims or demands on individuals whatsoever . . . and yet there is a collectivity with which one can identify and feel a part of in an individualistic and often atomistic society,"[14] the communities constructed at reunions require little investment. Class reunions are an integral part of American culture, allowing an appearance of community without the most minimal sacrifice of the competing (and dominant) values of individualism, thus speaking so well to the American dilemma of individualism and collectivism.[15] And yet if communities are important to contemporary Americans, high school reunions as a form of community constitute a rather telling comment on American culture.

The collective celebrated by the high school reunion has its foundation on shaky ground: the class as a social unit is invented and reified at the reunion, the event itself may not provide evidence that there was a collective in the past, past leaders may not take the roles other returnees expect of them, the notion of continuity is based on a partial foundation at best, and the entire collective may never meet again. Although Gans points out that "feelings of identity can be developed by allegiances to symbolic groups that never meet, or to collectivities that meet only occasionally,"[16] identities anchored to a community so tenuous are liable to be fragile and limited.

Nonetheless, the search for a community seems at least partially successful. Contemporary Americans may wish for more, but they are clearly willing to settle for even a very imperfect version and would not forgo it. Ten and twenty years later, a class that hardly existed as a unit in high school becomes a community. But the twist is, once we have invented this community, we are doomed to find out our place within it. In effect, this community ends up creating an informal process of social control. It is to this issue that I turn in the next chapter.

Reunions as Social Control

"Time is a friend, but mostly an enemy"
Refrain from a popular Israeli song

$\mathcal{H}$ere is evidence of another aspect of high school reunions, a display of one's achievements since graduation: "Paula Zahn can attend her reunion with pride," an airline magazine assures us. "Not only is she the co-anchor of *CBS This Morning*, she's married to a young, dynamic, and good-looking real estate developer and she has an adorable little girl."[1]

The organizers of class reunions suggest that those who attend will relive the "good old days." The motto of one company that organizes high school reunions is "to bring friends and memories together again." A high school reunion conjures up thoughts of nostalgia and a warm homecoming. When Greg spoke about his reunion, he kept mentioning the movie *Terms of Endearment*.

> [Shirley MacLaine] is a mom and [Jack Nicholson] is a neighbor, both of them in their 50s. There is a bed scene, and she is so prudish, and then just about ready to go to bed she is taking off her clothes and he's just taken off his shirt, and he's got a belly. But it doesn't matter anymore, he's going to bed with this lady, and finally she drops her guard. And this is what we are trying to do [at the reunion]. (Owner of a plumbing company, twentieth reunion, Garden High School)

However, although returnees may long for a support group, what they find instead is a reference group. Implicit in the invitation—and more importantly, within the occasion itself—is the fact that what attendees have done with their lives since high school will be on display. This concern is important in generating the agenda for a reunion, an agenda that

42

calls for self-reflection and self-evaluation along with the re-invention of a "reference group."[2] Thus, reunions are not—or are not simply—about bringing people together, but they involve contested evaluations in which individuals, consciously or not, attempt to protect and project their own way of life. The result is a pervasive process of social control.

Social control exists within almost every social interaction. Whether standing in a crowded elevator or ordering a meal in a restaurant, most people behave in expected and approved ways. Society rewards individuals for compliance with and conformity to social values and norms and, thereby, reinforces these values and norms. Yet the reunion is not just another everyday social interaction. It is ritualized, time-bounded, and, most importantly, culturally constructed as a vantage point from which individuals are called to account for their lives. Thus, the stakes here are much higher than in such social interactions as exercising elevator decorum. Reunions are not only about how one behaves within specific social situations, but also about the more serious matter of who one is. In this sense reunions are about the exercise of social control through the construction and definition of identities.

Like other observation points in life—such as retirement dinners, preparing curriculum vitae, psychotherapies, etc.—reunions force one to engage in self-reflection. Moreover, they compel one not only to create, but to share a life story. By inviting people to tell their life stories, reunions expose them to a group that feels it is its prerogative to investigate other people's lives. And knowledge about people, Michel Foucault notes, "makes it possible to qualify, to classify, and to punish."[3] Through conversations, hierarchies are established. Personal life becomes part of a public agenda and discourse. By obtaining access to a life, by acquiring knowledge, one exercises control.[4]

The special power of reunions as a form of social control lies in the contrived character of the social setting. Returnees are asked to state who they are after many years of separation, and to construct their autobiographies in the fullest form: an entire way of life including career choices, physical appearance, family status, and financial ability are evaluated, confirmed, or denigrated. The account that is given can be (and is) compared to expectations, memories, other people's achievements, and the value system of the group. More important yet, these comparisons are made by a special audience which includes ghosts from the past but, because it consists of people who all grew up in the same area and are the same age and at the same stage in life, it also constitutes a mirror of the present—one that often reflects a harsh light indeed. Almost everyone involved in a reunion ends up measuring himself or herself against classmates, coping with both the past and the present simultaneously. Thus the reunion superimposes two systems of social control on top of each other. One has to do with the original high school culture, with athletes and cheerleaders at the top of the hierarchy[5]—with the returnee's own situation in high school; the other has to do with everyone else's current situation—with a current hierarchy in which doctors, lawyers, and CEOs (preferably with a spouse, a house, and children) score much higher than anyone else. Moreover, asking what one is and what one has done with one's life since high school implies questions about what one is *not* and what one has *not* achieved since high school. High school reunions provide a social context in which the failures as well as the achievements of one's life are demonstrated and noted.

Reunions combine a process of self-evaluation with a more social process in which people judge each other. The latter process approximates what Durkheim implied when he stated that "moral remaking cannot be achieved [in modern society] except by the means of reunions, assemblies and meetings where the individuals, being closely united to one another, reaffirm in common their common sentiments."[6] High school reunions create an opportunity for modern society to regulate its members and reinforce the values of its culture, if only by making them create the measures by which they judge themselves.

One last word has to be said about the notion of social control. At first sight it might seem odd to talk about class reunions as a form of social control. Most often (for at least the last three decades), the study of social control has been dominated by the issue of "controlling" crime, deviant behavior, and social problems. As a result, the forms of social control examined and analyzed have been state-centered, coercive, formal, and purposive measures imposed by external agencies and aimed at what is defined as deviant behavior.[7] In effect, first-year sociology students studying "social control" often end up learning about "deviant behavior"; in many introductory textbooks the two are combined into one chapter.[8] Such an approach leaves very little room to imagine other forms of social control in everyday life. I would like to argue that what goes on in decorated catering halls, where former classmates evaluate and judge each other twenty years after their separation, can also be conceived as social control. Moreover, in modern culture many pervasive forms of social control are forms that are not state-centered.[9] Spitzer, for instance, addresses "the role of the market in interpreting how social control actually operates in capitalist societies."[10] They are informal,[11] nonpurposive and noncoercive,[12] external as well as internal,[13] and aimed at what is perceived as nondeviant populations.

The case of high school reunions exemplifies a form of social control which is not necessarily initiated or produced by the state. Reunions are noncoercive, informal, and deal with what is perceived as nonproblematic populations. This type of social control is not the responsibility of state agencies such as the police and the criminal justice system. But while it takes place in what Foucault calls the private self or what Rose calls the soul,[14] it is not an outcome of therapy or other work by paid professional technicians of the self. Neither does it use the mental health criteria of positive functioning, maturity, ego control, and the like. Rather, the criteria employed at high school reunions—wealth, family status, and occupation—are more old-fashioned ones. These are an integral part of American culture which emphasizes and cherishes "occupational or financial success,"[15] consumerism and its material symbols, marriage and parenthood, the need to progress, etc. In this sense, the very stuff from which people construct their identities is turned to the purposes of social control.

An Invitation to Think

The processes of social control start long before the actual reunion takes place, when the invitations arrive at former classmates' homes. The invitation itself generates a contemplation about one's life and a process of self-evaluation.

> [When I got the invitation I thought], twenty years have passed. I could not believe I was still single, and I could not believe I didn't have a family. . . . Time makes you look at things, it's twenty years, it's a reminder. (Evelyn, teacher, twentieth reunion, Garden High School)

The invitation intrudes on the life course and generates thoughts of accomplishments and failures. "I reflected on my life when I was called for my reunion," recalls Tom (chiropractor, twentieth reunion, Garden High School); "what have I achieved in life? I [usually] don't take a moment to think about that." Moreover, the organization of high school reunions around specific dates (ten years after graduation, twenty years after graduation, etc.) adds a sense of importance to the self-evaluation process. These are anniversaries of a sort and call loudly for summation. Although we all know that time passes, the invitation makes that passage too blatant to overlook.

> When you see that number, that it is twenty-five, that's a long time and you don't believe that so many years have gone. It's [the time

that passed] surrounding me but you don't want to say that it is that many years ... *and you want to see that you are somewhat successful.* (Grace, secretary, twenty-fifth reunion, Central High School; my emphasis)

In thinking about a reunion, one judges oneself, one becomes the subject of one's own social control, often ending by asking tough questions of oneself: "Is this the way I really wanted it to go?" Peter (tenth reunion, Main High School) asks himself upon receiving the invitation. He is working as a bus driver far from home and family, and dreaming about owning a business. "Have I made the right decisions?" wonders Mel (fundraiser, twentieth reunion).

This process of self-evaluation is not only internal but also mediated by the "audience" one is about to meet, an audience consisting of people who are the same age as oneself and with whom one grew up.[16] The criteria of judgment are clear to those who are invited. The agenda for comparisons at reunions consists mainly of physical appearance, family status, and job status. Thinking of how everybody else looks and what they do makes people wonder about the course of their own lives, their achievements, their failures, and the chances of their doing something about all of these things before the reunion.

I said to myself, "Oh I really don't feel like going. I don't know what the people are going to think. Everybody's going to be a millionaire, so much more successful." Whereas I hadn't made it as an actor. (Randy, bartender, twentieth reunion, Garden High School)

[Once I got the invitation] I said to myself, "Oh, God, get me something that will help me look skinny and like I'm successful." (Nicholas, business owner, twentieth reunion, Central High School)

So when it came time to send the money [to the reunion] I got a little nervous. . . . I didn't want to see people I hadn't seen in twenty years. . . . I've gained 90 pounds, I don't look the same at all. I figured they'd be better than me, thinner than me, prettier than me, more successful, more money, bigger houses. (Isabel, housewife, twentieth reunion, Garden High School)

People [would] say "Hi, I am an attorney," or "I am a teacher" or something important. Sometimes I do think, "My God, what am I gonna say?" (Sarah, housewife, twentieth reunion)

The anticipation of the reunion made me [nervous] because I knew people would ask me what have I done since [high school], and I wish I could say that I had pursued the things I studied in college

and brag. . . . But the fact is that I didn't. . . . That got me de-
pressed. . . . You know it's the truth and that bothered me cause I
didn't have anything impressive academically to say. (Frances,
housewife, twentieth reunion, Garden High School)

Former classmates see themselves as called to account for their past
and present. Moreover, their story is expected to have a special character:
there is a general anticipation in American culture of progress. Thus it is
little wonder that two systems of social control meet in the returnees'
minds, one based on evaluation of current achievements and the other
based on the norms that prevailed in high school. Consider Janice, for
instance, (receptionist at a jewelry company, tenth reunion, Central High
School), who had first to cope with the pressure of her current situation
in life: she was single and without a prestigious job. She had not become
the fashion designer she always wanted to be. No wonder she did not
want to attend her class reunion: "I'm not where I wanted to be in my
career, where I thought I would be; and I'm single. I felt I didn't have
much to say." Her failures, however, are made all the worse by the disappointment of once-high expectations: "[In high school] I was involved in
a lot of activities. . . . I was also in the honor society." As Laura (bookkeeper and business owner, twentieth reunion, Central High School) put
it, "it is much harder [to attend reunions] for those who were popular
because everybody is expecting so much from them."

The strength of reunions as social control is so embedded in the life
of my informants that it seems as if, even years before the arrival of the
invitation, people had been thinking about whether they would be able
to bring themselves to attend.

> That period of my life [before getting to law school] was the worst.
> I had been a manager of a restaurant for five years, and then a
> substitute teacher, and my self-esteem went down even farther. I
> thought, "Oh, I'm never gonna go to my reunion with this on my
> vitae." I even thought about it then. (Joanne, student, tenth re-
> union)

> Three years [before the tenth reunion] I said, "Oh, it's been seven
> years [since high school]. Oh my God, quick, do something." (Amy,
> student, tenth reunion, Main High School)

The process of social control does not stop with thinking. Many of
those who plan to attend their reunions are looking for the "magic pills,"
as Nicholas put it, that will make them look the way they think they
should look and be the way they think other people expect them to be.

The rush to buy new and sexy clothes before the reunion, the money spent at the beauty parlor, the diets, the rented limousine—all are part of an appearance one tries to project in anticipation of the process of measurement at the reunion.

Physical appearance is indeed a major concern at reunions. The way one wishes to look, the efforts to create that look, and the expense this entails are fundamental to reunions. Some returnees diet before the reunion, many more go through endless efforts to buy the "perfect dress" for the event.

> The biggest thing that I did [before the reunion] was probably make sure I lost my weight from the pregnancy. . . . I was thanking god that my reunion wasn't last year because I was pregnant. . . . I was always a very thin person and I was tremendous [during the pregnancy]. I bought this very sexy dress, size three, and I watched what I ate so I could fit into the dress. (Lesley, teacher, tenth reunion, Main High School)

Like many other informants, Lesley was very conscious of how she looked at her reunion. Later in the interview, she even admitted that she would have reconsidered attending her reunion if she were pregnant. Another informant told me that although she and her husband were considering having another baby, she herself was thinking about her reunion since "at a reunion there are some people you will not see again and you do not want them to see you pregnant" (Sarah). Not attending a reunion because one is pregnant is not idiosyncratic but part of a broader social process: while having children is an ideal (almost mandatory) in American culture, being pregnant is almost antithetical to "looking good."

It is worth noting that 69 percent of the returnees who reported dieting before the reunion and 80 percent who reported buying special clothes were female. Perhaps men were embarrassed to admit that they cared about their physical appearance. More likely, it reflects the special importance still given to the physical appearance of women. Women are still the ones who are overwhelmingly evaluated by this measure.[17] The reunion reinforces this gender-differentiated measure of "worth."

While the Music Plays

Before the reunion, most social control processes take place in one's own mind or, at the most, with some intimate friends or family members. But once one enters the catering hall, the process becomes more public.

The returnees are expected to provide personal information to a demanding audience, one with claims over a shared past as well as with a presumptive ability to judge present achievements. Through short casual conversation at the reunion, people sense how others are doing, who are the success or the failure stories of the class. Thus, at her twentieth reunion, Evelyn found herself talking with former classmates who wondered, "Why are you a teacher, you are not making enough money, why are you single, I cannot believe it."

Albeit informally, rewards and semisanctions obtain. No one tells returnees not to attend if they are unmarried or childless or hold insignificant jobs, but the message is nonetheless conveyed. And in fact, returnees tend to be people whose lives are "in order," congruent with the "American ideal-typical image."[18] As opposed to those who do not attend, reunion-goers are usually people who are married and have children and whose work is promising or successful.

Returnees who do not play according to the (informal) rules are liable to become the butt of gossip or raised eyebrows through which a message is conveyed.

> I was with a group of people . . . and then you get, "What are you doing?" and people say, "Hey, I am a doctor," "Well I am a lawyer on Wall Street," and then another person would say, "Well, I sell used cars," and I got the sense that people say, "Oh, used cars, ha, ha, ha." (Keith, artist, twentieth reunion, Central High School)

The process of social control at high school reunions can be formalized by awards ceremonies which affirm and reinforce the norms and values of the class. Some popular awards of this sort are those for the longest marriage or the most children. Being married and having children become "achievements." Responding to my question, "Did you think of giving anybody an award?" Maryellen (school employee, Central High School), the organizer of her twenty-fifth reunion, replied, "Yes, to the couple who was married the longest, because let's face it, people do not stay married long today, so that's kind of deserving an award."

Yet, ironically, the presence of formal awards for such matters as long marriage is a testimony not to the primacy of family values but to their secondary importance compared to career and material success. It is striking that returnees do not receive formal acknowledgment for the most successful careers; such awards are rarely given. Although organizers of reunions claim that it would be hard for them to decide who should win the prize, it is apparent that in each and every class reunion there is one person whose achievements are informally considered outstanding. The reason for not giving such awards for "most successful" is grounded in a prevalent feeling among many organizers that such an award is too blatant a statement. "Of course they do," says Michael (lawyer, twentieth reunion) referring to the process of comparison which is an integral part of the event, "absolutely, no question about it, we can't avoid it." But what Michael did try to do is to "minimize it. You can get people away from thinking about it by not giving awards. I wanted to eliminate the feeling that some people were better than others." It is worth noting that even Michael who so wanted to "minimize" the process of evaluation, could not resist the temptation; he ended up producing an elaborate re-union yearbook which included a distribution of occupations that even "broke down the number of doctors into specialties, because we had a large number of doctors. So everybody could see where people were." Ironically, if reunions do not give formal prizes for success, it is only because the process of evaluation is so pervasive that explicit recognition becomes altogether unnecessary.

Whether they came from a working class or middle class background, my respondents' definition of success was almost identical: "someone who made it in the business world, who is on top, a CEO, a good job, a lawyer, a professional, a doctor, making good money" (Barbara, house-wife, tenth reunion, Main High School). It is even better if there is also a spouse and children. Even the few who perceived success differently by defining it in terms of "being together with . . . life, feeling that my life is very meaningful" (Donna, student, tenth reunion, Central High School), or by putting wealth third on their list of what success means, after "being healthy and happy" (Sherry, dietician, twentieth reunion, Garden High School), ended up reaffirming the same cultural values. Thus Donna wanted her classmates to think of her as being successful in her job and, no less important, "good-looking," while Sherry thought that being successful consisted of "being a doctor or a lawyer."

The normative consensus about what is expected and desired was so strong among my informants that many were surprised to see people who fell far short of achieving the "American dream." "One woman," recalls Alicia (senior banker, twenty-fifth reunion, Central High School), "was at least one hundred pounds overweight, she never married, she had no make up on. Her hair was just not done . . . it took a lot of courage for her to go to that reunion." Mel had the same reaction to a former friend who had "just been divorced. She came to the reunion. I was very proud of her coming. I give her credit for coming, because people want to have their house in order when they show up."

Even if, before the reunion, returnees feel that their "house is in or-der," they still face a certain amount of risk; their encounters at the reunion might prove them wrong. Hope, who was very proud of being a mother and housewife, felt uncomfortable at her twentieth reunion at Central High School (which she organized). She was confronted with "all these other women who work and have families: so what's wrong with me? I felt that I should have been doing more in twenty years."

The process is reinforced yet more because all the returnees share the same past and are the same age and hence are expected to be at more or less the same stage in life. Such a position makes the reunions, as Daniel (college professor, twentieth reunion) put it, "benchmarks, a basis of comparison." He continued: "I have very few other yardsticks, how else or where else do you find a group of people who came from where you were coming from and who are the same age that you are?" In the interstices between the self-image with which attendees set out for the reunion and the reevaluation they make by comparing themselves with others, reunion-goers are forced to create more than a hierarchy; they create a "truth" about how things ought to look.[19]

Attempts to Escape or Avoid

Since the process of social control at high school reunions is informal, voluntary, and noncoercive, are there ways to avoid it? If there are, they derive first and foremost from the fact that there are two systems of social control at reunions, one in the name of "adult" values, the other in the name of the values of high school life of the past.

Most obviously, classmates can avoid current social control by not attending the reunion, keeping away from the judgmental process. "I didn't go to former reunions," says Grace, "because I was embarrassed at my marital status and life status. I was in the midst of a divorce and I felt I couldn't deal with that."

But staying away does not mean there is no public conversation. In fact, nonreturnees are often perceived by returnees as failures. Moreover, even if one is able to escape the control of the reunion itself, it may be harder to ignore the mailed invitation and the self-reflection process that follows. In addition, while they have many special features, reunions are also part of a larger phenomenon of time reminders, events that force, or at least stimulate, a process of self-reflection. By avoiding high school reunions, we avoid one type of time reminder, but not the others. Thus, when I asked Daniel whether he thought about his life following his reunion, he replied,

> Yes, I have, but it is a little bit hard to say [that it was because of the reunion] because I was also coming up for tenure, promotion,

and so I had to think through some of the same stuff in the same period . . . what I had been able to accomplish and what I hadn't. (Daniel)

The same process is described by Alicia, who said that she did not go through a self-reflection process around her reunion because, she said, "I went through a lot of that a few years ago, around my fortieth birthday." But even if personal observation points do not exist, people come across other collective time-reminders, public events that force them to contemplate the time that has passed:

> What contributed [to the self-reflection process] was actually the summer before [the reunion]. It was the twentieth anniversary of the Woodstock festival which I had attended and . . . the twentieth anniversary in the media caused me to reflect. (Erich, manager, twentieth reunion, Garden High School)

Time-reminders of different sorts make people think about their way of life, decisions they have made, and who they are now as distinct from who they were. Graduation ceremonies, retirement dinners, farewell parties, family reunions, and the like are all socially constructed observation points that call for summations, much in the same way class reunions do. While it is possible to ignore reunions to avoid embarrassing situations and painful questions, it is hard to evade the other autobiographical occasions in one's life, in which one is forced to subject oneself to self-reflection and self-evaluation processes.

Another way of escaping the social control of a reunion is to select an audience with whom one feels comfortable. Thus, Pamela (secretary, twenty-fifth reunion, Central High School) told me that "there was one area of people [at the reunion] and I didn't make any effort to go over and say 'Hi' to. I just stayed where I was comfortable." Unlike having one confessor or one psychologist before whom one has to account for a life, one has a variety of mediators at a reunion. Although there is a general sense of how things should look and of what success means, there are multiple versions of the truth, giving individuals some leeway in the midst of the self-reflection process forced on them. The problem, however, is that reunion-goers may be sufficiently self-aware to realize that in selecting an audience that does not pose a threat to their claims, they are going to great lengths to defend themselves. Moreover, it is difficult to avoid "meeting" the rest of the returnees, if not face-to-face, at least at a distance or through the reunion yearbook distributed at the end of the night. Although there may be various versions of the truth, there is still one dominant version of what present achievements should look like; avenues of escape from current social control, though available, are rather limited.

It may be easier to evade the values of high school by challenging past predictions, by witnessing their failures in triumph over a sometimes gloomy past. No formal ceremonies honor the "class failure," but many reunion-goers do feel a sense of poetic justice when the previous "stars" turn out to have dimmed in their brilliance. Even more, there is a strong feeling that the "old" system of social control has been challenged, if not overthrown, and that, for those who suffered from it in the past, "the time of their life" has come. Moreover, there is a sense that those who deserved it have gotten their come-uppance, that there is some relief for past growing pains. Not only have people managed to escape the past; they have returned to display their triumph. Consider the following examples:

> There is this one girl, she was the captain of the cheerleaders. The guy that she married was my best friend . . . and I had a mad crush on him. They got divorced and she gained a lot of weight and my girlfriend and I said, "Oh, God, we look so good." We felt really good. . . . and I got back [at her], revenge type of things, childish but . . . (Anna, nurse, twentieth reunion, Garden High School)

> All the very good-looking guys that were always so snooty and stuck-up and obnoxious, most of them lost their hair. It felt great, there is justice, you know. (Judith, lawyer, tenth reunion, Central High School)

These feelings are derived from the confluence of memories of ex-classmates and the complicated relations between past and present. The triumph of current social values over those of high school is apparent. The present is brought up so it can compensate for past deficiencies. But gloating as an attempt to escape from the process of social control is a telling comment on the ability to cope with social structure and culture. Moreover, although returnees attend their reunions looking for changes, actually they are struggling to ignore them. Thus, even the happily married multimillionaire, attending to make up for his high school image and show off his current success, may discover that some still see him as the sixteen-year-old nerd and refuse to acknowledge the change.

Naturally, not everybody shares the feeling that justice is served or that the hierarchy that should operate is actually in place. Reunions also attest to the failure of high school evaluations. Lila (social worker, twentieth reunion, Garden High School), for example, was frustrated by the fact that "the most idiotic person in our class is extremely wealthy now."

Witnessing the failure of past evaluations is harder on those who were at the top of the hierarchy, who have to cope with personal failures while watching former "underdogs" rise:

> Well, my friend Tom . . . I've known him since we were in grammar school. He was never really that bright. I was always in all of the smart classes and whenever I see Tom, who scholastically wasn't as bright as me, and now he's got the title "doctor," and I look up to him. (Greg, owner of a plumbing company, twentieth reunion, Garden High School)

What for Tom may constitute an escape from high school social control is for others not only a demonstration of its failure, but also of their own personal failure.

Another way to cast off high school social control is to acknowledge people who did not merit recognition in the past. Thus it is common at reunions to hold a ceremony awarding the person who traveled the farthest to attend—in many ways an indicator not only of commitment to the group but also of material success. This attempt to resist the past system, however, is limited insofar as it depends on the people who put the reunion together and organized the award ceremony. If the organizers are committed to acknowledging people for reasons not foreseen by the old value system, they can make returnees feel that, finally, the past hierarchy is gone. Yet often enough, the same people who were considered "all around" individuals in high school receive special attention again at the reunion, reinforcing the past value system—much to the chagrin of some returnees.

The convergence of the adult value system and the high school social hierarchy provides the opportunity to challenge both systems of social control. The contest, however, is not equal: people may invoke high school values to challenge those of adulthood, but adult values are far more often used to counter those of high school. The more successful attempts to escape social control are those that challenge the past. The social control inherent in current values and hierarchy is more difficult to evade.

It is important to note, however, that in certain respects the value systems of high school and adulthood are the same. People are still judged on their physical appearance, a major concern in high school. Those who had been deemed good-looking in high school may not be considered attractive in the present, but the importance of physical appearance is the same. Marital or partner status is another example. In high school, people were rated higher if they had a boyfriend or a girlfriend (something that was mentioned quite often during the interviews); at a reunion, people score higher if they are married. In high school, fame was often won in the sports arena; at reunions, this source of recognition is replaced by success as professionals or in well-to-do business. While the content might be slightly different, the form has not changed. Even if returnees feel that reunions turn the past value system on its head by rewarding people on their merit, the underlying logic of the contest remains the same. Different people might win this time, as professionals replace football players. The social order confirmed and endorsed at reunions seems more like "an older version," a more mature one (in the eyes of the returnees) than that of high school. The same system may have changed its titles and some of its content, so it can better suit today's "thirtysomething"-year-old but the notion of hierarchies remains.

Social Control and Modern Society

High school reunions do not obviously exert social control in the same way that executions, for example, or involuntary mental hospitalizations do. High school reunions are based on rewards for compliance, not on punishment for noncompliance. They do not involve the use of power, or even the threat to use power in the event of deviation from the norm. Informal and noncoercive social control proceeds subtly. Moreover, class reunions are voluntary; people need not attend if they do not wish to. And those that do are not objects of social control because of their real or imputed deviance. I have tried to show, however, that reunions may still be usefully analyzed as a form of social control. They call for a process of self-reflection that begins well in advance of the event itself, providing former classmates with a hierarchy and a reminder of the norms according to which they can judge and be judged.

Edward Shils claims that human beings need "categories and rules . . . they need criteria of judgment,"[20] and since they cannot construct those for themselves, their reference group provides them instead. Does a "need" therefore exist because people are judged and categorized? Such a conclusion is dangerous, as it involves assessments based on results: people are judged, hence there is a need. Traditionally, "problems" are perceived as preceding their "solutions." In the case of high school reunions, the "problem" might be translated as the need to remember what the norms are all about and what the hierarchy consists of, the need to be judged, to be punished and rewarded for one's way of life. The institution of high school reunions might be perceived as a possible "solution" to such "problems." But this functionalist explanation is inadequate;

needs are created by institutions and situations, which instead of solving problems may generate them. This only underscores the line of argument that runs from Durkheim through labeling theory, i.e., that social control produces deviance. Thus, rather than provide a solution for the need to be judged or normalized, reunions generate classification, hierarchy, and evaluation processes that might not otherwise appear. Reunions may create curiosity about "what ever happened to the class of 1965?" and about "who am I and where am I in regard to the people I grew up with?" An invitation to a reunion may provoke the self-reflection process. As a time reminder, class reunions may just evoke those difficult questions about identity.

The need to account for one's life at reunions is a force through which the social order is confirmed and, moreover, one's identity within that order is defined and assigned. Community is not easily created in a world where the more traditional groupings often disappear. High school reunions do create a community, but once created such a community controls its members, generating perspectives on identity, achievement, and failure. It elicits a hierarchy of norms according to which people are measured and judged. Different communities might create different orders and hierarchies; the process, however, remains the same.

Moreover, in the last century age has become an organizing principle in American culture.[21] Age has become a source for expectations, norms, and positions. Age-based peer groups, claims Howard Chudacoff, in many ways replace the more traditional forms of organizing social life such as families and communities, and thus enable individuals "to recapture a fading sense of identity."[22] How better can individuals gain perspective over their lives than by watching their own "contemporaries"[23] in a face-to-face interaction?

The question is, where can those age-based peer groups be found once adolescence is over? American culture is characterized by a rapid disappearance of communities from individuals' lives,[24] by the experience of "pseudo-events,"[25] and by the growth of communication between individuals without "meeting in the same place."[26] Class reunions create a rare opportunity for informal social control by re-creating one of the few groups—the group of high school peers—that retains its strength. "How else", as Adam (owner of business, tenth reunion, Central High School) put it, "are you gonna know if you do well? By looking at someone next to you and see what they do."

The sense of belonging may be so weak in contemporary America that the only place to which people feel a connection is their past. That shared past is used to legitimize the creation of a group—similar indeed to Hobsbawm's "invented tradition . . . which seeks to inculcate certain values and norms of behavior"[27]—against which and by which people are measured and defined. In some ways, high school reunions are relics, survivors of an old-fashioned "tradition-directed"[28] social control in which one's own community played a major part. Where tradition, communities, and the like are hard to find, reunions create a reference group for the returnees, a group within which their identities are defined and placed.

The shape of modern society encourages, even requires the invention of new forms of social control. And yet, while we are aware of formal forms of social control, we often overlook the informal ones that pervade modern society. Such informal forms of social control were powerful and dominant in traditional societies and have been perceived to be absent from modern societies. Indeed, this very absence is taken by classical sociological theorists, especially Emile Durkheim, as an inherent problem of modern society.[29] There is an obvious sense that modern postindustrial societies lack these traditional bonds and primary controls. But although difficult to identify and recognize, some equivalent informal forms of social controls and rituals remain with us. The social order and its culture do not only reproduce themselves through major social institutions. American society may be perceived today as postmodern and fragmented, but rituals and other cultural events remain. Through these rituals, the cultural values and the social order are recalled and reinforced. The high school reunion is such a form. It is perceived as voluntary; it has an appeal that makes people desire it. There is so little experience of the control as coercive that there is hardly any perceived need to resist or protest, both of which are more common responses where social control is formal and coercive.

Moreover, accounting for one's life is somewhat similar to a confession, and confession is an effective form of social control precisely because "it is so deeply ingrained in us, that we no longer perceive it as the effect of a power that constrains us."[30] Few resist or resent the reunion's agenda—none of my informants who attended their reunions challenged this component of the drama, by which I mean no one objected to the prerogative to investigate one another's lives; not even those of my informants who did not attend evinced any reluctance to talk about their lives in front of a demanding public. They might not want to share certain things, but they never challenged the agenda of telling one's life story, which is taken for granted.

The same process, of course, occurs in settings like the educational system, the medical profession, and the welfare organizations, all of which create settings in which and through which people are judged and normalized. In most institutions, however, such judgment concerns only one domain of life; high school reunions provide a site for an instant and condensed evaluation of every significant sphere of a person's life: family, career, place of residence, financial ability, and physical appearance. Moreover, all of the above is done in light of the past, its memories and expectations. In addition, even if people manage to avoid the reunion, it is a limited escape only. Other socially constructed observation points call for a similar process of summation, self-reflection, and self-government.

Instead of living one's life, one is forced to think about it in terms that have been set by a group of which one is a partial member. The consequences of modern forms of social control as demonstrated by this case study may be limited. People do not change significantly after their reunions; but the event does make them think and evaluate themselves, get a perspective over life as well as fit themselves into a hierarchy in which their identities are defined and assigned.

The type of social control discussed in this chapter takes place at the micro level. What the self has become is evaluated, and what one should desire for oneself is recalled. Still, the criteria employed at high school reunions are an integral part of American culture—a culture that emphasizes consumerism and its material symbols, marriages and parenthood, and the need to progress at all times: in other words, the fulfillment of the "American Dream."

Autobiography as a Social Endeavor

*A*utobiographies may appear to be personal matters, life stories that people tell themselves. In practice, however, autobiographies are social acts. Neither the discourse of the present nor that of the past can be detached from the audience before whom the story of one's life is told.[1] People construct their life stories within social occasions and in relation to a specific audience. We need an audience to listen to the story, to confirm it, to verify it, even to contest it. The audience is the subject of this chapter. The chapter focuses more on the structure of encounters and less on the actual outcomes of those encounters, which will be the subject of later chapters.

Although everyone has a personal past, a social past cannot be taken for granted. Before returnees can inform or recast their past, and before they can share the present, they must verify that they have some social standing in the specific social setting of high school. And the audience has the power to determine whether one did have a past within that setting. Unlike many other autobiographical occasions, the audience of a class reunion includes the author's "biographical others."[2] In effect, the presence of one's biographical others turns them into co-authors. Because this audience shares the "author's" past, it can help inform and enrich it. However, this is not a disinterested audience, and it can also challenge individuals' interpretations of the past, insisting on interpretations of its own or following an altogether different plot line. In the worst case, the audience will not even recognize the storyteller, in effect denying that there is any story at all. A great source of anxiety for many former classmates before they attend their reunions is the fear of not being recognized. Not to see any image at all of oneself in the eyes of the audience may mean that one had no social existence in the past. If identity requires first and foremost recognition by others,[3] not being recognized can be devastating.

Reunions testify to the social dynamics of autobiographies and, thus, the dynamic character of identities. This quality of reunions makes clear just how interactive autobiographies are. Each returnee is at the same time author of his or her own story, co-author of other people's stories, and audience. As authors, the returnees narrate to the audience who they were and what they have done with their lives. As co-authors, returnees help (or refuse to help) others to reminisce or sustain their performances. As audience, the returnees observe other people's presentations. More-over, the positions of actor and audience, even of star and supporting cast, are in constant flux. From one attendee's point of view, he or she may be the star of one particular drama, while from another reunion-goer's van-tage point, the same person may play little more than a supporting role in the enactment of another drama, or perhaps serve as nothing more than audience.

The time frame of participants' relationships varies. There are people who share the present as well as the past (oneself, classmates with whom one has stayed in touch, and spouses from the class). Others share only the present (spouses who are not classmates) or only the past (classmates with whom one is no longer in contact). Hence, some people may become a resource in discovering the past while others may become a resource in teaching about the present.

But the important quality that differentiates members of the audience is their power to validate one's autobiography and identity. "Some vali-dations are more significant than others. Every individual requires the ongoing validation of his world, including crucially the validation of his identity and place in this world, by those few who are his truly significant others."[4] The presence of just any class member at a reunion is not enough if one wants to maintain or change a certain image. In order to do such identity work, one needs the "right" audience.

The "truly significant others" at reunions are not returnees' inti-mates, such as spouses and close friends. They are former friends the returnees have not seen in years and former classmates who used to have public standing in the past. This is the "right" audience, the one with the power to legitimate the returnee's autobiography.

Yet, reunions are a remarkably concrete illustration of Cooley's "look-ing-glass self."[5] Those who attend reunions "play" to others but, as in the "looking-glass self," they do so to see themselves reflected in the approving eyes of the "right" audience. In that sense they are, ultimately, their own audience. Thus, while we need to acknowledge the importance of the audience and social experiences in constructing one's identity,[6] "in the last analysis we individually are the ones who decide" who we are.[7]

We attend reunions so we can put on a show, and thus reunions may be seen as a type of social drama in which various actors perform before various audiences. Thus Erving Goffman's dramaturgical metaphor may appropriately describe the scene.[8] But the show we put on is not just for entertainment; we put on a show to know who we once were, to display who we are now, to validate ourselves, or, at the very least, to protect ourselves from potential threats. The subject matter of the reunion's drama is almost always one's own identity.

When There Is No Mirror

Joseph was late for the first meeting of his thirtieth reunion organizing committee.[9] As soon as he entered Jack shouted out, "Hey, Joseph, how are you doing?" Joseph's sigh of relief was audible, and he said, "Whew! You recognized me!"

"A man's Social Self is the recognition which he gets from his mates . . . a man has as many social selves as there are individuals who recognize him and carry an image of him in their mind. To wound any one of these his images is to wound him," William James wrote over 100 years ago.[10] Although within modern life people move from one residence to another, change jobs, encounter new faces and, thus, must introduce themselves over and over again, when one enters an autobiographical occasion in which one expects to be known, being unrecognized has a different import, very much like the situation James describes.

Not being recognized at a class reunion can be the result of two different causes. First, one's appearance may have changed dramatically since high school. Not to be recognized because of such markers of age as wrinkles, pot bellies, gray hair, or no hair at all is dramatic evidence that one has aged, but giving one's name and entering into a brief conversation usually establishes one's identity.

On the other hand, some reunion-goers may not be remembered because they were "nobodies" in high school, someone few people knew or cared to know—in short, people of no particular social significance. "I was shaking," Joanne (a law school student) said, recalling her fears before her tenth reunion; "what if I get there and no one even looks at me?

Maybe I was nothing." Going unrecognized for this reason can be devastating.

> I can't tell you how many people looked at me, read my name tag, and shook their head, like "I don't remember you." And you know what? It still hurts. In cases where I recognized people but they obviously didn't recognize me, it was like a curtain just dropped, it was a stone wall. (Frances, housewife, twentieth reunion, Garden High School)

What Frances learns about her past is harsh, and the implication is not easy to bear. Lack of recognition means that Frances was, in fact, "nobody" in high school, where she spent three years of her life. Within this social context, Frances can hardly find either a past or an identity. To be sure, she does have a personal past and a biographical identity, but she found no one to support or confirm it. Frances is left, in effect, without a social identity. More important, like others who went through the same realization, Frances must confront discontinuities between past and present, at least when it comes to their high school years. Where we are unknown, we have no biography, we are apparently nonexistent.[11] This is not only hard to accept but also portends that there is little chance of managing the gaps it creates for our autobiography.

No wonder, then, that returnees who find themselves with no past to encounter withdraw from the event. Vanessa (journalist, twenty-fifth reunion, Central High School) stood on the sidelines with her lone girl friend, hardly mingling with the other classmates who "didn't remember me"; Frances clung to her husband, walked only with him, or sat with him at the table throughout the event. The experience caused Vanessa, who before the reunion had perceived her high school years as an important part of her life, to "sever whatever very thin thread I had to my past, cut whatever very thin thread or tie it was to the past—I think that that's what the reunion did to me."

By not acknowledging Vanessa and Frances, their former classmates taught them that they were not part of what they thought they were. It may even be a much more significant and stronger lesson than in cases where people are remembered. With that in mind, no wonder my informants frequently mentioned how happy other people made them by recognizing them. Jonathan (lawyer, twentieth reunion, Central High School) describes himself in high school as "fairly shy and quiet, really unrecognizable." Taking into account his social invisibility in high school, it comes as no surprise that the best part of his twentieth reunion was the fact that he did in fact find a mirror he could look into: "It's so nice to be remembered."

The "With": Spouses

Although spouses are often invited to class reunions, only about half of married returnees bring them.[12] All of my informants who did not bring their spouses to their reunions claimed that, unless the spouses had graduated from the same class or at least from the same school, they felt there was no reason to drag them to an event at which they knew hardly anyone. Some had had bad experiences at prior class reunions or at their spouses' reunions and did not want to repeat them.

> [At] the first [reunion] my wife came with me, I wanted to meet more guys and more girls that I had gone to school with. I felt that she wasn't part of it because she did not grow up in Garden. She didn't feel uncomfortable. My wife is very friendly, but I wanted to talk more with my friends. I didn't want to leave her at the table, so I got up and then I went back to her, and then got up again. This time I said, "Don't come" . . . so she didn't . . . and I was glad she didn't because I was able to talk to friends, hug and kiss my buddies. (Tom, chiropractor, twentieth reunion, Garden High School)

Tom's description of his wife's role at his tenth reunion exemplifies the major concern of returnees whose spouses join them at reunions: the spouse's lack of interest leaves returnees torn between commitments to spouses and the wish to be with former friends.

Couples enter and leave the reunion together. They spend some time with each other at the beginning of the evening, while the classmates introduce them to other classmates, while having dinner at the tables, and in the last hours when the dancing begins. Many of the spouses I have observed at class reunions simply sit around the tables, drinking and eating, while their husbands and wives circle the hall, sometimes alone, more often with close friends from the class. Too often, the spouses grow bored. When spouses do make the circuit of the hall with returnees, it often has to do with the returnees' sense of being out of place, unrecognized, or lonely. Even then, spouses seldom become involved in prolonged conversations with returnees or other spouses.

While only a few of my respondents who had brought their spouses said that they did so because they were "a very important part of my life today" (David, lawyer, twenty-fifth reunion, Central High School), it seems that bringing spouses to reunions has less to do with the essence of reunions and more to do with relationships between couples and a general understanding and expectation of married life in contemporary America. Many of my informants said that they brought their spouses to their reunions because "I wouldn't even go near telling her that I don't want her to come. She would take it as 'Hey, are you embarrassed by me? What are you trying to do?'" (Greg, owner of plumbing company, twentieth reunion, Garden High School). Mel (fundraiser, twentieth reunion) explained why she had brought her husband along simply by saying, "I just couldn't hurt his feelings." Connie (housewife, tenth reunion, Main High School) was laughing when I asked her why she brought her husband to the reunion. "He is my husband," she answered. "It was the right thing to do," replied Nicholas (businessman, twentieth reunion, Central High School) to my question, while Tracy (bank employee, tenth reunion, Central High School) said that she does not "go to parties without my husband, social events like that, you know. You kind of create a problem with your image."[13] Tracy also said she would "feel bad if he went to his reunion and didn't ask me." Spouses bracket the event. The presence of spouses at reunions is a constant reminder of the present and its privileged status. It is the present and its representatives reasserting their claim over the past, marking the reunion as no more than a temporary suspension of usual priorities.

Some returnees brought their spouses as part of their autobiographies. Together with cars, clothes, and other material artifacts perceived and treated as an extension of the ego,[14] the returnees' spouses could be considered a prop used to represent one's present life. Spouses are one's current "with"—"a party of more than one whose members are perceived to be 'together'"[15]—and by introducing them to old classmates, attendees are also consciously presenting themselves.

But what is the role of these "with" biographical others at class reunions? Above all, a spouse means that one is married and has thus fulfilled at least one significant part of mainstream American social values. Judith, an unmarried lawyer (tenth reunion, Central High School), expressed this clearly: "I know that if I am married [at the next reunion], I will bring my husband to show him off, to show them that I got it all, that I have a career and that I am successful in my family life." A few reunion-goers, however, had a more specific agenda in mind, part of which involved using a spouse not only as a prop of current life but also in an attempt to transform past images:

> I had such a reputation in high school so bringing my wife was kind of giving the impression that I didn't marry a fat pig. (Greg)

In effect, spouses can be observed and can thus provide clues about classmates' identities; who one has married is as important as the fact of being married. Returnees tend to associate the spouse's occupation and physical appearance with their classmate. Thus, a spouse is a piece of information that can confirm or change past impressions. In general, returnees obtain very little information about the spouses they meet, but they tend to treat these few fragments of information as if it represented their former classmates' identity.[16]

> There was this girl who was very shy and quiet [in high school]. She is such a success . . . she became prettier and more popular. . . . She is now married to a doctor, and he was there that night. (Joanne)

> I think that some of them [the "nerds"] turned out socially more popular and successful than we thought they would be. . . . One guy, Steven, was always very smart, but he was not very good looking. But he came with this young honey and I thought, "Oh, God, where did this guy pick up this one?" (Anna, nurse, twentieth reunion, Garden High School)

Both Joanne's and Anna's accounts illustrate the tendency to generalize from the spouse to the classmate. While Joanne's classmate's success centered on a combination of her physical appearance and her husband's occupation, it was Steven's good-looking and provocative young wife who made Anna look at Steven differently. Although she did not change her mind about Steven's having been a "nerd" in high school, he made a strong impression through his wife's physical appearance. The perception of a couple as a unit encourages returnees to attribute to former classmates their spouse's traits and characteristics. Such perception implies the privileged status of the present over the past. If someone is married to a doctor, that someone is successful; if someone is married to a good-looking young wife, that someone is socially successful.

Only a very small minority of my respondents perceived their reunions as an occasion for their spouses to encounter their past, using their former classmates as co-authors in the reenactment of the past, and thus perhaps to help their spouses "understand more of my life" (Jonathan). In general, however, spouses actually learn little at the reunions, the consequence being that reunions provide only a limited amount of information. Even Jonathan reported that his wife learned nothing about him at his reunion and was, for the most part, bored.

Even when spouses do learn about the returnees' past, the result is not always desirable. The revealed past may be sad, even embarrassing.

Spouses may discover that their husbands and wives meant very little to their class. Frances' husband found himself telling her former classmates, who seemed to recognize him but not her, that "my wife is the one who went to school with you." His presence at her twentieth reunion exposed to him her drab past. Frances' husband knew she was shy, but there is a difference between having that knowledge and seeing it made concrete by the fact that hardly anyone remembered her from high school.

A drab past is not the only kind that can be discovered at reunions. Spouses may find a glorious one, as in the case of Lesley. Curiously, though, a glorious past does not necessarily make spouses proud and happy.

> My husband told me afterwards that a lot of the guys were coming up to him saying, "You married Lesley Blair? Well, I was in love with her in high school." He said to me, "I was so sick of hearing how everybody was in love with you in high school," and I said, "Oh, that makes me feel good!" (Lesley, teacher, tenth reunion, Main High School)

Thus our most intimate biographical others function at a reunion as people to be observed from a distance, to be available when things go wrong, or to help with purposes of impression management—and to be ignored when everything is under control. As props, spouses constitute an important but limited resource in establishing an identity. Former classmates hardly get a chance to talk to them; the impression they leave and their implications for current identity are based on physical appearance, in some cases their occupations, and very little else. As audience for one's past, a spouse's learning is limited and selective. Moreover, the reunion as an occasion is in most cases not understood as an event from which spouses can learn something, and thus, the spouses themselves may perceive their role as that of a prop. In addition, spouses are hardly talked to; in order to become an audience for the past, spouses need to take an active role in the drama. But the drama is not their own. While returnees are busy enacting their own scripts, they rarely find the time or energy to play to other people's spouses.

One last word about the most peculiar group at class reunions—never too large but always there—consisting of spouses from the class: unlike spouses who are not from the class, spouses from the class are people with a reputation. Former classmates knew them in the past. Such prior knowledge bears implications for one's identity, including threats to it. Significant others from the class are vested with potential power to make others validate, confirm, or even change past identities in ways that other spouses cannot. And that is exactly what makes spouses from the class critical co-authors.[17]

Every reunion is attended by a few couples from the class. High school sweethearts who married each other do not generate much surprise, but classmates whose relationship developed after high school do tend to surprise. "It was kind of a novelty [for the class]: 'Oh, you married Lenore? Oh, my God'" (Michael, lawyer, twentieth reunion). Classmates' prior knowledge of a spouse may limit one's ability to manage impressions, maintain a past image, or recast one's past and present. There is more at stake and less leeway in identity work. The following two examples illustrate the fears and hopes that accompany presenting a spouse who was part of the class.

While Michael was one of the most popular students in high school, active in different sports and cliques, his wife Lenore was not part of the "in crowd." Michael was nervous about what people would think of him now. Would his wife change the way his clique perceived his past? Would they think that he had changed completely? When I asked him what it was like to have a wife who was a classmate he answered in a whisper, making sure Lenore could not hear us, "I think that I was more proud than embarrassed [that Lenore is my wife]. I had both those feelings, but I think more the former than the latter."

The other side of the coin is illustrated in Hope's story. Hope (housewife, twentieth reunion, Central High School) describes herself as a "nerd" in high school. But, twenty years later, she was married to someone who had been part of the most popular clique of her class, the "jocks." At her reunion she approached "many of these jocks" and said, "Hi, I'm Hope Mitchell, you know my husband is Rick." Through her marriage to someone who had been part of the "in crowd," Hope tried to make a statement about her past: she had not been part of the popular clique, but she could have been—after all, Rick married her.

By presenting a spouse who is a classmate, one makes a statement about the present as well as the past. Seeing Michael with Lenore and Hope with Rick might make their former classmates wonder whether Michael and Rick were really part of the "best" clique in the class or never really fit in. Seeing Lenore and Hope might generate a sense of having missed out on them, of their being more than what they appeared to be. While Hope was proud to have her popular husband as a coauthor, and convinced that such a prop could only benefit her, Michael was concerned whether his prop (Lenore) might undermine his identity.

Escorts

Apart from the rare instances of classmates who have married each other, former classmates who have remained close friends are the sole witnesses to both past and present. Yet no more than spouses are, close friends are not the primary audience for the enactment of oneself, either in regard to the past or the present. Returnees do not attend their reunions to see and inform their close friends, and close friends do not need to hear each other's life stories, since they already know them well and are often part of them.

The importance of close friends lies elsewhere. As we saw in chapter 1, those who maintain close friends from high school are more likely to attend their reunions. So, although close friends are not the ones returnees come to see, they facilitate attendance (sometimes even force it), making returnees more comfortable while facing a curiously unfamiliar past and present. Returnees do not attend reunions in order to see their close friends, but they attend reunions with them. The close friends serve as escorts. They act as a kind of bridge between the two different times as well as answering the problem of recognition; close friends can witness that we were actually there.

In addition, close friends can do what neither the returnee nor his or her spouse can do: they can comfortably and without embarrassment praise a reunion-goer's achievements at those times when returnees feel uncomfortable praising their own achievements. Implicit and explicit "deals" among friends help carry the right messages to the right audiences. In that sense, more than spouses, close friends become collaborators in the production of biographies and thus create what Goffman calls "a performance team."[18] Phil (twentieth reunion), who owns a very successful reunion company, illustrates this point. Phil was very frustrated at his twentieth reunion, finding it difficult to explain his financial success to his former classmates. "When I tell people what I do," recalled Phil, "they give me this look, as if they want to say, 'Can you make a living out of that?' They don't know how well we are doing." It was important to Phil, who had been considered immensely popular but not very serious, to show his classmates that he had changed since high school, but he did not know how to do it. The solution that presented itself was "some of my friends walking around, telling everybody that I was a millionaire." Susan (twenty-fifth reunion, student, Garden High School), who grew up in a lower middle class neighborhood and went on to graduate school, expressed a similar frustration. "I was embarrassed to walk around and tell people what I do, but my friend Pat did it; she was all over telling people that I was getting a Ph.D."

Friends could say what Phil and Susan could not, acting in effect as their supporting casts. But close friends are authors in their own right as well, with their own past and present to manage. Thus their commitment to assist other people's presentations is often limited. Moreover, "while a team-performance is in progress, any member of the team has the power to give the show away or to disrupt it by inappropriate conduct."[19] Thus, close friends pose a threat to one's presentation of identity when one wishes to hide certain parts of that autobiography. On such occasions, close friends must be notified and prepared and must be willing to cooperate. Donna's account illustrates this point. After high school, she dated someone who was a member of her class. According to her account, both she and her former boyfriend wished to revise their past identity. Hiding their past romantic relationship seemed just as necessary to both of them in carrying out their agendas. But Donna still feared that her former boyfriend would disclose the secret, thereby jeopardizing her attempts to revise her identity.

In Donna's case (student, tenth reunion, Central High School), the threat of her friend exposing their past was minimal since both of them were well aware of the price of disclosure: "because he knew my reputation in school, and I knew his reputation" which, needless to say, was not a good one. What they did was "pretend that it didn't happened. We pretended we were friends." Both had an interest in keeping this part of their autobiography concealed. Yet one cannot always control what close friends—even those with the best intentions, let alone those without them—can reveal.

The Critical Other

"I was looking forward to seeing the people I hadn't seen in many years" (Lenny, owner of a chain of stores, twentieth reunion, Central High School)—this was the most common response elicited when I asked my informants what prompted them to attend their class reunions. The people Lenny and others wish to meet are what I call objects of curiosity. They include former friends with whom the returnee has lost touch, and class celebrities. By class celebrities I mean those visible classmates who were known to most people yet rarely knew everyone else, who were often the objects of a certain envy, and who typically represented the core values of the class. The central positions these classmates held in high school makes other returnees eager to know what happened to, for example, the former football player, the class president, the boy voted best looking, or the girl voted most likely to succeed. However, with more than curiosity, returnees attend reunions in the spirit of actors and authors. Many seek to inform their past with their present, in effect to change or to confirm their past. To validate these changes, they require the corroboration of former friends and class celebrities. Thus, objects of curiosity become the most important audience before whom a life story is enacted and an identity recreated.

Both former friends and class celebrities are potential informants of the past, since they were part of it. But because their past relationships with a returnee are different, the returnee's expectations of them are similarly distinct. While being recognized by a class celebrity may often be enough, former friends are required to deliver much more than mere recognition.

CLASS CELEBRITIES

Class celebrities are like theater critics vested with a special ability to consecrate. Everyone wants to talk to them, since they can confirm old identities or, even better, atone for "past mistakes." Judith, for instance, could not wait to talk to Anthony Porto, who was

> this popular guy. Every time I wanted to run for an election or an office [in high school], he always had to run against me, because he had to prove to them that he could beat me. And he always did beat me, and it aggravated me. I was hoping he would be [at the reunion] since he is a lawyer now also. But he didn't come. . . . You know, finally we are at this stage of our life where there is no longer that popularity business.

After becoming a lawyer herself, Judith found the courage to talk to a class celebrity who had been a longtime rival. She wanted to talk to him as she had not been able to in high school, precisely because a new relationship, however brief, would validate the changes she herself had gone through. Judith felt that her time had come. Finally she had the courage (and the degrees) to make the class celebrities grant her the attention she could not get in high school. Acknowledgement of her success by class celebrities was important to Judith. She could validate changes and revise identities in a way that few others could; Anthony was the "right" audience for her. Unfortunately, for Judith, she was stymied by a common frustration: the voluntary character of class reunions. Anthony, like many other former classmates was not there and his absence from the reunion meant that Judith could not pursue her agenda.

By acknowledging those who were unacknowledged in high school, class celebrities have the power to transform past identities, even to make people revise who they were. Let me refer again to Joanne's account. Joanne was astonished to see that class celebrities who she thought "had nothing to do with me" approached her at the reunion with great interest.

> The highlight of my night was this guy I didn't really know. He was *very, very popular.* He was standing there with a bunch of people and he called me over: "Joanne, look Joanne is here!" I thought "Wow, I guess I rate now." He even wanted a picture with me, so I had to take a picture with him and three other very popular guys I thought had nothing to do with me. But I guess I've made it!"

Whether the former class celebrities' reaction at the reunion was a response to her own performance at the reunion, or whether it indicates that she had always been well liked (something she was not sure of), the power held by class celebrities is patent. Before her reunion, Joanne had not thought of them as potential co-authors, but their reaction toward her made them the most important audience for her that night. She had believed that they neither knew her nor wanted anything to do with her; being treated like someone with whom they did indeed want to associate prompted her to rethink her perception of both her past and her present. Not only may her past have been different from what she had thought, but her present at the reunion also emerged as something she could be proud of. The important point, however, is that a status bestowed earlier continues to exert its force; certain people remain powerful and much sought after at reunions. But their power is two-edged: precisely because they are much sought after, as a result of having been most visible during high school, they cannot acknowledge everyone who wants to be acknowledged. If they can confirm identities, or even make people revise them, so too can they disprove them.

FORMER FRIENDS

Former friends may have less prestige than class celebrities but they can inform and enlighten returnees by recalling memories which had been forgotten. In fact, former friends may confirm or change returnees' own impressions of themselves. Less powerful than class celebrities, perhaps, they are potentially more threatening; because of the presumed intimacy of their past relationships with a classmate, the potential harm caused by their failure to evince interest in a former friend can be devastating. Former friends are critical biographical others for any returnee at any class reunion. No wonder, then, that returnees as actors often direct their performances towards former friends, while at the same time functioning as an audience for those same people.

The potential exists for the objects of curiosity to inform the present with material from the past. Moreover, returnees may discover that they themselves are of interest to unexpected others, that they had more friends than they realized, and, thus, that they may enact themselves before a larger audience than anticipated. By the same token, returnees may discover that they are performing before a smaller audience than expected and that those in whom they are interested do not reciprocate that interest. They may find out that their "looking-glass self" has been reduced. The people Maria (secretary, tenth reunion, Main High School) "was waiting all night to see . . . didn't care about anybody." Moreover, the nature of the encounter with the past, its selectiveness, the lack of time, the agenda of reunions which center around the present, the fact that reunions are voluntary events and therefore may not be attended by specific objects of curiosity—the only ones who can inform the present and confirm change—all these factors limit the options of reliving the past or even of sustaining it, informing the present, or validating change. These limitations are echoed in Monica's account. At the age of twenty-eight, Monica, a graduate student, wanted to exhibit how different she was from her high school persona. "A big issue for me in high school was that I was perceived as a 'dumb blond.'" At her reunion, Monica was curious to know what happened to those who shared with her "the drug culture," but more than this she wanted to change her past image. However, her reunion turned out to be a big disappointment, as the people who were supposed to see and confirm the change did not attend. Those that did

> didn't have that impression of me. They just said "she liked sports." They didn't say what I knew about myself then, maybe because they weren't close to me. . . None of my close friends were there. (Monica)

Monica's account underscores the need for the "right" audience, the right "looking-glass," in order to maintain a certain image or to change it. In Monica's case, the absence of her clique elicited disappointment. She could not achieve the goal she set for herself because "the right crowd" was not there. And the crowd that was there remembered aspects of her identity she neither cared about nor wished to revise. Only the presence of classmates who remembered her as part of the drug culture would have enabled her to confirm her departure from that subculture. "Because of the ones who weren't there," says Jonathan, "[it is] like a piece of you is gone." Moreover, the absence of objects of curiosity may imply that they care little about their classmates, a disturbing thought indeed for people who made the effort to attend only to learn that others considered the event, and them, of little import.

There are other obstacles at class reunions that are shared by many other social presentations of the self, problems that were well observed and analyzed by Goffman. When it comes to the past, classmates often wish they and their former friends could perform as a "team"—meaning "any set of individuals who co-operate in staging a single routine."[20] But, unlike spouses and close friends, former friends are hard to control. Moreover, they are never props nor even necessarily a supporting cast. They can talk, and they are either an audience or, more often, authors of their own life stories with their own agendas. While others may play out the author's script, they may also improvise, miss their lines, or act out a drama entirely of their own making, thereby undermining another actor's efforts to enact him- or herself. In the worst cases, an object of curiosity may ignore the attempts of returnees to be acknowledged or may refuse to become an audience.

> One classmate was in my English class and I thought he was pretty interesting in high school. But at the reunion he went on about stuff that was boring, standing there and talking for 20 minutes. You have to be almost an egomaniac to just stand there and talk without saying to the other person "and what about you?" (Vanessa)

Vanessa became an audience for someone who refused to reciprocate and allow her be an author. For him, she was not an object of curiosity. He may have felt that she could not tell him anything of interest, either about his past or about his present or Vanessa's. He might have been, in Vanessa's words, an "egomaniac." In either case, such encounters are usually unpleasant, often signaling that someone seen as a friend in high school had perceived the relationship differently. Returnees are willing to become an audience for other people's stories, but they refuse to be deprived of their right to act and talk as well.

The Author as Audience

Although the autobiography is a social enterprise, and although returnees are curious about other people whose presence is critical to the process, the ultimate audience at reunions is oneself. "I was curious about
my *own feelings*," explains Monica about her attendance at her tenth reunion, while Erich (manager, twentieth reunion, Garden High School)
wanted to know "what type of a person I was at the time. [The reunion]
contributed to [my] thinking about the changes that happened in my
life." In presenting ourselves to other audiences, we see ourselves in the
mirror of their reactions. Through what spouses see, through what objects of curiosity say, through the attention (or lack of it) of class celebrities, returnees become their own audience. When I asked Annie (social
worker, twentieth reunion, Garden High School) why she attended her
reunion, she answered: "It is making contact with that eighteen-year-old
girl. It's reconnecting with yourself. . . . It's not me versus [other class-
mates] as much as it's me versus me. It was measuring myself against
myself." The reunion is ultimately about ourselves, about who we were
and who we are.

If one wants to learn about the past, one must encounter that past. If
one wonders about who one was in high school, one must let that social
setting speak across the years. By listening to stories and conversations
about ourselves in high school, we become our own audience, reflecting
on our lives through other people's eyes.

In attending reunions we not only become an audience to our past but
also to our present. Returnees wish to know not only who they were but
also who they are, allowing both past and present to inform the present.
Thus, Carol (physical therapist, tenth reunion, Central High School) attended her reunion to "tell myself, not that I wanted to tell other people,
I wanted to tell myself," and Keith (artist, Central High School) arrived
at his twentieth reunion so that he could get a perspective on his life:

> You lead your own life, and you have very narrow perspectives
> about what is normal, what it is to be thirty-eight years old, about
> how much you have accomplished, about a lot of things, about what
> it means to come from where I came from. . . . And you need to get
> out of your life in order to get a perspective on it. . . . The reunion
> was sort of stepping back from my life and putting it alongside of
> the lives of all these other people who came from the same place,
> who have grown the same amount. It is a better sense of where
> I was.

Even the returnees' observations about other people prompt a closer look at their own lives. Through the telling of other people's life stories, and their responses to their own stories, from a general impression of their class, reunion-goers gain a perspective on their own identity. Listen to Mel:

> [at the reunion] the thing that stared back at me when I looked at these people, was the realization that I was getting old. I looked at these people and thought to myself, "Gee, they look older," but then, "wait a minute, they look older? I guess I look older." It is a reflection . . . you don't really see their life as much as you see your life."

We look at an audience looking at us and thus become our very own audience. "It is a reflection of you," says Tom; "you look at them and you really look at yourself."

Not about "Them" but about "Us": Authors and Audiences

Goffman has discussed problems of organizing and controlling the performances played out by oneself and by others.[21] Class reunions which are beset by problems inherent in the nature of the event demonstrate the complexity of Goffman's dramaturgical framework. Authors and audiences exchange places, authors become supporting cast members, and some of the props may become burdens. The script is not fixed but rather improvisational. People may go to a reunion expecting close friends to provide teamwork or a supporting cast, only to find that their cast is unwilling to support them, busy with its own drama or, worse yet, that the cast poses the threat of revealing intimate secrets. Some returnees may attempt to enlist new recruits in their dramas, most often class celebrities, only to discover that they are unwilling to play along. The "right audience," the one that can confirm past images or validate changes, may be missing, may hold different interpretations of the past, may be uninterested in the play or in the actor. But new and unanticipated audiences may be interested in both. The ever-changing character of an audience may generate pleasant surprises for reunion-goers who discover they have more friends than they thought, enabling them to play to a larger audience than they had anticipated. But it may also reveal that they did not have friends at all, or that nobody recognizes them. This drama is a multidimensional one in which different autobiographies (some of which may be hard to decipher) are presented by different authors and before different audiences, all at one and the same time. The stage is crowded, as every reunion-goer is author, producer, prop, reviewer, and audience.

The sense of identity that is anchored in such an ever changing and sometimes out of control audience can be as dynamic and unfixed as the occasion is. At the same time, it also means that returnees can choose to a certain extent to whom they will listen and before whom they will perform. Such options allow identities to be constructed selectively; and yet the characteristics that facilitate such selection are the same ones that limit the freedom. The audiences can be chosen, but the selection ultimately depends on attendance and on the problems inherent in the encounters with the past, assessment of the present, and other people's agendas. Thus, the audience which gives the dialogue between the past and the present its opportunity, its strength, and its social character (let alone drama) also can threaten and undermine one's identity.

By introducing the participants in the social drama called "high school reunions," in their relations to and relevance insofar as they speak to the self, in this chapter I have tried to demonstrate the social character of autobiographies, and thus the notion that identity is bound up with social processes. Yet while there is no life story without an audience, the ultimate and most important audience and actor or actress at reunions is oneself. Thus, however ultimately bound up with social processes, identity is still primarily an individual possession.

Moreover, the construction of identities within autobiographical occasions involves a relationship of past and present, a relationship that first we have to establish. Thus, even if the past is not what one wished, one "must not repudiate it, for it is a proof that we have really lived."[22] Not being recognized poses a threat to our sense of continuity, as we have no social past that we can count on or relate to. Moreover, since situated identity and personal identity affect each other, the absence of the former affects the latter.

People attend their reunions in order to inform their past with the present and their present with their past. Others wish to confirm their past or even transform it. At reunions we construct our autobiographies or, more accurately, attempt to protect our identities with material acquired through social encounters with different types of audiences. But on occasions which are surrounded by past and present, which are dependent on the existence of an audience made up of people with prior knowledge about us, many of whom we have not seen in years, not every participant is as important as every other. Former friends and class celebrities are the ones returnees come to see since they are vested with the ability to confirm past images, correct past mistakes, and validate present changes. These critical biographical others are the ones who carry the potential of solving the puzzle with which returnees are faced at their reunions. However, with the frequent absence of "the right audience," the problems inherent in all encounters with the past and the present, the agenda of the objects of curiosity, the potential for change which may threaten one's sense of continuity, and the difficulties common to all social events where one is busy presenting oneself, at the end of reunions too many returnees are left with little knowledge about either the past or the present, and with more questions than answers.

The types of audience matter, of course, but only insofar as they provide the "actor" with a means of seeing himself or herself through the eyes of that audience. Although the presence of an audience is crucial, the reunion is not so much about other people as it is about ourselves. Even when one hears other people's accounts and stories, shows an interest in whatever happened to past class celebrities, is impressed by current success stories, like a boomerang, everything ultimately returns to oneself and leaves one with the tension between a situated identity and a biographical-personal one, as well as with the problems of attempting to encounter the past, and with a threat to one's sense of continuity. What could have been a source of enlightenment about identity may appear at the same time as a potential threat. The agenda ahead, then, will follow all of those themes that were only implied by the presentation of the participants, both actors and audiences.

A Memory of a Collective

*B*y definition, autobiographical occasions involve encounters with the past. The character of those encounters and the nature of the material available on autobiographical occasions form the subject of chapters 5 and 6.

Our relations with former times are effected through memories. As Shils states, "memory is the vessel which retains in the present the records of the experiences undergone in the past."[1] It is clear, however, that memories are neither fixed nor necessarily accurate.[2] Although oriented toward the past, memories in general and changes in memory in particular have a great deal to do with present needs and circumstances.[3] Thus, although the past informs the present, the former is affected by the latter. Concretely, one may discover things that had been forgotten. Things that seemed negligible at the time they happened may gain significance in the present; so too, things that once seemed portentous may lose their importance. The end product is thus not necessarily an accurate description of the past but rather a biographical account that may fit the demands and needs of a specific present.

There are two schools of thought among sociologists about the nature of memory.[4] According to the constructionist view represented mainly by Halbwachs, perceptions and conceptions of the past are affected by present needs and circumstances.[5] Other scholars, notably Michael Schudson, emphasize the power the past possesses to shape the present and thus its memory of the past.[6] My view is in line with the "golden path" offered by Barry Schwartz, who states that "the past cannot be literally constructed; it can only be selectively exploited. Moreover, the basis of the exploitation cannot be arbitrary. [It] must have some factual significance to begin with."[7]

Insofar as memory involves more than one person and reminiscing takes place in a social setting such as high school reunions, it should be called "collective memory." Following Howard Schuman and Jacqueline Scott, I define collective memory as containing "memories of a shared past that are retained by members of the group, large or small, that experience it."[8] Thus, collective memory includes the way in which the collective remembers itself, common events and specific individuals who are (or were) part of the collective, as well as the way in which individuals remember a shared past (what Halbwachs calls "autobiographical memory").[9] The latter type of collective memory, which centers around encounters with the past that take place when returnees interact with each other during the course of the event, is the subject of the chapter 6. This chapter addresses the former type of collective memory—often manifest in some form of public enactment—by focusing on how class reunions are organized and structured.

The notion of collective memory has recently gained attention within sociology; scholars have "discovered" Halbwachs' neglected terminology and his work on the subject years after it was originally published. Most of this research and discussion concerns national memory, or what Halbwachs has defined as "historical memory."[10] This kind of memory, which reflects the way in which the nation chooses to remember its leaders, heroes, wars, etc.,[11] deals to a large extent with people and events sufficiently distant in time not to be part of the individual memories of today's citizenry. Of necessity, it derives most of its substance from secondary sources, such as old newspapers, history books, and museums.[12] Commemorations of these individuals or events are controlled by a relatively small number of historians, politicians, archaeologists, etc., who wield a significant amount of political and social power, indicating their view of how things used to be and suggesting, perhaps, how they should be.[13] Even when the events being commemorated are within current memory, the expression of collective memory at the macro (national) level is largely in the control of a limited number of people. Wagner-Pacifici and Schwartz's detailed analysis of how the Vietnam Veterans Memorial in Washington, D.C., emerged serves as an example.[14] Although many Americans experienced the war and its consequences, the decisions over the type of memorial to represent the Vietnam War appear to be the work of a small group of "moral entrepreneurs."[15]

In contrast, the present study stresses the microsocial collective memory of events personally experienced by all commemorators. Although one might expect that where the memory is experienced directly—as it is by returning graduates—participants would be more involved in this collective creation and presentation than they are at the national level. But this is not the case. Through a discussion of the construction and organization of the memory of the collective at class reunions, I will argue that, much as in the case of the macrosocial collective memory, the collective memory at the microsocial level is selective as far as who does the remembering and what is remembered. While all members of the collective remember, only segments of the collective—the reunion organizers—get to construct the public and formal embodiment of those memories. Thus, despite the terminology, the collective *per se* does not recall and cannot recall; more accurately, it is not invited to recall. What actually takes place is that specific agents—working under substantial constraints—evoke the memory of the collective for an entire population and thus exercise disproportionate power over the manner in which the past is performed and perceived.

Before elaborating on the constraints and concerns with which reunion organizers work and the type of microsocial collective memory that results from their efforts, I will briefly describe the process of putting a class reunion together.

Putting a Reunion Together

Organizing a class reunion begins about a year in advance. Generally, a few former classmates who still live in the area of the school and are often still socially connected get together and decide to hold (and run) the event. While in some cases former "class celebrities" (former class officers, the "all around" people, and so on) are involved in the organizational process, this is not a predictable feature. The first meeting of the organizing committee often brings twelve or even more people, but as the process continues, the dropout rate rises. Not uncommonly, a single person makes most of the decisions on the structure and the content of the event. Even if the committee continues to meet, there are always one or two dominant personalities who are more decisive than the others and can thus impose their own perception of the event on the group. Where a commercial company (e.g., "Reunions Unlimited," "Reunions of America") takes over the organization—a phenomenon that increases in frequency every year[16]—the organizing committee is left with even less to do.

The two main areas of logistics discussed at the level of the organizing committee are fundamental to any reunion. One area is technical, and includes locating the former graduates, selecting the site, and choosing a caterer. This technical domain is where the entrance of commercial companies into the sphere of high school reunions is felt the most. These companies will locate the graduates, manage the correspondence, collect the money, and make catering arrangements. The second area concerns the content of the reunion: deciding issues such as whether to hold a program, invite teachers, put together a reunion yearbook, and so forth. At the reunion itself, the organizers are the "people in charge" who welcome the returnees and, if there is a program, lead and control it from beginning to end.

The role and input of reunion planners in the organization of reunions is crucial to its outcome. As stated by Don Handelman, public events "are constituted through their ... design ... and through their practice."[17] Moreover, in cases where events are invented, as class reunions in many ways are, the "design usually has temporal priority over its enactment."[18] Thus the power of organizers in shaping the structure and the collective content of the event makes them not only key informants,[19] but also people whose voices need to be heard in order to gain a better insight into the phenomenon studied.[20]

Organizers are not completely free agents, however. They are bounded by a number of constraints (real and perceived) that shape the event and the collective it commemorates. In particular, several elements in the actual preparation and construction of high school reunions conspire to reconstruct a selective past in which the academic character of high school is underrepresented.[21] These include (1) structural constraints, (2) financial constraints, (3) the voluntary character of the event and, most important, (4) the concerns and the preferences of the organizing committees themselves.

However, one should distinguish between what organizers perceive as external constraints beyond their control—some form of cultural "key scenarios which provide strategies for organizing action experience"[22]—that bind them long before they begin to make their decisions regarding the event, and what they perceive as their own latitude, their own freedom to choose and act. The length of a class reunion is an example of the former, while the content of the reunion program is an example of the latter. It is, of course, somewhat arbitrary to make a sharp distinction between the two domains. What might appear as a standardization of events bounded by culture, or circumstances which are beyond one's control, may still hold a few other options that could have been chosen; and what might seem to be the organizers' "free choices" may actually be less open-ended than they appear. What is important, however, is not so much the distinction itself but how the organizers perceive the cultural framework within which they must operate, the liberty to act, and, of course, the effect this has on the public enactment of the past, the reunion party itself.

STRUCTURAL CONSTRAINTS

As far as memory of a collective is concerned, the resources at the disposal of high school class reunion organizers are scarce. The cohort—the class as a whole whose collective past is supposed to be commemorated—is not a substantial social unit in most American high schools, and was not in any of the schools that were part of my study. Organizers face the same difficulty that returnees face when they try to recall "their class" as a whole (see chapter 2). The dimness of memories of a collective leaves organizers rather narrow margins within which to work. This testifies to what Schwartz or Schudson claim about the limitations of commemoration that is rooted in the past. According to Schudson, "there is much that can still be done to bend interpretation to one's will—*but the available materials still set limits*" (my emphasis).[23] In effect, what should fascinate us is not so much what the organizers fail to do, but what they actually succeed in doing with the very little substance at hand.

FINANCIAL CONSTRAINTS

Financial constraints are an integral part of life in general, and, naturally enough, high school reunions are no exception. The "key scenarios"[24] with which organizers work are in most cases composites of other class reunions (their own or their spouses', siblings', etc.) which they have either attended or heard about, as well as wedding parties and other "formal events" at catering halls, with music, food, and alcohol.[25] By the time organizers take the above ingredients into account and calculate what would make ticket prices attractive to potential returnees, they are left with a limited budget. This restriction forces organizers to make particular decisions and set priorities, resulting in a past shaped by the possibilities available to the organizers. The question of whether to invite former teachers—which invariably crops up in the course of organizing a class reunion—illustrates this point.

Teachers were an integral component of the high school experience, but at many reunions their presence depends on the amount of money at the organizing committee's disposal. Given that a ticket costs sixty to seventy dollars per person and that teachers cannot afford to attend and pay for several reunions each year, the only way teachers can be included is if they are invited as guests. But the reunion budget is limited: "If it was for free [I would have invited them], but how many can I absorb?" (Jimmy, fireman, twentieth reunion, Garden High School). In this situation the decision of which teachers to invite or whether to invite them at all is made by the committee members who organize the reunion; former classmates are never consulted. By selecting only a few teachers, reunion organizers re-create a memory of a collective which might mean very little to many of the returnees.

The organizing committee at Maryellen's twenty-fifth reunion did not have enough money to pay for teachers to come, but the commercial company that organized the event provided three complimentary tickets. These were distributed to the class guidance counselor, a math teacher, and Maryellen's uncle, who was the principal of her *junior high school*. When I asked Maryellen how she chose those teachers out of the dozens who taught the class, she responded,

> Roy [the other committee member] and I talked about it, and we thought it would be nice to have some teachers that were with us in high school. I think he chose Paul, the math teacher, because Paul was cool. Then Agnes was the guidance counselor, another cool teacher, and my uncle. I felt that there were many junior high [school] students whose principal he had been. *And I said "Gee, I am doing it, I'll ask him."* (Maryellen, school attendance officer, twenty-fifth reunion, Central High School; my emphasis)

Here, the memory of the collective is shaped by Maryellen and Roy, who organized their reunion: two teachers whom Roy and Maryellen thought were "cool" in high school, and Maryellen's uncle, who had nothing to do with the high school. One can only hope that people who had not gone to Maryellen's junior high school (Central High School absorbed students from four different junior high schools in the area) did not wrack their brains trying to remember who Maryellen's uncle was.

Judith's frustrated account of the decisions she and the rest of her committee members had to make illustrates how financial constraints can shape the very memory of the collective as well as how the decisions are made. Responding to my question about why they did not have a class reunion directory, she said,

> It cost extra, that's why we didn't have a directory. The company [that organized the reunion] wanted to charge us a significant amount of money per person. I think it was three dollars for a directory, and then if we wanted buttons with our old pictures, that was more, and *we* felt that for a ten-year reunion, sixty-five dollars was a lot as it was. If we went up to seventy or seventy-five dollars,

people might shy away, because we are not that successful at this
point that we can just throw away seventy-five dollars, or one hundred fifty dollars if you bring a guest. But I would hope that for the
next reunion, even if it is one hundred dollars per person, I'd like
to have it more complete. (Lawyer, tenth reunion, Central High
School)

Although people are willing to spend considerable amounts of money on
their class reunions (flying in, buying expensive clothes, etc.), organizers
feel that it is hard to know at what point the ticket price becomes "too
much."

The decisions that organizers make on this issue have an impact not
only on shaping the memory of a collective and its past, but also on potential personal reminiscing at the event itself. For instance, many of the
returnees felt that name tags incorporating old yearbook pictures would
help them recognize former friends and that, without them, some potential to recover personal memories of former friends might be lost. Moreover, although most reunion directories are oriented towards the present
by providing current personal information about the returnees, some of
the content does relate to the past. The directories as a souvenir, as a trace
of a trace, carry the potential of reminding people not only of their class
reunion but also of their past. The lack of such documents might take
away from the memory of a collective, as well as from specific memories
of former classmates.

THE VOLUNTARY CHARACTER OF REUNIONS AS A CONSTRAINT

A public enactment of a collective requires a public to be present. Because
reunions are voluntary events, organizers are very limited in their power
to make people attend. Although almost everyone is located and invited,
in most cases only one-third to two-fifths of the class attends. While
what encourages attendance is linked to resources anchored in both the
past and present as well as contacts with former classmates (see chapter
1), I suspect that organizers can make a difference in the ratio of attendance. The best turnout I ever came across was Michael's twentieth reunion, with some 80 percent of the original class attending. For Michael,
a reunion was "worthless" without the entire class:

You want to see the whole picture, you don't want to see half of the
picture. . . . It's an informational function as well as an emotional
function. If you are standing in a room and you have the sense that
absolutely everyone is there from that time, that's a much greater
sensation than if you know that half of the class is there. [demon-

strates in a different voice] "It's too bad so-and-so couldn't come," and then again, "Oh, it's too bad so-and-so couldn't come," right? So if they're all there, you get the magic of that fact alone, everybody sort of saying, "My gosh, I can't believe it, they are all here!" (Lawyer, twentieth reunion)

Michael's account of his almost fanatic determination to "get everybody" is a fascinating look into an organizational process that aimed at getting the entire original class under one roof for a reunion. Sitting in his spacious law office, Michael described how he had first looked for potential organizers for his reunion among people he remembered with "the broadest number of contacts [in the class]." The second criteria was "to recognize that we have various cliques or groups, like the athletes, the academics, and try to get people on the committee that were part of these groups." Michael's committee met once a month for an entire year. "I was religious about this; if we didn't make some progress, we used to sort of beat ourselves." The committee had its own stationery printed and kept up correspondence with the classmates. "I wanted it to be an event that you had to go to, either out of a moral obligation to attend or because it appeared so great that you wouldn't want to pass it up." Moreover, Michael and the other committee members phoned each and every classmate who did not respond by mail. He even pressured people to come by "offering to buy their plane tickets." When I asked him if anybody asked for money, Michael replied,

> Nobody would ask that way, but we called everybody and we found out—you can find out from a phone call if they're on the defensive because of financial reasons—and so we offered them some way to get them out. [Did they take up the offer?] Well, they were proud about that and felt embarrassed when we offered . . . and then they found the money.

While there may be other reasons for the impressive turnout at Michael's reunion, it is clear that the organizers did put a lot of effort into reaching almost the entire class. But this is not the case at most reunions, and the entire collective generally cannot be reconstituted. The collective as a whole—as it used to be—is never there. "The whole picture," as Michael puts it, is rarely found.

THE VALUES AND CONCERNS OF ORGANIZERS

The most influential component in the construction of the memory of the collective involves the values and concerns of the people who put the reunion together. The organizing committees have the power to decide where the event takes place, whether former teachers constitute an important part of the current presentation of the past, if and when former class celebrities will be acknowledged, and so forth. More important, the organizers have the power to decide whether to include a public enactment of their class in a formal program. As with many of the previous constraints, here too some of the organizers felt restricted. They felt unsure about enforcing a program. As Maryellen put it, "People just don't seem to want to be bothered with that, they just want to go and have a good party." But Maryellen, the organizer, never consulted her former classmates about their preferences. Her perception of what a reunion should be made the event look "like a party," lacking any formal memory of a collective—something which, in fact, bothered most of the attendees. While the class may not have been an important part of the returnees' actual past, at their reunions they want and expect a public enactment of their cohort. Where a program was held (as at Garden and Central High Schools' twentieth reunions and Main High School's tenth reunion), most returnees wished it had lasted longer. Where there was no formal program (as at Central High School's tenth and twenty-fifth reunions), returnees complained. The absence of some kind of agenda bothered the reunion-goers, who were anxious to experience something transcending their personal conversations, something that would present a collective past.

Where they thought a formal program should be held, the organizers thought it should last no more than ten to fifteen minutes. We will see shortly that even in this short span of time, and within a problematic framework that suffers from many constraints, organizers can point the memory of the collective in a particular direction, even creating a specific memory where one hardly existed.

One of Hope's acquaintances in high school was Alex, a Vietnam MIA for nearly twenty years at the time of her reunion. As the twentieth reunion of Central High School approached, Hope "wanted to do something about it." She wrote to Alex's mother, who was very moved by the gesture. Two months before the event, Hope received a letter from Alex's brother, informing her that the family had purchased an art print (whose subject was the Vietnam Veterans Memorial in Washington, D.C.) with Alex's name on a small plaque affixed to it. The brother asked her to give the painting to the principal at the reunion so it could be hung in the school.

Hope presented the print to the principal at a little ceremony in the course of the reunion. Interestingly, that was when most returnees first learned about Alex. For some of them the name rang a bell, but to most he had been unknown. They had not even been aware that someone by this name had been part of the class, let alone that he was still missing in Vietnam.

> [Until the reunion] I didn't even realize he graduated with my class. His name had been in the papers, and the name never clicked. The picture never clicked. I knew that he was from Central, [but] I never realized that he was from our class. (Eve, beauty consultant, twentieth reunion, Central High School)

> I thought that was wonderful [the ceremony for the MIA] and when I got home, I looked at the guy's picture and I remembered him. I didn't remember his name at the time of the reunion. (Beth, optician, twentieth reunion, Central High School)

If not for Hope, her memory of Alex, her strong will to commemorate him, and her ability to do so, few would have recalled that Alex was a member of the class. Fewer still would have known what happened to him. Hope's efforts created a memory that would not otherwise have existed.

Less dramatic but also pertinent is Susan's (student) experience at her twenty-fifth reunion. After the band leader "announced something . . . Alice sang the class song. I didn't even know we had one. I don't think people remembered the song." Maria's (secretary, tenth reunion, Main High School) bitter account of her reunion also speaks to the power organizers have over the memory of the collective. At her reunion the organizing committee decided to acknowledge the "longest sweethearts," i.e., a class "couple" that was still married. While all of my other informants from that class thought that the ceremony was nice and even appropriate, Maria resented it:

> I don't think it was fair because the same clique [that organized the reunion] won all the prizes. The longest lasting couple? But they broke up every other month, they never even went steady or anything [in school]. I'm sure that if they looked, they could have found a couple that deserved it, but they didn't. *Nobody asked me how long I was dating,* they really didn't investigate. They really didn't know. (my emphasis)

At Garden High School, Jimmy, the organizer of the twentieth reunion, presented a table display of memorabilia that *he* had kept throughout the years. This memorabilia did represent the past, but one organized according to Jimmy, on the basis of what the past meant to him. The display included artifacts that might have meant very little to people who were not part of his own high school experience (e.g., the football team). And in fact, Jimmy's classmate, Ruth (housewife), complained that no one had asked her to bring her own memorabilia from high school. "I would have brought some of my things from the prom." Jimmy's recollection of the past is not to be discredited; past memories are not only "sustained by the world of objects and artifacts, but [are] . . . in part, shaped through the ways in which the world of things is ordered."[26] In this sense, Jimmy's memorabilia not only represented the past, but helped create it.

Though no one can take away Maria's or Ruth's memories of their past, their voices are silenced in the face of a formal enactment of their collective past, an enactment organized by a specific clique or by specific people.

Encountering a Collective Past

Despite the paucity of resources at the disposal of reunion organizers, they succeed in constructing a public enactment of a collective and its memory. No doubt returnees reminisce about topics other than the ones chosen by their organizing committees. But as we will see, the conditions for the micro "memory lane" are difficult, and the topics seldom transcend personal encounters with former classmates and teachers. Whether or not class reunions and their organization alter personal reminiscing, they definitely add a new dimension: a memory of a collective. And the memories of the collective, of the class, are primarily in the hands of reunion organizers. This is true even when class reunions are based on much richer resources—when the collective as such constituted a significant social entity in the past. A reunion organizing committee that does not include a representative of a particular clique or set of experiences within that collective is liable to construct a public enactment of shared past experiences that totally overlooks the existence of that particularity.[27]

The public enactment of a collective memory created at class reunions is different from the past from which it is supposed to derive and which it proposes to commemorate. It is no coincidence that many of my informants used the word "prom" when they referred to their class reunions. More than anything else, a class reunion resembles a prom and thus lacks many significant features of the experiences of a group of people when they were in high school: it takes the form of a party; it scarcely involves students from other cohorts; it lasts only a few hours. The teachers and high school academic experience are hardly to be found at class reunions.

Too many members of the original cohort are missing. The high school itself is often nowhere to be seen. By meeting in a banquet hall which has no special meaning to the class, the class remembers selectively. The class regroups—albeit with qualifications—but it does not relive. It commemorates the past, but it does so under conditions that acknowledge the limits of commemoration rooted in the present.

To a significant degree, the collective memories of the past are shaped by reunion organizers and by the structure of the event itself. Structural and financial constraints, the voluntary character of the event, and, most important, the values and concerns of the organizing committees themselves all conspire to reconstruct a collective past and its memory. The memory that is created is not a literal or photographic memory of the past, but one created in the present.

Microsocial collective memory is shaped and organized in a way similar to the shaping and organization of its macrosocial counterpart. It is selective insofar as who remembers and what is remembered. Moreover, those in charge of organizing the memory of the collective exercise disproportionate power over the way the past is publicly perceived, while the voices of the majority of the participants are ignored.

Though we might not be able to remember our past without the right social context—as suggested by Halbwachs[28]—the right social context (or its closest approximation) is not sufficient for reliving the past as it really was. It evokes some specific memories but not others, while it exploits the past according to present needs and circumstances.

And yet, although it is clear that the present has a privileged status, the past is not merely invented; it sets limits on its reconstruction. Although the present search for a community could benefit from a fuller and richer presentation of a collective past, the dimness of memories at the group level not only limits the ability of people in the present to construct the past, but also testifies to the power of the latter. Thus, this work neither altogether supports the constructionist views of the past-shaped-by-the-present, nor altogether testifies to the power of the past in shaping the present. My view follows Schwartz, who claims that the present exploits the past but does not invent it.[29]

Public discourse, however, does not provide the only encounter with the past that returnees experience. Autobiographical occasions encompass an informal discourse whose subject is also the past. It is to this issue that I turn in the next chapter.

Encountering a Personal Past

We speak so much of memory because
there is so little of it left.
Pierre Nora

$\mathcal{S}$ituations in which we remember, claims Hewitt, "are critical to our construction of the self."[1] High school reunions illustrate a fundamental way in which a window to one's past may be opened. As stated long ago by Halbwachs, memories are more often than not unfolded and sustained within "the right" social and spatial context.[2] Hence rejoining people who shared past times, as well as returning to one's childhood districts (in this case the high school building), provide a locus from which questions about who one was stand a chance of being answered. Unlike other autobiographical occasions, such as job interviews or first dates, reunions provide returnees with companions who share at least some aspects of the same past and thus carry the potential of becoming a resource in constructing one's autobiography and identity.

This chapter addresses such encounters with the past by examining what *prima facie* seem to be promising vessels for an odyssey to one's past. By focusing on the casual and informal conversations returnees engage in with each other during the course of the event—attempting to know "who I was"—we will see that many of the problems inherent at the level of the public discourse with the past (which were the subject of chapter 5) are also an integral part of the personal discourse. The structure of the occasion—which involves the lack of the "right" space, time, and audience—shapes the framework within which returnees must manage, making the revelation of the past a rather ambitious task. The structure allows some room for reminiscing, but even within this framework the past is elusive, the agenda concerns changes, and the knowledge that is transferred is marred by insincerity. Though Lowenthal claims that "yesterday is a time . . . when no one can answer back,"[3] the audience at high school reunions can and sometimes does answer back, not always with what one wishes to hear. Although returnees attempt to inform, confirm, transform, or learn about the past, all too often their efforts culminate in the creation of identities that are threatened and puzzling. If "the self with which . . . we ourselves are concerned is constituted, defined, and articulated through its history,"[4] then the resources about one's history provided by reunions are partial at best.

Although public enactment of the past and personal reminiscing are analytically distinct, they are not altogether unconnected. Both discourses are based on the notion of memory and thus share many of the problems inherent in that notion. Furthermore, while the content of the public enactment of the past is at least partially based on an informal discourse among the organizers before the reunion, the public enactment of the past—an integral part of which is the way the event itself is structured—in many ways affects the conditions under which casual reminiscing takes place.

External Constraints
SPATIAL CONSTRAINTS

Following Halbwachs' logic regarding the spatial component of memory, one would expect high school reunions to take place at the schools themselves. Many of my informants did also:

> In my fantasy of a high school reunion, [it] would not take place in one of these stupid hotels, these plastic places. They are like ridiculous places from a bad movie. I would have had it in the high school gym because the whole idea is for me to have a high school reunion. (Jeffrey, social worker, twenty-fifth reunion, Central High School)

> I wanted to have the reunion at the high school. I thought it was going to be a real nostalgia thing. . . . I thought that it would blow people's minds to just walk into that school and have that feeling, just that feeling. I think it would have put you in the correct frame of mind. [What is it?] To bring yourself back, back in time. To be nostalgic you have to try to get into that type of environment. (Greg, owner of plumbing company, twentieth reunion, Garden High School)

"What's wrong," Vanessa (journalist, twenty-fifth reunion, Central High School) asks rhetorically, "with having it in the place you're supposed to reminisce about?" But there are many things "wrong" with holding reunions in the school. First, serving alcohol on school premises is prohibited by law in the area of my field study, and "alcohol is a big thing at reunions" (Phil, professional reunion planner). "I couldn't care less if they have liquor or not," says Maryellen, a school attendance officer who organized both her twentieth and her twenty-fifth reunions at Central High School, "but I think that for some reason people want to have beer just as a social crutch; it makes you feel a little bit looser when you meet new people. I don't mean new people, I mean people you haven't seen in a long time." Second, most reunions are held during the summer and many schools do not have proper air-conditioning systems. Third, "most schools do not want to have the affairs there because it means additional liability costs and we would have to pick up the liability insurance" (Phil). Fourth, in order to prepare food, permission must be obtained from the school cafeteria.

Although most of my informants thought that going back to the old gym "could have been nice" (Adam, owner of business, tenth reunion, Central High School) or "more fun" (David, lawyer, twenty-fifth reunion, Central High School), considerations other than returnees' wishes lie behind the decision to hold reunions at catering halls. In fact, the one principal I interviewed told me that no one had ever approached him with the request to hold a reunion in the school, and none of the organizers I interviewed ever even considered that option seriously. Like most decisions about the structure of reunions (see chapter 5), the location of the event is a decision made by the organizing committees; no one ever sends questionnaires to potential reunion-goers asking them about their preferences for the site of their reunion.

I can only speculate whether the amount of reminiscing would have changed had the reunions taken place at the actual schools. But, if one follows Halbwachs' argument about the importance of the spatial element in the construction of memory, one may conclude that, by having high school reunions at catering halls, something is taken from the memory and the options for its rediscovery.

TIME CONSTRAINTS

Time also is an issue that affects personal reminiscing. Most reunions are scheduled for no more than five hours. Although some continue the following day in a family-picnic type of setting, the only time people get to see each other without the encumbrance of children is during those five hours. In reality, the reunion experience lasts for much less than five hours. Many attendees arrive fashionably late, some a half-hour after the time specified on the invitation, in order to make a "grand entrance." It takes time to register, look for one's name tag, and "settle" one's spouse. When a group picture is taken or when a videographer asks to interview people, more time is lost. It takes time to get the food and eat it (returnees usually eat with their spouses as well as with other people). Many reunions include a ten-to-fifteen-minute program. The last hour is usually reserved for dancing. Thus, the time for conversations, for face-to-face interaction, is narrowed to three hours or even less. Within that time span, only a limited amount of reminiscing can take place. Moreover, the large number of people with whom one wishes "to catch up" and the brevity of the opportunity to do so limit the options to carry on intimate and in-depth conversations. Irene's impression of her reunion (nurse, tenth reunion, Central High School) is representative: "It reminded me of my wedding," she says; "it went very fast, it was like a big ball of energy. There were so many faces, I don't think I spoke to any particular person for more than five or ten minutes." Moreover, many reuniongoers said that they did not want to "be stuck" with any one person for more than a few minutes, since they would miss many other people with whom they wanted to touch base: "They only gave us five hours and that's not a lot of time, you've got so many people to see" (Brian, technician, tenth reunion, Main High School). "Two or three hours of reunion," says Annie (social worker, twentieth reunion, Garden High School), "where there's a lot of noise, is not much of a chance to really talk with each other." Mel's account of her conversation at the reunion neatly portrays what most returnees experience: "There were three minutes of " 'what are you doing?' " There is only so much reminiscing that can take place in the course of such brief conversations in which one is expected to update ex-classmates about where one lives, where one works, and how many children one has (while showing their pictures), as well as to listen to the same information from others.

THE VOLUNTARY CHARACTER OF THE REUNION

The voluntary character of reunions also has an impact on both the public enactment of the past and potential reminiscing. Obviously, when only one-third to two-fifths of the graduate class attends, many former classmates are missed, depriving returnees of the opportunity to reminisce, resolve unfinished business, be informed about the past while informing the present. "I thought," says Laura (bookkeeper and owner of business, twentieth reunion, Central High School), "that some of my friends would be there, but they didn't show up. I mean, there were people there that I was friendly with, but the ones I really wanted to see didn't show up." The problems inherent in the absence of so many people are echoed in the accounts of several reunion-goers I interviewed:

> There was this one person that I had a crush on [in high school] and I really wanted to see him, but he didn't come. (Judith, lawyer, tenth reunion, Central High School)

> My friends from the music program weren't there and I was very disappointed. (Jonathan, lawyer, twentieth reunion, Central High School)

> You know, I didn't get a high school yearbook. I didn't have my picture taken. [Why?] At that point I was a little bit withdrawn. I didn't have problems with school or anything like that, but I just got to the point [where] I couldn't wait to get out. . . . I wanted [at the reunion] to introduce my wife and tell them that I was married and live in Main and that I work—you know, to show them that I made my mark. You see, I wasn't part of the yearbook. I wish I could have seen five more people but they weren't there. I would like to see more people. (Vincent, technician, tenth reunion, Main High School)

> There were a number of kids I used to hang out with in high school who were interesting. One of them was homosexual. He was a writer. . . . In junior high school we wrote a book together. He didn't come to the reunion and I was so disappointed. . . . And there was this other guy who was voted "the most artistic" [in high school]. But most people who were involved in the yearbook were not Jewish and so the non-Jewish kids got all the prizes—and he was the non-Jewish artist. He didn't come to the reunion. I heard that he has a drug problem . . . and he doesn't do art anymore. (Keith, artist, twentieth reunion, Central High School)

Judith, Jonathan, Keith, and especially Vincent attended their reunions with a specific agenda in mind; there were certain people they wanted to see and talk to, whether about the past or about the changes they had experienced since high school. Judith had some unfinished romantic business she wished to resolve. Jonathan missed the most important clique for him, the only one he had been part of. Keith, who says he was considered "an outcast" in high school and who clearly felt he was the victim of anti-Semitism, was curious about several people but especially about the one voted "most artistic." Since Keith was a well-known artist by the time of his twentieth reunion, one can only assume that exhibiting the present contrast between himself and his former rival would have given him some satisfaction. Vincent probably had the most ambitious agenda. He wanted to mark the huge change in his life: from being a nobody to becoming what he defines as someone who "knows what I'm doing with my life."

For Vincent, as for so many other returnees, the voluntary nature of the event imposed drawbacks. If one wishes to change a memory that has to do with a collective, one needs that same collective, "the right audience," to attend and confirm the change. It was not enough that Vincent felt he was leading a successful life and had made the mark he had not made in the yearbook; he needed the collective to witness the change and affirm it. The absence of the "right" collective might leave reunion-goers such as Vincent and others disappointed.

Within the Framework of the Reunion
THE ELUSIVE PAST

For many who attend their reunions the point is to relive the past. "I wish we could go back just for one day, one day," said Sarah (housewife), who organized her twentieth reunion. A few succeed in doing this, as was the case with Greg:

> I was dancing with my wife. The room was large and there was some music that was very popular back in our time, The Temptations. I looked down the room and I saw Al, and he still looked the same. He looked about fifty years old when we were sixteen and he still does. He aged back then. And I looked down there and I saw him dancing and I just felt that I was sixteen or seventeen years old. I just felt I was back then, that I didn't age. I was back, sixteen years old, and I said to my wife, "It blows my mind." And she said, "Greg, you are not going to believe this, but you're dancing with me and I was thirteen then." And she said, "I felt the same way, as if I haven't aged." It was really a weird situation where I felt that the clock was back then.

Greg's experience, however, is rare. For most people there are factors inherent in reunions that do not permit the past to overwhelm the present. For some it is the appearance of former classmates who "look old" (Daniel, college professor, twentieth reunion), or worse yet, "look like what their fathers used to look like" (Jeffrey). More than anything else, reunions demonstrate how time flies, how people do age.

For others, it is the present agenda of the organizers that determines the reunion-goer's experience of the past. Christine (student, twentieth reunion), who had been a member of the elite clique of her class, had expected to be treated as she had been in high school, "as a member of the elite. And I found that people [who did not belong to the elite] had more to do with the event. They just didn't care [about me]."

Moreover, in attempting to relive the past, one runs the risk of losing a fantasy. Jeffrey, a forty-three-year-old social worker, tried hard to relive his past at his twenty-fifth reunion. He wished the reunion had taken place at the school and wanted a program that would focus on the past. But present constraints refused to let Jeffrey's vision of what a class reunion should be materialize. First, there was the presence of his wife:

> I had a crush on this girl in high school. And she was there [at the reunion]. She was an intelligent Jewish girl and I was pretty heavily into her. At the beginning of the evening, I wished Elizabeth [my wife] wasn't with me because I wanted to put the move on this girl . . . to flirt and maybe to even sleep with her.

Then there was the present reality of his old flame:

> Then [my wife] left. But [the woman] turned out to be such a weirdo. She looked overly made-up . . . totally ridiculous. I couldn't even . . . relate to this girl.

Jeffrey was like the homecomer described by Schutz, who "expects to return to an environment of which he always had and—so he thinks—still has intimate knowledge . . . [but] what belongs to the past can never be reinstated in another present exactly as it was."[5]

One way or another, present reality is insistent and cannot be ignored. People look different from how you remember them. There are wives and husbands, either at the reunion or waiting at home. There are babysitters who need to be relieved of their duties. There is work that has to be done the following day. However much returnees thought that by attending their class reunions they would be able to go back in time, reality convinces them otherwise. Not only do returnees look at their former classmates with "1990 eyes" (Randy, bartender, twentieth reunion, Garden High School), reunions take place in the present, and the present has a privileged status.

"Basically, you know," concedes Sarah, "it can't be the same, it's never going to be the same." "You can't really stay at that point of your life," adds Anna (nurse, twentieth reunion, Garden High School). Randy wonderfully sums up what happens at the intersection between past and present:

I think that the spirit of high school was a seventeen-year-old spirit, so that it really couldn't be captured. But the spirit of the reunion was captured. Just touching all bases, meaning "Hi, how are you? How have you been? You look great" ... You're not actually capturing the high school spirit, you're capturing the spirit of the meaning of the reunion.

THE AGENDA

Dwelling on the past, however, is not the prime concern for most returnees. In the mailed questionnaires, returnees were asked to check off the reasons they were coming to the reunion. They could check off as many as they wished. Of those who responded, 29 percent were "more interested in reminiscing," while 85 percent were "interested in what [their classmates] have done since high school."[6] Leo's description of conversations at his tenth reunion illustrates many people's experience:

> It is really funny because you think that you have so many things to talk about with people, and then it's, like, "So, what's new in your life? What have you been doing the last ten years?" It was: job, whether you are married or not, where you live, major things that happened to you since then. (Car dealer, Main High School)

The same notion is expressed in the accounts of both Dana and Adam. Although it seems that they talk about the time constraints, there is more than a technical issue in their narratives.

> [What did you talk with them about?] Mostly it was what we are doing now, you don't have the opportunity to talk about old times because you try to catch up on what is going on now, and you want to do that with as many people as possible because everybody was trying to talk to a lot of people, everybody. You know, you would talk to somebody and then somebody else would interrupt, it wasn't like sitting around a table for an hour. (Dana, executive, tenth reunion, Main High School)

> We wouldn't get a full understanding of what each of us is all about, or what they are really doing. It was more like [he says the following very quickly to demonstrate], "What are you doing?" "What are you doing?" By the time you get to talk about what's going on, the next person would be there, so you talk about the same thing, or you listen to the same thing, and then you can't finish with that person before the next one says hello to you, because it was so fast. (Adam)

When past events are brought up, they often only trigger a discussion of their aftermath. For instance, Keith's high school girlfriend committed suicide after high school. Keith admits that her death strongly affected him and his art work. At his twentieth reunion he met a woman who was a mutual friend of his and his girlfriend. Yet they did not discuss "the past," but rather "the aftermath, the effect on the family, and how we both felt about it now, because [the mutual friend] had gone back to see the girl's mother recently."

Even those who, like Eve (beauty consultant, twentieth reunion, Central High School), said that they liked to reminisce, admitted that they did not focus exclusively on memories of the past at the reunion, "because you are trying to catch up—married, kids—so it was a combination of both." Later in the interview Eve complained of a lack of time at her reunion. When I asked her, "Time for what?" she replied:

> To catch up on where you have been, where you went after high school, did you get married, how many kids do you have, where are you living, what happened. I know a lot of the girls were married and then got divorced. I mean, there were some juicy stories and you want to hear them. There is so much that goes on.

Although Eve spoke specifically of "reminiscing, reversing back, remembering when," she was interested in seeing "where did you go from there when I went my way?" Beth (optician, twentieth reunion, Central High School) also spoke about reminiscing and capturing the past; but what she wanted from her reunion was "to see if their dreams came true." In fact, the overwhelming majority of returnees are not interested in an annual reunion "because there is no real progress" (Marcia, owner of a small business, twenty-fifth reunion, Central High School). "People don't change that much," adds Lisa (psychologist, twenty-fifth reunion, Central High School), "so there will not be that much new information about them." "If you see them every day, it's the same old thing. If you have five years in between, then we can have a conversation" (Laura). The time that most returnees feel is missing is not time for reminiscing, for reliving their past, but rather time to see and learn about what has happened between graduation and the present, time for autobiographies that start at the point of departure from high school.

A PAST TO REMEMBER, A PAST TO INFORM

While it is clear that the past cannot be relived, that there is not enough time to reminisce, that there may be scarcely any former friends to reminisce with, and that reminiscing is not even the chief focus of reunions, nonetheless, returnees find themselves touching the past. But what do their encounters with the past consist of? First and foremost there is a general feeling of remembrance. Its impact on returnees is not clear, but it is certainly there.

> When I went [to the reunion] I realized how many friends I had in high school. I kept walking and saying to myself, "I was friendly with this guy for at least a year." There was this feeling in the air. (Nicholas, owner of a business, twentieth reunion, Central High School)

> You go there and you realize how close you were to a lot of these people, and then you never saw them again [after graduation]. A lot of these feelings had sort of rekindled when you [saw] them again. [What sort of feelings?] Friends. (Mark, physician, twentieth reunion, Central High School)

> I went [to the reunion] and I realized that there were so many people I forgot about. (Peter, bus driver, tenth reunion, Main High School)

> I was surprised to see so many people that I had liked and I had forgotten about. (Lisa)

> I celebrated that I hadn't remembered what a good time it was and that for years I didn't think it was a good time. And I celebrated being wrong. (Randy)

However, "feeling" the past is not limited to good experiences such as these; returnees may find themselves feeling a past they wished would not be revived. At her twentieth reunion, Annie, who describes herself as "shy and quiet"—a phrase I have learned is often a euphemism for "a nerd"—and who had a "hard time" in high school, found herself going through the same motions, without anybody actually saying anything specific to her. "It came back to me . . . remembering how I was and finding myself *again* just sometimes standing there, not knowing what to say to people, feeling awkward and feeling very much like I felt back then."

More than just feelings, encounters with the past encompass two concurrent activities. The first is the process of teaching, which involves an active individual who reveals and/or reminds others about his or her past. The second is a learning process in which the returnees take a more passive role while waiting for others to refresh their memories or teach them things they never knew about themselves. Often the goal of these processes is to either confirm the past or change it, not by changing actual events but by transforming their meanings. Having an active audience is crucial to all these processes. Not having anyone whom we can teach about the past is as frustrating as not having anyone who can remind us who we were. In any case, whether individuals are busy affirming the past or altering it, recalling memories of others or memories they shared with others, or the way they think they functioned in that collective, or the way they think others remember them, the memory work is a social enterprise and thus attests to the social character of autobiographies.

Teaching about the Past. Reunion-goers rarely find themselves in a teaching position. If there is a process of teaching about the past, it most commonly has to do with revealing feelings to the objects of long-past crushes. Jonathan recalls telling the pianist, "I always had a crush on you." And when he said good-bye to her, she said, "Thank you for telling me that." Through the teaching process, however, one might not only help others recast their past; one might also learn about oneself.

> When you are in third grade[7] and you have a girlfriend, you don't tell her. You write her initials all over the place, but you don't discuss it with her. All of a sudden [at the reunion] I could tell this girl, "You know, I had a crush on you in third grade." And she said, "You know, I liked you too." And I felt like "holy shit" and we were talking about it thirty years later. . . . (Greg)

In the process of teaching his ex-classmate something about their past which she did not know, Greg also learned something about his past. The revelation left him with bittersweet feelings, gratified yet also inevitably experiencing the regret of opportunities missed long ago and the recognition that very little could be done now. And it is sad:

> We were six girls [at the reunion] and all of us told this guy the same thing, that we had a crush on him. [What did he say?] He said, "Nobody told me [at the time] and now it's too late." (Laura)

Even a benign revelation like this is frequently not made because of present circumstances. For instance, Donna (student, tenth reunion, Central High School) did not tell any of the men she had a crush on in high school about her feelings since "they didn't look that great [at the reunion]." Mario (garbage collector, twenty-fifth reunion, Central High School) did not reveal his past emotions to the woman he had a crush on in fifth grade "because she is kind of laid back," and Judith said that she would tell the fellow she used to have a crush on "depending upon what he was like; if he had grown up and was an adult about it, yes, but if he was . . . the same little kid he was back then, I wouldn't do it, I wouldn't boost his ego." Others did not reveal their past emotions because of their shyness. "There was one guy," recalls Anna, who came over

> and kissed me. . . . I thought he was really cute in high school. Although at this point of my life, I feel I could walk up to him and say, "Gee, Tony, I really thought you were cute," I didn't do it. With the girls you were pretty much forward all along and you could say pretty much everything.

While I am not certain that "with the girls" women were indeed able to "say pretty much everything," it is clear that the challenge of revealing emotions to the opposite sex is complicated.

Present circumstances in the form of spouses may also limit the option of revealing the past.[8] In high school, Mel wanted a certain boy to ask her to their senior prom. "In those days, girls couldn't ask boys out, and when the time for the prom came, I thought he would never ask me out . . . so I asked the guy I was going out with, and then a week later [the other boy] called me up and asked me to go out with him." But it was too late, and Mel felt she could not break her promise to the boy she was dating. At her reunion, twenty years later, she met the boy she had wanted to go to the prom with. He "looked so distinguished, very witty, he is a professor who may or may not get tenure." Mel wanted to talk with him and tell him "the truth, to tell him the story, and to close it, but I didn't have the opportunity because his wife was there, and she was very nervous. She probably heard about me; the families knew each other. We all traveled in the same circles."

The teaching process also takes place when returnees do not reveal past information but remind people of past encounters and experiences, either as part of a recognition process or as a way to contrast past and present. Greg reminded a former classmate how "we used her hair for a science project," calling out, "Hey, Lillian, we can't use your hair for the barometer anymore," referring to her current short hair cut. Jonathan met a woman and "could see that she didn't remember me until I finally said, 'You went to my Bar Mitzvah.' And then she said, 'Oh, yes, I rode your bike once, I swam in your pool once.'" Arlene reports a similar experience. She also brought up a specific memory only after she had tried to make people remember her by introducing herself.

> If they didn't recognize my name, or my face, I said "BAGELS," and then their mouths would drop open because my father had just started his business back in the '60s and he kept overbaking and I would bring ten dozen bagels every other day, and by the third period everybody was munching half a bagel. People were saying,

"If it wasn't for your bagels, we would be starving right now." [Did you remind them of the bagels?] I reminded them in case they didn't remember my name. (owner of a small business, twenty-fifth reunion, Central High School)

Although most of the teaching process involves fond memories, and although returnees are on their best behavior and usually control the information they choose to release, there are still cases where reminiscing ends in embarrassment. Consider the following accounts:

One girl came up to me and said, "Hi, remember me?" I said "Oh, yeah, you're the one who got better grades than me." [Laugh]. It just came out, because she used to leave the room with the teacher and get her tests back. And then she would announce loudly, "95?" So I always hated her for that, and it just came out when I saw her. (Carol, physical therapist, tenth reunion, Central High School)

There was this woman. I remembered how she used to brush her hair. She had a unique hair style, static electricity, her hair used to stand up, and she used to brush her hair, and that was the first thing that popped into my mind [when I saw her]. (Susan, student, twenty-fifth reunion, Garden High School)

I had gone out with this guy and had broken it off, probably not in a ceremonious way. I was very glad to see him [at the reunion] and I felt bad about the way I [had] dumped him. I talked to him and introduced my husband and the man said to my husband, "Mel must have told you about me," and he said, "No!" (Mel)

One can only guess how Carol's, Susan's, and Mel's former classmates felt, listening to what people remembered about them and how important they were in their pasts. It is probably safe to say that it did not please them. It is worth mentioning that Carol, Susan, and Mel felt bad about the content of which their memories consisted (or, in Mel's case, the absence of any content), but while Carol did not pursue the conversation, Susan later approached the woman and said, "Gee, I remember other things, not only that. I didn't want to make it seem like that's all I remembered about you." Mel did the same: "Later on, . . . I talked to him, I apologized, and I think he appreciated it and he said, 'Thank you for telling me.'"

Learning about the Past. Through encounters with other classmates, individuals gain an opportunity to refresh their memories about things that are long forgotten and sometimes even learn things they never knew. As Halbwachs says, "A man must often appeal to others' remembrance to evoke his own past."[9] Thus, reunions may provide critical resources for constructing an identity. But the resources provided by reunions are problematic. The reciprocity of the audience is crucial for the learning process. However, although returnees may actively search for people who might teach them about their past, their role is passive. For instance, Maria (secretary, tenth reunion, Main High School) came back from her reunion very disappointed. She expected "more reminiscing" but the people she "was waiting all night to see . . . didn't care about anybody." In other cases, however, the audience cooperates; and Paul's story testifies to its power in bringing up the past, a past that might have been erased had the audience kept silent. Paul's story was told to me first by Anna, his former classmate.

> We were in the honor society. This other fellow was not very good looking or socially popular and he was not accepted into the honor society. Academically he should have been in the honor society. We had a meeting in the basement of the school and he made a speech about how [the honor society] was a farce, because it should be on academic merit only and it was not. I remember him giving the speech and, looking back, I think he was really right. At that point he was more mature than us, to pick up on this kind of thing.

When I interviewed Paul himself about his reunion, he mentioned a person who had made him very happy. In general his answers were shorter than my questions, but the story about the honor society was exceptionally long.

> After I wasn't admitted to the honor society, I addressed a meeting at the honor society. I'm not much of a public speaker. This is all from another classmate's account of what happened, because I had forgotten about it. . . . She remembered that I came up and I told them that I think that when they choose members of the honor society, they should consider the work and the academic achievement of these people before the social status . . . [How did you feel when this person reminded you?] Oh, I felt great. I felt that it was worth it, I felt it lasted, and she told me that she was so impressed by it, and I had no idea. And I felt good, so good. (podiatrist, twentieth reunion, Garden High School)

Not only did Paul not have any idea of the impact his speech had on the honor society, he did not even remember giving it. What makes this encounter with the past even more significant is that Paul was not very outstanding or popular in school, something he mentioned often during the interview. His speech to the honor society was the only time, throughout his school years, that he became visible. Yet he needed his former classmates to recall this part of his biography for him. And if it had not been for Anna's memory of the event and her wish to share it with him, Paul would have had no knowledge of a past that, in the present, gained significance.

The learning process involves negotiations. Returnees do not deny and fight for their version of the past if past memories are fond ones, but they only feel satisfied by what they are taught if it sparks some recollections of their own. Maria was eager to talk to a man at her tenth reunion. Finally he approached her and said,

> "Maria, Maria, how are you doing?" But I didn't know who he was. He told me who he was and that we used to hang out together, and I said, "I used to hang out with you? I have no idea, I have no idea who you are." And then he named everyone I hung out with and I was like "I don't know who you are."

Although this was someone Maria wanted to be associated with ("I was praying that he would come and talk to me"), she did not remember any of their past relations; and though he had tried to convince her by naming other people who used to socialize with them, she remained skeptical. The memory that was offered was hardly a problematic one, but one needs at least some sort of recollection in order to "remember." Laura went through a similar experience when a former classmate at her twentieth reunion told her that he had kissed her in tenth grade. Laura could not recall the event; all she could say was, "I'm surprised, I hope so." She did not deny the memory, but she certainly did not confirm it.

Other and more significant problems with the learning process concern the obvious fact that reunion-attendees have little control over the information they obtain. Although people may ignore certain aspects of their past, "things that we have ignored may be thrust upon our consciousness by someone who points them out to us."[10] Revealed knowledge about the past may please returnees, as it did Paul, or it may just as easily prove to be unwelcome. And reunions fail to distinguish between what one wishes to hear and what one wishes to forget. Evelyn (teacher, twentieth reunion, Garden High School) attended her reunion under uncomfortable circumstances. In high school she was very popular, was an excellent student, and had dated another popular classmate whom she had married and later divorced. One of the most embarrassing moments of her reunion took place when another classmate danced with her while insisting that, "as far as I am concerned, you and Michael [her ex-husband] will always be together." Although she tried desperately to let the past go and told him, "I'm divorced for so many years and Michael is remarried and has three children, he couldn't let it go." And because he could not "let it go," he forced her to be reminded of a past she would rather have forgotten.

Less dramatic but no less indicative is Joanne's account. Joanne—whom we met in the introduction of this book—had a very ambitious agenda for her tenth reunion. One reason she attended was to finally know "what I was like." She had some indications that she was not the popular girl she had wanted to be. At some points in high school she thought she had changed her image and become "popular," but "the only problem was I didn't really know." Her tenth reunion thus presented the time and the place to check what her past had consisted of.

Preparing herself for the big night, Joanne bought the "perfect" black, sexy, "figure-flattering and classy" dress, and new lipstick and nail polish. She brought her very good-looking husband with her. At her reunion she became (according to her account) one of the stars. Many people recognized her and were very happy to see her. To her great surprise, she discovered that she had had many friends in high school. Nevertheless, Joanne was left disappointed at the end of her reunion. Although she learned that "maybe they did like me" and that she was more popular than she thought, "people made it sound like I was a flower that blossomed." A new-future memory of Joanne may have been created among her classmates, but if she was a "flower that blossomed," then she was not a "shining star" in the past. Joanne had to face reality. Though she is doing well in the present, and though she had more friends than she thought she did in high school, she had not been as pretty or as popular as she wished she had been. Joanne's learning experience confirmed what she was afraid of and in effect reaffirmed her past image—an image she had wished was different. Although Joanne stated that the reunion was "a medicine for my insecurities, medicine for not believing in myself," at the same time she says that she "made it *at the reunion.*" The very same process of "making it" in the present implies that she had not "made it" in the past. And there is little she can do about it. Even the successful creation of a new-future memory of ourselves may not resolve past growing pains.

Even when the lesson about the past seems more favorable, it might end up in a bittersweet discovery.

I ran into one of my friends. He said, "I was in love with you," and
I said, "You were my friend, what are you talking about?" (Eve)

Although Eve was "excited" and "felt great" about the revelation, she
felt sad "because he never told me and I never realized it. He was my
buddy." She felt bad for him, for herself, for not having recognized his
feelings towards her at the time. In a way, Eve learned that she was not
the sensitive person she thought she had been at the time. "You feel bad
when you don't recognize someone else's feelings, when you are just
aware of your own."

Confirming or Transforming the Past. Just as some returnees wish to encounter their past in general and thus inform their present, others are
much more specific in what they expect from this informational process:
they wish to either confirm or transform their past identities by enacting
their present. Although affirming past identities or altering them are different in content, they are actually just two sides of the same coin and
thus suffer from the same problems.

It is perhaps obvious that those returnees who wish to confirm their
past identity are the ones who are proud of it. At the same time, however,
they hope to show that they lived up to past expectations. Ernie, an art
director (twenty-fifth reunion, Central High School), could not wait for
his reunion so that he could show his former classmates that he had indeed met the expectations that they (and he) had had for him in the world
of art: "A lot of people knew I was a great artist [in school] and they came
up to me [at the reunion] and asked me if I fulfilled my talent." Ernie
was proud to demonstrate his current success within the art field, especially since "at the beginning of almost every conversation, they asked
me whether I did anything with art . . . absolutely right down the line."

No less obviously, people who were not happy with their high school
identities wanted to transform the image they had had in high school—
or that they thought they had had. Vanessa (twenty-fifth reunion, Central High School), who became a journalist for a well-known newspaper
without any formal higher education, hoped to show that "despite
my horrible record in high school, I still managed to get ahead in life,"
implying that her classmates were wrong about her. Margaret (college
professor, twenty-fifth reunion, Central High School), who defines herself in the past as someone who was "shy and quiet, very strange, never
went to a dance, never dated anybody, never talked to anyone," wanted
to show that twenty-five years later, she "can get up in front of 500
people and teach." Hope (housewife, twentieth reunion, Central High
School) even used the fact that she organized her own reunion as a way

of showing "everybody that I can do what [they thought] I couldn't in the past."

Whether we attempt to confirm a past or change it, the most fundamental issue that is raised is how one can be sure that the message is transferred to other people. The structure and the nature of the event leave too many returnees skeptical about the success of their mission. Jonathan, for instance, felt that although he kept his past "promises" by becoming a lawyer, his former classmates "cannot think anything of me now because they haven't seen me in twenty years." "What they [former classmates] think of me would be very superficial because they really don't know me" (David). "At the reunion you really didn't get into some of the details—you know, behind 'You look great,' and 'How many kids do you have?'" adds Grace (secretary, twentieth reunion, Garden High School). Beth sums up her conversations at her twentieth reunion, "It was very shallow, it wasn't very deep. . . . For five hours . . . you don't really know what's going on." Even Joanne, who was so determined to convey the news of her current success, did not accomplish her mission: "No one asked me what I was doing. No one! I was so disappointed. . . . I was so shocked that it never got past how I looked."

Alicia's account also exemplifies the difficulty of conveying information and constructing knowledge during a class reunion. In school, Alicia (senior banker, twenty-fifth reunion, Central High School) had been part of a clique known for being "elitist." The members of that clique were all excellent students, and widely considered to have great potential for successful careers in life. Twenty-five years later, Alicia holds a top position in a commercial bank, is married, has two children, owns a home, and travels all over the world on business. "And it all falls together," she says with much pride. At her reunion she was out to confirm her past while conveying the message that her success in high school had carried on into adult life. She had been part of the elite of her class and she is part of an elite in her present life. "It goes back to being an elitist [in high school]," she explains. "You want to demonstrate your success, that we were an elite group." Nevertheless, she was not sure that it had been possible to convey the desired image to her former classmates. Sitting in her well-appointed office, she could not get over one particular encounter she had at her reunion:

One fellow I hadn't seen in twenty years said to me, "So what do you do?" And I said, "Well, I'm in banking." He said, "Ha-ha," and his reaction was almost an attack on me—why would he even question that I went to college? . . . He looked down on me. There is no question about that. The response was, "Oh, you poor thing, you are only in a bank!"

Although Alicia's close friends were amused by her encounter with her former friend, now an attorney, and told her that she was the most "successful woman in this group," Alicia remained bothered by the incident, an encounter she defined as the "most personally emotionally devastating experience." While Alicia was trying to use the present to confirm her glorious past as a promising person who did not betray the group she belonged to, she felt very frustrated because, at least in one instance, she could not deliver the right message.

Because Alicia's former friend apparently did not appreciate her current success, he seemed skeptical about her really having deserved to be part of the elite group she had belonged to in the past. Not only did she have problems extending her past identity into the present, but her claims regarding her past identity themselves seemed to be in question. Unlike Alicia, Donna wanted to revise her past identity, to "fight an image," as Joanne puts it. Although Donna was provided with ample clues to her current success, as "a lot of the guys who wouldn't even pay attention to me when they were in high school were looking at me and kind of coming over to me [at the reunion]," the reinforcement from people who made her feel "popular, for the first time," led her to wonder about the ultimate success of her mission. Perhaps—and only perhaps—she successfully conveyed a message about her present, but she has no assurance whatsoever that she actually succeeded in revising her past.

In order to maintain a certain identity within a specific group, one needs an audience to approve it.[11] Although no one can deny Alicia her current success, or her sense of continuity, the class reunion taught Alicia that "identity is always subject to challenge."[12]

Alicia and Donna had different agendas: Alicia was seeking to confirm her past and Donna was seeking to revise it. Both faced the same problem of conveying the right message and shared the same risk of uncertainty about whether the desired message had been conveyed.

THE PROBLEM OF SINCERITY

It was a hot summer afternoon when I observed the first meeting of an Israeli committee of former classmates that had decided to hold a reunion on the impending thirtieth anniversary of their graduation. To my right sat a well-known stage director who was the center of attention throughout the meeting. At a certain point I asked him if he had been a celebrity in high school. Before he had a chance to answer a woman near him said,

"Yes." He looked at her and asked "Yes?" and then he looked at me and said, "Yes." Later I asked the hostess whether the director had in fact been a celebrity in the past and she answered quickly and firmly: "Him? No. No one knew him, and [the woman] certainly didn't know him." This short anecdote speaks to the problem of sincerity posed by reunions.[13] Even if the right audience attends and cooperates, in some cases and for different reasons, people are not willing to reveal what they perceive to be the truth about the past. As a result, the past and the present may be falsely informed.

> We [Donna and her friend] used to send Jake notes in high school, but it was a joke. We used to tell him that we had a crush on him. We made him believe that it was one person [who sent the notes] and he didn't know that it was my friend and [me]. At the reunion we told him, "We were the ones who sent you the notes," and he said, "Oh, that was cute." But it was a joke. [Did you tell him that it was a joke?] No, we didn't tell him that it was a joke, we left it at this point. (Donna)

We can assume that in high school Jake thought, falsely, that someone had a crush on him. At his reunion, Jake discovered that it was two women who had sent him love notes; the catch was that neither Donna nor her friend actually had a crush on him, and that neither of them told him it had been a joke. In a sense they made him believe in a past that was not there. As far as Jake is concerned, his past is filled with women who had crushes on him. This is a "make believe" past. The process of learning and teaching need not be sincere, and the discovery of the past may not necessarily reveal a "real past." The truth is irrelevant to people who do not know otherwise. Yet, Donna's account makes one wonder about the character of the revelations that take place when one encounters the past.

Facing a false past is in many ways inevitable at high school reunions. Following unwritten rules, most people neither take up fights that occurred twenty years earlier, nor do they reveal the negative things they "really" thought of people. In most cases, people are on their best behavior. "After twenty years," says Jonathan, "[former classmates] will be on their guard. And a lot of the time you can be selective about your reminiscing, so you see only the good memories." Even when the reminiscing goes beyond the level of courtesy, returnees are not certain about the honesty of the accounts they hear. When Adam was in fourth grade, someone who used to be his friend started a fight:

He called me "a Jew bastard." It was offensive and I couldn't believe it. If it had been anybody else, I would have said "nuts," and that's that. But I cried and I didn't fight. I never forgot that and I haven't spoken to him since. . . . It was never resolved. And then we saw each other at the reunion. We looked at each other, and I felt bad, and I'm sure he felt bad. . . . I brought it [the incident] up. I took him aside. I had to do it. . . . It was late, time to go, and he didn't remember what he did. But, I don't know, because otherwise, why we would look at each other and never say a word? So he kind of recollected what had happened. . . . And we talked about it. . . . Not that I was ready to fight him then [at the reunion]. We were joking and I said I wasn't going to fight about it now. . . . Then he made a comment, that I wasn't sure was truthful or just something to say. He said, "It was worth coming to the reunion just to get this off my chest." But I got a mixed signal. I didn't feel it came from here [points to heart]. (Owner of small business, tenth reunion, Central High School)

Joanne expressed it beautifully: what she did not like about her reunion was that "people who never liked each other then, got together and pretended they liked each other now."

If sincerity is important when one encounters one's past, reunion experiences pose a threat to the attempts to know who we were, to the identity-work that is carried out at those events. Reunions breed skepticism; the information about the past which is supposed to inform people about themselves is problematic. While probably no one wants to hear the completely unvarnished truth, it is safe to say that the little shreds of truth that emerge at reunions leave the returnees puzzled about the information they have obtained, clouding the quality of the knowledge they sought.

THE PAST IN THE PRESENT

High school reunions promise to bring "friends and memories together."[14] Many returnees, however, find the trip down the time tunnel disappointing and inconclusive. The spatial context is not "right"; the time is too short; the "right" audience is often missing; and those who do come are often more interested in the present than in the past; the wish to relive the past can never be realized and present encounters may end in the loss of one's fantasies.

Yet, returnees attempt to exchange knowledge about the past, though it is often less than what they expected and more than they bargained for. Generally, returnees feel the existence of their past, but this past contains people in general and nobody in particular, events, places, encounters in general and nothing in particular. Even when the "right" audience is present, offering the possibility for particulars to emerge out of one's past, the encounters are hectic and rushed and thus the information obtained about the past is partial and superficial at best. Moreover, while the cooperation of an audience is crucial, it is not always forthcoming. If returnees can control the information they provide to others, they have less control over what others tell them and the end result may be a past that is not what one hoped to encounter. In addition, when the event is over and former classmates return home, they can never be sure whether the knowledge they wanted to convey has been received in the manner they hoped for. It remains a moot point whether they were successful in their efforts to confirm their past images or transform them.

Hovering over it all is the problem of a lack of sincerity among returnees, thus making class reunions a questionable resource for knowing who one was. And if sincerity is important for constructing one's identity, reunions are a problematic social setting for such a task. The promise to encounter the past at reunions seems less a resource for constructing one's identity and autobiography and more like an assault on this process.

Although the public enactment of the past and the personal reminiscing are carried out at distinct analytical levels, they are not entirely independent. The values, concerns, and personal memories of organizers affect to some degree the content of the formal presentation of the past; the structure of the event and its constraints have an impact on the personal reminiscing. The framework that awaits the returnees would have looked different had the organizers considered the implications for potential reminiscing.

Moreover, both the microsocial collective memory and the personal reminiscing share some common problematic grounds. First, just as the memory of a collective is at least partially driven by a search for community in the present, so, too, is personal reminiscing driven by the present; more than looking back, we look forward or, perhaps, sideways. Second, the voluntary character of reunions has an impact on both levels: the entire collective "as it used to be" is never there, and too many people who could have become key personal informants for returnees are absent. Third, the short span of time that limits the option of presenting a more elaborated version of the collective past also threatens the personal reminiscing. Fourth, much as organizers exercise disproportionate power over the way the public enactment of the past will be presented, at the personal level the audience holds power over whether, if, and how the past will be told and recalled. Yet, while at the microsocial level the organizers point the memory of the collective in a particular direction, even creating a specific memory where one hardly existed, at the personal level returnees are more suspicious of memories they feel they cannot intimately confirm. While Alex's former classmates "remembered" him after the ceremony, they were less eager to acknowledge past information about themselves. It seems, after all, that a public and formal discourse about the past holds more power and is less open for negotiation than the informal and personal one.

But what is so fascinating about encounters with the past is that, although people are disappointed about what they see and how little they learn, they still believe that things will be different next time. In effect, 79 percent of the informants who had been to their reunions stated that they intended to attend future reunions.[15] They continue to hope that the "right audience" will be there to testify, that there will be more time, that people will not look as old as they do, and so forth. But reality is always different than what we expect or hope for. Jeffrey expressed it well: "The second time [I went to a reunion] I should have known better; you'd think I would have learned. . . ." But we never do. There is something about the past that tempts us try to touch it, to know it from within or at least to know it better. Though we might not be able to remember our pasts without the right social context—as suggested by Halbwachs— the right social context (or its closest approximation) is not sufficient for reliving the past as it really was.

Reunions as a resource for one's identity are partial at best. To rephrase Pierre Nora, we speak so much of the past because there is so little of it left, and whatever is left is enigmatic.

Managing Discontinuity

> Life is messy but autobiography is linear and orderly,
> with coherence imposed less by the facts of life than by
> the autobiographer's need to make sense of them.
> (Pierre Bourdieu cited in Berger, *Authors of Their Own Lives,* xvii)

$\mathcal{T}$he ultimate, often the only, question that returnees ask and are asked during their reunions is, "What have you done with your life since high school?" This question creates the setting in which people enact their present, provide a narrative of their post-high school life, and most accurately create a version of their biographical identity. Where we are unknown, there is no past to take into consideration. But our past is an integral part of class reunions. Thus, depicting one's present at high school reunions is embedded in returnees' past dreams for a now-present future, in their former classmates' expectations (or lack of them), and in their own success or failure at meeting those expectations. In short, returnees must deal with who they are in light of both who they once were and what they (and others) expected of them.

Such a task confronts one with the issue of the continuity of one's identity. Identity involves, in William James's phrase, the perception that we are at any given moment "in some peculiarly subtle sense the same" as before,[1] and in Erikson's terms, "self-sameness and continuity in time."[2] It may seem almost archaic to speak of continuity in the age of postmodernism. The self, we learn, is "fragmented," "saturated," and sometimes hard to locate at all.[3] Still, contrary to some postmodernist claims, I found in this study that there is still a notion of continuity in our understanding of processes of identity formation. It confirms Hewitt's description of human beings as "meaning-driven creatures, [who] look for connections between things and events *over time.*"[4] Moreover, "continuity over time is a main criterion of identity."[5] We assume continuity; we assume that we are a continuation of who we were. We may not be exactly the same persons we were in the past, but we often think we are. Feelings of fear and meaninglessness, even madness, can be generated by inconsistencies and chaos in one's life story.[6] Autobiographical occasions give us the chance to enhance a sense of continuous identity. Returnees have the opportunity to show whether they and others did or did not fulfill their promise. If we are fortunate, our past identity is something we are proud of and can confirm in the present. But we are not always so fortunate. One's past may consist of images and prospects one wishes to ignore or forget altogether. One's present may not live up to past promises and predictions. Thus the very same setting that can reinforce one's sense of continuity may also pose a threat to it. Here, we face our own past dreams and expectations as well as those of others, together with their realization in the present. "Identity begins to become a problem in life when a person first notices incongruencies between who he or she was at one time and who he or she is now."[7] Class reunions are a classic case for documenting the efforts individuals make in order to resolve this problem. Put concretely, if I was "the most likely to succeed" in high school, how can I account for all the failures in my adult life? If I am a success story in the present, how can I explain my having been the "class clown" in the past? How can we make our current success legitimate in light of who we were in the past? Moreover, how can we maintain a sense of continuity in the face of the American cultural value placed on "making progress," and in the face of the inevitable passage of time?

Returnees do not attend reunions only to be actors; they want to be audience too, to see "how people turned out. You had certain feelings about certain people and think that they are going to be . . . writers or doctors and be very successful, and you want to see if they made it" (Donna, student, tenth reunion, Central High School). Our sense of continuity may be disturbed not only if *we* did not follow through on past promises, but also if *others* did not. Although we do not assume that people stay exactly the same over the years—and the American dream and expectations of progress discourage people from staying exactly the same—we are disturbed when we cannot recognize the oak tree that has sprouted from the acorn. We allow for growth and development, but with qualifications. Explaining away discontinuities in other people's lives goes beyond maintaining a sense of continuity for others. This tendency to explain away discontinuities also responds to the construction of congruency and consistency between our past perceptions and present impressions, as well as to our ability to make good judgements. Concretely, how can we justify past impressions of former friends when the present does not conform? Were we wrong to admire our past celebrities who did not fulfill our dreams? Were our past predictions misguided and our idols unworthy?

This chapter focuses on the efforts people make to align past and present in the context of an assumed continuity of identity. Whenever possible, returnees denied the existence of change, maintaining continuity based on the notion of a "true self"[8]—some form of inner essence of oneself that has not changed—which is independent of both appearance and behavior. When this continuity was not easily accomplished, returnees employed a variety of strategies that differed depending on whose continuity needed to be maintained, and on the relationship between past and present.

When it comes to oneself, the assumption of continuity never breaks down, and returnees are able to align their past and present while maintaining a sense of continuity. They do so by invoking the notion of a "true self," while revising the past and only the past, a fact that demonstrates the privileged status of the present whether or not it is perceived as good or bad.[9]

When it comes to maintaining a sense of continuity with regard to other people's life stories, the notion of a "true self" is raised as well, but the relationship between the past and the present is not always resolved in favor of the present. On most occasions, and when the changes people went through are easy to absorb, there is a tendency to revise the past— much as the case is for oneself. When the past contains traumas whose revisions may raise difficult questions for oneself, one tends to refuse to look at the present.[10] In effect, in this kind of situation one raises the notion of the "true self," but this time it is independent of evidence. Only rarely and under specific circumstances—when former class celebrities disillusion them—do returnees acknowledge discontinuities and dismiss the notion of the "true self" that has not and cannot change.

While actual continuity "may not in fact exist," what is important to returnees is the existence of "a *sense* or perception" of continuity.[11] It is clear that over twenty-five, twenty, or even ten years, people undergo changes, some of which are dramatic by most criteria; what is important to observe is how individuals maintain a sense of coherence in their lives and the lives of those around them when they talk or listen to autobiography.[12] This chapter is about such efforts, about the "accounts"[13] returnees use in order to make sense of their own and others' life stories.

The Assumption of Continuity: Plus ça change . . .

Although the agenda at class reunions focuses on the present and although people attend them ostensibly to view the changes that have occurred, often they are actually struggling to ignore them. Despite the patent indicators of change exposed at reunions—divorce, widowhood, twists in career tracks, parenthood, unlikely success, mobility, and so forth—more often than not, returnees insist that they have not changed at all:

> I'm still me. I haven't changed. (Arlene, housewife, twenty-fifth reunion, Central High School)

> Basically, I'm the same type of person. (Susan, student, twenty-fifth reunion, Garden High School)

> Basically there is something very similar. (Monica, student, tenth reunion)

> Maybe they changed physically, but we are kind of who we were. (Randy, bartender, twentieth reunion, Garden High School)

> They probably saw me fat. That's about the only difference in me. I have the same personality. (Fran, housewife, tenth reunion, Main High School)

This insistence on continuity in oneself is impressive, considering how dramatically many people in fact did change: Arlene recently had to cope with her son's serious medical problems; Susan began university studies at the age of thirty-five, and is married for the third time; from being "a burn out," Monica became a graduate student living in the suburbs; Randy lost his property taking temporary jobs as a bartender; Frann kept talking about how far removed her current life was from the dreams she had in high school, while her husband, out of work at the time, was sitting in the living room watching television. And yet, they all claim that they stayed "the same."

Returnees also insist that former classmates stayed the same:

> People don't change that much. They basically have the same personalities . . . Their personality is still there. If they bullshitted in high school, they're bullshitting now. If they were shy then, they're shy now. (Sherry, dietician, twentieth reunion, Garden High School)

> Nothing has changed. Nobody changes. Everybody is still the same. (Beth, optician, twentieth reunion, Central High School)

I looked at everybody the way I saw them in high school. They had basically the same personality. (Tom, chiropractor, twentieth reunion, Garden High School)

The little boy is a big guy. He is a man, but you see that little boy in him. (Adam, owner of business, tenth reunion, Central High School)

A lot of the girls got skinnier, a lot of them got fatter, but . . . their personalities didn't change. (Peter, executive, twenty-fifth reunion, Central High School)

They have changed physically, appearance-wise. I don't think they have changed inside. (Eve, beauty consultant, twentieth reunion, Central High School)

In the face of obvious change, returnees nonetheless quite easily found the connection between past and present. At times the connection seems almost obvious: "This particular guy," recalls Jonathan (lawyer, twentieth reunion, Central High School), "was very bright in high school and now he's a doctor. We knew he'd make it." But even when the similarities between past and present are more tenuous, returnees seem to grasp at minimal and superficial knowledge obtained through their encounters with the present, so that they can confirm their past impressions and maintain a sense of continuity. A "soft and sexy" voice confirms that a woman is "still a bimbo" (Carol, occupational therapist, tenth reunion, Central High School). If a man remembered as "a womanizer" in the past is still "single" (Beth), this is a sign of continuity. Being "a flirt" in high school can almost explain how someone became "a gynecologist" (Donna). Bragging about children—an inevitable part of any social interaction involving young parents—is understood as continuity of identity for someone who used "to like announcing [her grades]. . . . She was always like that" (Carol). And a comment about cigarette smoking, a comment that could be perceived as merely politically correct and health-conscious, validates a sense of continuity in other people's lives: "I mean, this is something she would have done twenty-five years ago [laughs]. She didn't change that much" (Susan). Those who were active in the drama club "are now teachers. It's sort of performing" (Donna).

Moreover, returnees maintain a sense of continuity even when it is independent of any evidence, making assumptions based on no knowledge at all.[14] From watching his former classmates who used to wear "gold chains and shirts unbuttoned, walking around as if they were hot stuff," and from "sensing the same air about them at the reunion," Chuck (policeman, twenty-fifth reunion, Central High School) inferred that they "are still wise guys trying to figure out a way to wheel and deal out of the system. They are still wheeling and dealing, buying and selling, maybe even into some illegal activities . . . looking always for the easy way"—none of which surprised him. The same goes for Jonathan, who looked "at the list of the deceased" and, apart from one case in which he knew how a former classmate had died, claimed he "could *guess* why they died: some had drug problems, some were criminals. Because they were criminals in high school . . ." It is worth noting that the list of the deceased did not contain information regarding the circumstances under which those people died. They may have died from overdose. But they may as well have died in Vietnam, in a car accident, or from cancer. As we can see from all of these illustrations, people are willing to compromise a good deal on what constitutes good evidence in order to maintain a sense of continuous identity.

Some cases, however, are more challenging. How can we legitimize our current success in light of past failures while maintaining continuity? How can we maintain continuity while acknowledging changes in current behavior? Current failure may also seem too hard to ignore, even for those who refuse to acknowledge discontinuity. Moreover, certain situations may involve such dramatic changes that threats to past predictions are unavoidable. Let me turn now to those challenges and the way returnees manage them.

MAINTAINING CONTINUITY IN ONESELF: THE "TRUE SELF"

Maintaining continuity in oneself is challenged during class reunions on two levels. First, returnees have to cope with the fact that class reunions are a harsh mirror. More than anything else, returnees witness the "nature of the beast" (Judith, lawyer, tenth reunion, Central High School), how former youngsters—including themselves—"look like a bunch of people who belong in a PTA, no zest" (Vanessa, journalist, twenty-fifth reunion, Central High School), and how it is "amazing what time does to some people" (Brian, technician, tenth reunion, Main High School). Although it bothered returnees to see wrinkles, pot bellies, gray hair, or no hair at all, none of these signs of aging generated any feelings of discontinuity. An overwhelming majority of reunion-goers insisted that the changes were external. Signs of aging in themselves were by no means signs of "real change." Raising the notion of a "true self" which is independent of appearance and behavior enables the returnees to maintain a sense of continuity.

Lenny beautifully portrays the struggle to maintain continuity in the face of change, distinguishing over and over again between what he perceived as external changes and some inner core that remained the same. Well aware of his current success as the owner of a chain of stores, where many of his former friends do their shopping, Lenny was very conscious of the possibility that his present achievements would be attributed to major changes in his personality, changes he thought he had not experienced, he did not want to experience, and certainly did not want to admit.

> I haven't changed. . . . I am doing a lot of the same things, going to concerts. I still enjoy myself. . . . [I didn't] become very stodgy, you know, joining the country club, playing golf, concerned about paying the mortgage, putting the kids to bed on time, very parental type of responsibilities. (twentieth reunion, Central High School)

It may be hard to claim continuity and still feel young when one's children are teenagers themselves and one's mortgages are twenty years old. Not becoming part of the establishment was especially critical for those who grew up in the 1960s, as Lenny did.

> The group of students I went to high school with were rebellious. We rebelled against the school, we rebelled against our parents, and we rebelled against society in general. I think a lot of them wanted to see that [I have not changed] because I was definitely one of the rebellious people.

At his twentieth reunion, however, "there was a question whether fatherhood and being married and becoming a business man had made me that much less rebellious and . . . part of the establishment." Lenny wants to show himself and his former classmates that he had never betrayed their past way of life and that he maintains a sense of continuity. However, age alone takes its toll. And even Lenny admits at a certain point that,

> I don't go to as many rock concerts. I don't do the same amount of drugs that I did. I don't stay up all night the way we used to. . . Not that we don't enjoy it, but your body does not let you stay up all night anymore.

Yet Lenny claims that he has not "changed at all. I remained youthful in my approach," insisting that the changes are external and not internal. By accomplishing adult tasks and at the same time maintaining a "youthful approach," as well as a specific past value system, Lenny copes with what may appear to be discontinuities in his life.

The second level at which the assumption of continuity is challenged

goes deeper than changes in mere physical appearance and apparent behavior. How can returnees demonstrate and legitimize current success in
light of a not-so-glorious past? How can one expect to be respected for
present fame when one showed "no promise" in high school? How can
one be certain that present success will not be discredited in light of past
failures? Is it "once a nerd, always a nerd?" How do people cope with
threats to their own positive present identities and still maintain continuity? Phil, for example, was "part of the fast crowd, the jocks" and, moreover, had "a horrible reputation in high school because [after I broke up
with my girlfriend] I never had a relationship in high school, [only] one-
night stands" (reunion planner, twentieth reunion). How can he now
convince his classmates (and himself) that he is a serious businessman
and a loving husband and father while at the same time maintaining a
sense of continuity, at least in his own eyes?

Donna's account beautifully illustrates how continuity is maintained.
When she was in high school, she used to "do silly things, just to get
attention. I was acting like I was out of it." While Donna seems unable
to dismiss her past performance in school, the difference between her
past and her current life as a graduate student at New York University
calls attention to the discontinuities in her life. She resolves this problem
by distinguishing between her "true self"—what she knew all along
about herself—and the role she played in high school: "I was just pursu-
ing a role. I wasn't really myself," she explains. Thus she is able to acknowledge past performances and dissociate herself from them without
generating any discontinuities.

A common variation of recasting the past involves blaming others for
not seeing through exteriors and for past misjudgments: "I'm not as
crazy as you thought I was. I guess that's pretty much why it was important for me [to attend]" (Nicholas, businessman, twentieth reunion, Central High School). And yet, underlying the blame there exists the notion
of a "true self" that has not changed. That "true self" may have been
buried but it was always there: Ron (lawyer, tenth reunion, Central High
School) wanted to say [to former classmates] "I haven't changed but if
you had known me better then. . ." Anna's account is similar. Twenty
years after graduation she is out to make a statement. She wants the
opportunity to tell many of her former classmates that they "missed out
on" her in high school. "Gee, I would have been fun to be with, if they
had taken the time, twenty years ago, to see me, to be more friendly"
(nurse, Garden High School). The same idea is echoed in Frances's account:

I was shy but they thought I was stuck up, but I wasn't and people just wouldn't accept me. . . . If they only knew how afraid of them I was. . . . They really didn't know me twenty years ago. That Frances they knew was not really who they thought. . . . And if I didn't look them eye-to-eye it wasn't because I was better than they were, but because I was afraid of them, and I wish they knew I wasn't looking to compete with them. I wasn't stuck up. (Frances, housewife, twentieth reunion, Garden High School)

By blaming former classmates, Nicholas acknowledges the fact that in high school people did not take him seriously, and at the same time makes his current success legitimate. Frances was never "stuck up" the way people thought she was. She was shy and not arrogant. Anna knew how outgoing and friendly she was, but no one seemed to notice that. Nicholas now claims that he always knew he would make it. It is only "they" who were wrong in judging him as they did since they were not aware of his "true self."

Even when returnees admit that they have changed—"I'm not shy anymore," claims Jonathan—they find a way to create continuity by resorting to the "true self" that was always there. Jonathan distinguished between former classmates who "really" knew him and thus "wouldn't consider me shy and not outgoing, because for them I was outgoing," and a larger circle who did not know him and thus thought him shy. Being "outgoing" in the present does not pose a threat to Jonathan's sense of continuity, since the only people who thought of him differently were those who did not know him and his "true self."

Although former class celebrities who turn into failures are not a common phenomenon at reunions,[15] they present the strongest—and saddest—testimony of the need people have for a coherent life story as well as of the privileged status of the present. By revising their past, and thus aligning it with a less than glorious present, they explain (mainly to themselves) why they never fulfilled the high expectations everyone had for them. When I asked Evelyn (teacher, twentieth reunion, Garden High School) if she had come across any past "stars" who were present failures, she answered sadly, "If you want an example of a failure, you can take me." In high school Evelyn was the captain of the cheerleaders, well known, and very popular. Currently she was divorced (from another former class celebrity), quite unhappy with her job, and overweight. Evelyn's way of explaining away the discontinuity was by revising her past while claiming that her "true self" has not changed.

Most people thought I had everything. They really didn't know how I was feeling, they expected me to be real happy. I had it all. Everybody wanted to go out with me. I could go out with everybody, but I wasn't emotionally secure.

Although Evelyn does not dismiss the past ("everybody wanted to go out with me"), she revises its meanings, thus reinterpreting her past in a way that enables her to create a coherent story of her life: she was never what they had thought her to be. In that sense, her present life is no surprise.

The same type of argument is used by Christine, another "happy-go-lucky [person], part of the elite," as she describes herself in high school. At the time of the interview Christine was in her mid-forties, divorced from someone who "looked like Tom Cruise," raising two kids on her own, and struggling to make ends meet while going to school. Like Evelyn, she revised her past: "Everybody thought I was happy, but I faked it, because I really wasn't happy though I knew that everybody thought I was" (student, twenty-fifth reunion). Christine does not revise past impressions of her character, but she clearly distinguishes between her role in high school and the "real Christine," which enables her to create a sense of continuity in her autobiography.

Mario's account is similar. In high school he was a football star who used to be "invited to parties . . . because I played football and football was big in school. We won a lot of games" (twenty-fifth reunion, Central High School). Now a garbage collector, Mario is recovering from alcoholism, an addiction that cost him dearly. While he reads in his yearbook that he "was popular," he states that he "never saw that. . . . I felt I was an outsider. I have low self-esteem. . . ." We might expect people to hang on to their glorious past, especially when the present is bleak, and acknowledge discontinuity, but people seem to prefer continuity, sad though it may be.

MAINTAINING CONTINUITY IN OTHERS

As I have mentioned, it is important to returnees to maintain a sense of continuity not only for themselves, but also for their former classmates. Here, however, the process gets more complicated. It is not only other people's life stories that need to be coherent and consistent; returnees seek to maintain continuity in what they thought of others as well. Were we wrong to expect what we expected? How can past expectations be aligned with present performances?

In general, changes that one likes and can sympathize with are easy to welcome. And yet, even such changes require some account that will make both past and present congruent, that will not undermine what we see now as opposed to how we perceive the past. On such occasions, returnees once again make claims based on a "true self," that has not changed. Most often they do this by revising the past. Alicia, for instance, recasts past relationships:

> One fellow, whom I never thought would be successful as he was. He is an attorney. He is well spoken and he seems interesting. But I didn't know him very well back then. (Senior banker, twenty-fifth reunion, Central High School)

By making a "disclaimer,"[16] i.e., by saying "I didn't know him very well back then," Alicia can explain her past inability to predict her classmate's future ("I never thought he would be successful"), implying that, had she known his "true self" better, she would have been able to predict his success later in life. In this way, she creates a sense of continuity.

Judith exemplifies returnees who recast others' pasts while distinguishing between an inner core that was always promising and an outer appearance that was misleading. Judith came across a fellow who "you would picture hanging out on the steps of the high school with a cigarette hanging out of his mouth." When she met him ten years later, he was a professional like herself. She explains the incongruencies and copes with discontinuities by claiming that "he always had the ability inside of him to be a good person, and then it came out. He matured. He grew up." However, if Judith's friend always had the ability to achieve what he did achieve, why hadn't she seen it before? Judith's response is to blame him. It is not that she could not see him for what he was, but that he "grew up." The combination of maturity and an inner core that "was always there" is also echoed in Ron's account of a former classmate he met.

> This guy was my friend and then we grew apart. He was hanging around with the crowd, getting into trouble, and now he has a business and owns a house. But it was always there.

Even when present performances are described as "a surprise," returnees attempt to minimize the astonishment and thus create a sense of continuity. Margaret, a college professor (twenty-fifth reunion, Central High School), met a former friend who became a physician—a profession Margaret can relate to—whom she used as her example of someone who "surprised" her. Although she said that she "never thought he had the drive [to become a doctor] but I guess he did." She added that "she knew he was smart." Ron encountered a former classmate who was "very quiet and . . . [who] is now a politician in the district." Like Margaret, Ron says "maybe he changed later," in the same breath adding a disclaimer: "[I] didn't know him too well." Even Judith, who claimed that the changes her friend went through were not real ones since he "always had the ability inside," added that "she really didn't know him in high school."

Even when the present contains elements that we cannot sympathize with, returnees revise the past while bringing up the notion of a "true self." Consider Leslie (teacher, tenth reunion, Main High School), who describes a former classmate at her tenth reunion: "About every other girl [at the reunion] she said, 'Look at her, she got fat,' or, 'She is not as ugly as she used to be.' She was saying this in front of . . . other people. . . . I was saying to myself, 'I didn't know that she was that critical,'" touching on incongruencies between past and present. And yet two seconds later, Leslie rejected that option by saying, "she was always like that." Listen to Lisa meeting a former graduate who

> was in my English class. He was a "school spirit" type. I sort of liked him. He was a nice guy and I had been sorry for not being more friendly to him. (Psychologist, twenty-fifth reunion, Central High School)

She met him at her twenty-fifth reunion, but "he was very cool" towards her. How could his current behavior be explained in light of Lisa's past perception of him? Had he changed? Was she wrong to like him? To cope with the discontinuity, she revised the past: "I found myself saying, 'Gee, maybe my first impression of him was a little more on the bottom.' [But still] I was so disappointed because I was hoping to see a nice person because I liked him so much." She concluded her discourse with herself by declaring that "I think he probably was like this [cool], and I talked myself into thinking he was a little nicer than he was, and then my initial impression was reconfirmed." The past is revised, some "true self" was always there and "an initial impression" which was never mentioned before is now being "reconfirmed."

Although it is the past that is revised most often—suggesting that the present has a privileged status—when returnees struggle to maintain a sense of continuity in others' life stories, that is not always the case. When the acknowledgment of a change not only threatens the consistency of other people's life stories but also forces one to reconsider past judgments—especially those that were harsh or based on painful experiences—returnees refuse to learn about the present altogether. Keith's account illustrates this point.

Keith was considered an "outcast" in high school, someone nobody liked and with whom nobody wanted to associate. At a certain point, he befriended a classmate who had just moved into the neighborhood. When she abandoned him, Keith was devastated.

> She wanted to join a sorority, and they have to be, like, slaves for weeks [to be accepted by the sorority]. So they created tortures for [the new members]: they had to kiss me in public, which, of course, was a terrible thing because I was an outcast. I was sitting in the corner of the cafeteria when I suddenly felt that something was going on, and then I saw 150 kids around my table . . . laughing and pushing two girls [the friend and another girl]. They had to come and kiss me. And they were crying. One of them gave me a kiss on top of my head and ran away in tears and the other one broke down completely and they let her go. (Artist, twentieth reunion, Central High School)

Keith met this woman at his twentieth reunion. Although she came to him and tried to "flirt with me," he would not forgive her. On the contrary, her whole appearance confirmed her past identity in his eyes. Although Keith assured me that he "judge[s] people on what I see in front of me" and not on what they did to him in the past, the very short encounter with her was sufficient for him to decide that she had not changed since she had humiliated him in the cafeteria:

> She was still someone who needs to be approved by other people, and was interested in superficial things. She looks like somebody who hangs out in singles bars trying to get picked up by men. She hasn't changed at all.

Their past was never brought up at their reunion; in fact, they barely talked. Yet their very short encounter was enough for Keith to reach many conclusions about this woman's current life, none of which were complimentary. Keith creates a sense of continuity in regard to his former friend's identity and at the same time reassures his own. He could not expect much of her in the past (as proved by the humiliating incident in the cafeteria), and he cannot expect much of her in the present. If we accept Schudson's views about past traumas that will not go away,[17] as well as the assumption about continuity, Keith had no choice but to ignore any changes that may have taken place in his former friend since high school. He cannot claim that she was a decent person in the past; this might imply some merit in how she had treated him in high school, an implication that Keith refuses to accept. Thus he can adopt a positive opinion of her current character only at the risk of confirming his own low status in high school. By refusing to encounter the present alto-

gether—and, in effect, any positive sign she may have tried to convey—
Keith overcomes a threat to his identity.

Even when there is much less at stake, returnees do not let in information about other people's present that might threaten their negative
memories about those people, thereby preserving their assumption of
continuity. For example, when Lisa was in sixth grade, one of the girls in
her class "made some racist comment about a black teacher and it put a
mark on her for me ever since." Twenty-five years later Lisa met the girl
again, now a woman at their reunion: "I saw her again and she just looked
[like] the same person. . . . I don't know what she does. I'm sure she does
nothing important to me. It seems she stayed the same." Lisa would not
let any current information revise the past or create discontinuity. She
makes the present, about which she knows virtually nothing, confirm
the past.

On rare occasions the present is not ignored but turned into a farce.
One story I heard several times when I interviewed former Main High
School graduates concerned Scott. Scott was described as "a real wild
person [in high school]. We thought he would never make it" (Vincent,
mechanic, tenth reunion). To their astonishment, ten years later, Scott
was a pilot who owned a helicopter company on the West Coast. Vincent
recalls that "everybody was saying, 'I wouldn't take a helicopter from
him.' Ten years later, he's got a company, and you still don't trust him . . .
because you know how he was in high school." Knowing the background
of Main High School, where many former graduates are now working as
city employees, mechanics, and in other blue-collar jobs, one would expect that Scott's present success—the fulfillment of the American dream
which " 'promised' unlimited social mobility for everyone" [18]—would be
a source of pride. Nevertheless, Scott's achievement did him little good.
Not only did he not manage to change the way people viewed him in the
past, but people even made jokes about his present.

Scott's success menaced the coherence of past and present. Acknowledging the unexpected changes in Scott's life, while maintaining a sense
of continuity, might have forced his former classmates to revise their past
perceptions of him and ask themselves why they had misjudged him, or
else acknowledge discontinuity. Aligning the past and the present meant
that either Scott's past or his present had to be altered. But altering Scott's
past entailed a considerable price for his classmates and, as we have seen,
only rarely are people willing to acknowledge past misjudgments. By
not letting the present inform the past, let alone revise it, a sense of
continuity is maintained. If we turn the present into a farce, we need not
question ourselves and both past and present are comfortably aligned.

Although once again we can see here the notion of Scott's "true self" which has not changed throughout the years, the question is why his former classmates were not willing to do what they did in many other cases and revise the past. Unlike Keith's story and even Lisa's, it does not seem that painful traumas were attached to Scott's history. Turning Scott's success into an anomaly may have to do with the fact that his was a type of success story that his former classmates could not relate to. Scott's success story went way beyond the dreams of his past cohort, and was therefore something they could not welcome.

As we have seen, it is rare for people to revise the past by blaming themselves in order to explain away incongruencies between past and present. "There were a couple of guys who were really into drugs [in school]," says Brian. At his tenth reunion he saw them "coming down to earth. They are married. They have kids." Their change, which was easier for Brian to absorb than Scott's, made him think, "Maybe I was wrong about these guys." Admitting that his past judgments could have been wrong has the effect of a double-edged sword. The admission does create a sense of continuity for other people's life stories—if they are "coming down to earth now," they must have been decent young people at the time—but it threatens Brian's continuity of perceptions of people. No wonder then, that even Brian, a rare example of someone willing to admit a lack of coherency between past judgments and present perceptions, adds another possible solution to the enigma by concluding his story of the entire encounter with "these guys" by saying, "Maybe that's the way things happen." Brian allows for change as part of growth and development and thus restores a sense of continuity.

ACKNOWLEDGING CHANGE

As we have seen, whenever possible and regardless of the evidence, returnees tend to explain away any possible discontinuities in their own or other people's lives. However, under specific circumstances the assumption of continuity breaks down, and returnees acknowledge change. Those specific circumstances occur when former class celebrities—the ones we envied and watched—let us down. In part, acknowledging change is a function of a natural inclination for "poetic justice," hoping "that the perfect cheerleader had gained thirty pounds. . . . There is always this little other person that goes, 'Oh, good for you, something went wrong in your life too!'" (Eve).

But beyond this, the "failure" of former class celebrities forces returnees to contend with disillusion, to question their own standards and models, their ability to judge. Were we so ignorant of the "true facts" about

them in the past? Were we so blind? Did we choose the wrong idols?
Admitting that we may have misjudged people in the past may also undermine our present confidence in our competence to evaluate people. No
wonder then that returnees tend to refuse to admit that they may have
been wrong in choosing their past heroes, even at the price of acknowledging discontinuity in other people's life stories as well as incongruence
between their own past and present perceptions. Class celebrities' current
stories are not ignored; only rarely do returnees cling to insignificant bits
of information—as they do with other returnees—in order to maintain
a sense of continuity.[19]

> The leader of my gang was like a part of me that I wished I was.
> He could beat the shit out of anybody. He had a lot of athletic prow-
> ess and he was very popular. He was the head of my club, my gang.
> So I thought pretty highly of him. . . . I had come to be disap-
> pointed in him a while ago because I saw him and thought he was
> an asshole. It was very disappointing to see him becoming very
> belligerent. And other people confirmed to me that yes, he became
> a very belligerent kind of guy. (Jeffrey, social worker, twenty-fifth
> reunion, Central High School)

> The captain of the cheerleaders . . . became a teacher, but I had seen
> her in a couple of other places—a manager in a restaurant, seating
> people at tables. She got divorced, and you felt that she had more
> potential. It is kind of depressing, because I think that they [people
> like her] never lived up to their potential. It seems that, "Gee,
> maybe high school was the highlight of their life." They peak at
> seventeen or eighteen, and then what do you do for the rest of
> forty, fifty years? What is it, all downhill since then? It's kind of
> scary. (Anna)

> You know the football players? When you're fourteen it means ev-
> erything. And I had this crush on this guy and I used to write his
> name one hundred times on my books. . . . He worked in the drug
> store so I used to buy stuff there just to go in and say "looseleaf,
> please." I would buy and buy. My locker was full of junk just to
> talk to him. And then I saw him at the reunion, and nobody both-
> ered with him. He had no life, and no wife, and no kids, and nothing
> to brag about. . . . But you feel sad, you feel bad. (Isabel, housewife,
> twentieth reunion, Garden High School)

Michael was voted "best looking in the class. In high school he was everything. He was good looking, an A student, and he was always dressed

properly" (Eve). Although Michael became a physician—clearly considered an achievement in American culture—he did not live up to his classmates' expectations. "We expected him to come in a three-piece suit with his hair all combed back, with a beautiful wife, but he was by himself." Worse yet, Michael attended his reunion "with a long beard and long hair pulled back in a pony tail. The girls were dying" (Eve). Physical changes that were somewhat acceptable in other returnees elicited disappointment, even anger when they happened to class celebrities. Pointing with excitement to her reunion picture, Hope could not get over how "shocked" she was "to see [Michael]. He looks so much worse."

> I thought he would have lived up to the idea of what a best-looking guy should look like. In your own mind you expect the best looking guy, like Miss America. She is supposed to be the embodiment of beauty throughout the United States. . . . I was surprised because you would have thought that the guy would have kept himself better. . . (Hope, housewife, twentieth reunion, Central High School)

Both Eve and Hope wanted Michael to remain "Miss America" for the rest of his life, and even his professional success was not enough for them. He was supposed to look the way they envisioned him, and he was supposed to be married. Nothing less than that was sufficient to maintain continuity for past idols.

Only in one case, where "the fellow who was the class president didn't turn out to be as talented as he was supposed to be," did a returnee admit that his perception may have changed. "He was never as good as . . . we all thought he was" (David, lawyer, twenty-fifth reunion, Central High School). Although admitting past misjudgments creates a sense of continuity as far as other people's biographies are concerned, it leaves David uncomfortable regarding his ability to see through people and thus, later in the interview, David raises an option that lets him off the hook: "he must have had an inherently good P.R. He must have been a good P.R. person." Here David maintains a sense of continuity that explains the class president's lack of present success while confirming David as a person who is competent to judge. After all, the president had impressive public relations skills. Therefore, no one can blame David for not being able to see through it to what this class president "really" was. It is worth noting that even here David reacts as if there is some "true self" that may have been different from what he perceived.

Revising the past in order to align it with the present exacts a heavy price, challenging our past choices and preferences. When the present cannot be overlooked, we are left with an acknowledgment of change and a realization of discontinuities in other people's lives. And even if return-ees are gratified, as Isabel is, to see that "every dog has its day," the reaction to the current failures of former idols is always sadness, commis-eration, and even pity: "You feel bad," "it's so sad," "what a waste." Anna goes so far as to say "it's kind of scary." Discontinuities are frightening not only because they force one to admit that past potential may mean little for the present, but also because they highlight the fragility of one's own current successes.

High school celebrities embody the ideals we held at an earlier time, and the pinnacles to which we aspired. When their present lives are not congruent with our expectations, we are faced with a harsh challenge. We don't want to admit that we were wrong, yet we refuse to dismiss present reality, especially when this "little other person" delights in a sense of poetic justice. Only in this situation does the assumption of continuity break down and returnees cease to fight for it, experiencing sadness, dis-appointment, even anger.

The Present in the Past: Struggling to Maintain Continuity

The intersection between past and present confronts returnees with the issue of continuity of identity. Postmodernist thinkers argue (among other things) that "as rational coherence is increasingly questioned, so does the traditional view of identity as fixed by cross-time continuity lose its appeal."[20] However, this study calls into question those claims regarding identity over time, supporting the notion that the continuity of identity is something we attempt to construct and affirm under almost all circumstances. Whether in our very own life stories or in others' ac-counts, discontinuities are explained away, often quite easily.

Although people attend their reunions ostensibly looking for changes, actually they ignore them, claiming over and over again that they and their (former) friends have stayed the same. On the basis of fragmented information, past impressions and predictions are confirmed and a sense of continuous identity is maintained. However, some situations are more challenging in this regard than others requiring more effort on the part of returnees to create a coherent life story. Some individuals want to legitimize current success in light of an unpromising past. Some former classmates have surprised us. Some changes may undermine our past im-pressions and competence to evaluate people. Thus, the social context that may enhance a sense of continuity is the same one that threatens it.

If we lived in a world where discontinuities were endorsed, the prob-lem of incongruency between past and present would be more easily resolved. Individuals would be able to acknowledge that they and others could be different in the past and in the present, that change actually takes place, and that life is full of surprises. But the returnees are unwilling to embrace such a resolution, engaging instead in almost frantic efforts to align past and present and to make them congruent with each other. While invoking the notion of a "true self" they claim that the changes are only external, distinguishing between an inner core that has remained the same and external appearance that has changed. When acknowledging change may threaten one's sense of continuity, generate reconsideration of past evaluations, exert an emotional price, or undermine current achievements, they revise the past—thus implying the privileged status of the present—and sometimes refuse to look at the present at all. Whatever the motivation, the returnees are preoccupied with such constructions and with a belief in the notion of a "true self." They struggle to create a world where almost everything makes sense, is consistent, is coherent. Even when returnees must cope with current failures in light of glorious pasts, they prefer to revise their past to suit their dismal present instead of acknowledging change. The effort to create a sense of continuity even when it is undesirable says much about the importance we attach to continuity of identity. Only under specific circumstances does the assumption of continuity break down, leading people to consider discontinuity: when class celebrities fail to fulfill their former admirers' dreams, the former admirers acknowledge change. An inclination toward "poetic justice," coupled with a reluctance to admit that we may have chosen the wrong idols in the past, propels returnees to acknowledge change as a last resort, evoking disappointment and sadness.

The impressive struggle to maintain a sense of continuity says something about current American culture, in which changes are much talked about while its members fight to ignore them when their own identities are involved. Even at a high school reunion, when confronted starkly with the discontinuities of their own lives and those of their classmates, returnees seem to be insisting that they are nonetheless "in some peculiarly subtle sense the same" as before.

Between Situated Identity
and Personal Identity

$\mathcal{T}$he threat to a sense of continuity is not the sole problem faced by returnees. The intersection between one's past and present within a social context generates an almost inevitable tension between situated identities—enacted, held, and understood in a social setting—and personal identities, which are those that returnees bring to the situation and with which they leave the reunion, identities that are (or are believed to be) internally felt.

Although they are analytically distinct, situated identity and personal identity are not independent. Situated identity affects personal identity; who we are, or who we think of ourselves as, is affected by social situations. Similarly, personal identities are brought into social situations. At the same time, personal and situated identities are often in conflict. If we are fortunate, if the person we would like to think of ourselves as corresponds with the person we seem to be, then there is no conflict between situated identity and personal identity. But we are rarely so fortunate; more often than not, there is at least some tension between who we would like to be and who we seem to be. In this chapter, I first examine how the tension between two distinct (albeit not separate) facets of identity is coped with.

But to make things still more complicated, the techniques of self-presentation used at a class reunion go beyond the present setting and the need to survive it. It is, for example, problematic indeed for the most popular cheerleader in high school to find herself overweight and divorced twenty years later, or for the boy voted most likely to succeed to be on the brink of professional failure twenty-five years later. The same goes for the boy and girl, unnoticed and unpopular in high school, who grew prosperous and prominent. These problems, however, are not simply problems of the present and its presentation, of specific situations and the identity that may emerge out of them. Reunions bring men and women into contact with others who remember appearances those men and women have since lost or abandoned, appearances that are no longer part of their self-perception. Thus, in confronting attendees with discontinuities over time, reunions also confront them with discontinuities between what they appear to be (or appeared to be) and what they believe themselves to be. Put somewhat differently, reunions raise fundamental issues about the possibilities of the alignment and misalignment of different aspects of identity.[1]

Over and above management techniques used by returnees as an attempt to resolve (at least to a certain degree) the tension between the different facets of identity—techniques similar to those identified by Goffman and others[2]—this chapter examines the relationship between situated identity and personal identity, as well as the implications of this relationship for the latter. In order to maintain a situated identity with which we can feel comfortable, we may have to sacrifice personal identity. This may involve admitting to ourselves that we are lying. What is important about how one manages the reunion itself is whether the show is convincing, not whether one lies or exaggerates. However, for an internally felt credibility, for matters of personal identity, these issues are critical. Successful techniques in terms of situated identity may exact a heavy price in terms of personal identity. "It is far more unsettling to discover that we have fooled ourselves than to discover that we have been fooling others," states Hochschild.[3] More important, if we stray too far from who we "know" we are, situated identity can be severed from personal identity. In most instances, situated identity is a source of personal identity because we see ourselves reflected in the responses and reactions of others to us.[4] But if we lie, even if we simply stretch the truth, we can no longer see ourselves in the reflections of others, because we know that the reflection has been distorted by the misinformation we have proffered. Thus, impression management is most effective as a set of techniques in the construction of those aspects of identity that depend on the responses of others. But it is not, for the most part, successful in helping construct internally held beliefs about the self.

Similarly, we may sacrifice situated identity for the sake of personal identity, although not in an exactly parallel process. We cannot, for example, so clearly sever situated identity from personal identity in order to protect the latter as we can to enhance the former. Nonetheless, we might, as some do, insist on presenting ourselves as blemished, if only to convince ourselves that we are honest and, even more, to reassure ourselves that the responses we generate are responses to ourselves as we believe ourselves really to be. Reunions are case studies in the possibilities and limits of self-aggrandizement.

To many critics of contemporary American culture, the tension between the different aspects of identity seems one that is increasingly resolved in favor of appearance. It is the claim, albeit often implicit, of a long line of social criticism that the conditions of contemporary life have made the production of stable, deeply held, inner beliefs about the self unusually difficult. Thus, in Riesman's assessment of a shift from "inner directed" to "other directed" personality types, in Lasch's claims about the development of a "culture of narcissism," in Gergen's description of the emergence of a "segmented self," in Bellah and his colleagues' discussion of the waning of "communities of memory," and—perhaps most powerfully, if least explicitly—in Goffman's insistent recourse to dramaturgical imagery, we are confronted with claims that identities, internally felt and integrated across situations and over time, are fast disappearing from American society.[5]

My position is different from any of these. Although reunions tempt those who attend to sacrifice their inner understandings to the dramaturgical exigencies of the moment, the techniques they use reveal the efforts ordinary Americans exert to maintain a level of personal integrity in the face of a culture often deeply hostile to those efforts. Although we will see that many of the returnees did indeed stretch the truth—and a few may even have practiced outright deception—I argue that it is far more striking to observe those who attempted to provide more or less honest accounts of what they had done in the ten or twenty years since high school graduation. Given the choice between embellishing their situated identities and fortifying their personal identities, some returnees chose the latter path, or at least felt unease in choosing the former. Thus, despite the premium placed not only on success but on the appearance of success in American culture,[6] the returnees furnish an illustration testifying to the even greater felt need for integrity. In addition, we shall return in this chapter to the issue—already raised in the preceding chapter—of maintaining continuity. In the preceding chapter I discussed the desire for coherency and consistency between past and present, between the way we were and the way we are. Here I shall discuss the similar desire for consistency between who we appear to be and who we feel ourselves to be.

First, I show how the contingencies of constructing a personal identity place limits on the management of information in the service of appearances. But I do not mean to imply that personal identity is itself entirely innocent. Thus I show, second, how inner beliefs are constructed at high school reunions, albeit in forms different from those usually remarked on by social scientists interested in impression management.

Facets of Identity

The concept of identity enjoys a widespread acceptance. It is "both a cultural cliche and a technical term."[7] And yet, there is little agreement or shared understanding as to what it actually means.[8]

The notion of identity that emerges in this work is within the symbolic interaction sociological perspective.[9] Identity, as generations of symbolic interactionists have argued, emerges out of the reactions of others, which are, in turn, based on appearance broadly understood.[10] Within this perspective there is a distinction between two major forms of identity, in particular: between personal identity and situated identity.[11] My distinction between identities that are publicly enacted and those that are internally felt is for the most part parallel to the distinction between situated and personal identity.[12]

"To have a situated identity is to have an organized set of impulsive responses within a defined situation, responses that are more or less shared with others and that are brought under conscious control as people utilize their own and others' perspectives to form conduct."[13] For the purpose of this study, situated identity refers to those understandings of the self that are public in the sense that they are socially enacted and negotiated, and that they are also bounded in time and place.

It is often the case that who we believe ourselves to be depends heavily on the appearance we foster and on understandings that are socially enacted and shared with others. But this is not always so. Identity also refers to those deep, inner understandings of the self that transcend both time and situation and are independent, at least in the short run, of the responses of others. It is this sort of understanding that I call personal identity. Personal identity, as Hewitt observed, involves a sense of continuity "constructed by the person not in relation to a community and its culture but in relation to the self and its projects."[14] To be more concrete, Ralph Turner defines personal identity as "self conception . . . I-myself as I really am,"[15] and it goes beyond "mere social identity or the subjective reflection of a social role."[16] It is a felt idea of who one is. Moreover, the definition of personal identity emphasizes the notion of identities "brought into play or asserted during the course of interaction,"[17] and thus provides actors with power that is not always acknowledged even within the symbolic interaction perspective.

The Management of Situated Identity

In popular culture, reunions are a stock element of comedy. In episodes of the television shows *Taxi* and *Laverne and Shirley*, for example, plots revolve around the protagonists' convoluted (and unsuccessful) efforts to hide their failures in adult life from former classmates. In the curious reality of actual reunions, something of the same sort often happens, although only rarely in the same tone of comedic hysteria found on television. In particular, those who attend reunions practice various forms of what Goffman, with characteristic understatement, called "information control."[18] Information control does not, of course, alter an underlying "reality," but it is critical to the management of those impressions out of which some aspects of identity are constructed. Yet information control as a technique for the management of identity ultimately fails—not simply, as is typically the case in representations of reunions on television, because of the danger of discovery, but also because of a more basic conflict with exigencies of managing an inner sense of selfhood.

Although I do distinguish the different techniques used—avoidance and omission, half-truths and exaggerations—it is worth noting that these practices differ in degree with regard to two characteristics. First, all of the practices involve limiting information that is, at least potentially, discoverable and that, if discovered, discredits those who have limited the information. Second, all of the practices involve representations of the self the practitioner himself or herself believes to be untrue.

AVOIDANCE

Perhaps the most obvious means of limiting information at a reunion is to avoid the event altogether. By staying away, people can safeguard the past, avoiding impressions they do not want to make, questions they do not want to answer. In fact, some returnees said that if they had been unhappy with their lives, they would not have attended. "If I was not happy with myself . . . why would I want to put myself in the position of meeting 150 or 200 people that I knew twenty-five years ago?" wonders Alicia (senior banker, twenty-fifth reunion, Central High School), in a comment typical of many.

This strategy is perhaps most tempting to those who have recently experienced a major, potentially discrediting life event. Roberta (executive, twenty-fifth reunion, Central High School) had enjoyed former reunions but did not want to attend her twenty-fifth. She had just been separated from her husband but, "mainly," she wrote me, "it would be too emotional to discuss the death of my oldest son who was almost twenty-three." Lisa (psychologist, twenty-fifth reunion, Central High School) did not attend her tenth reunion because "I had so many problems that it was too hard." Listen to Harvey, who organized his thirtieth reunion:

> I called this guy. He is an astrophysicist. He got a Ph.D., something which is really prestigious in the eyes of society. He has this nice house too, but now he is out of a job and refused to come. He was embarrassed, so he didn't come. He told me, "What am I gonna say, that I'm unemployed, that I'm looking for a job?" (Administrator, thirtieth reunion).

Another reunion-goer's story about her class president is similar. She met him shortly before their twenty-fifth reunion:

> Our class president was very popular and he had a lot of friends, but he became very, very heavy. I saw him at a family gathering and I said, "Are you going to the reunion, Joseph?" and he said "No." He had this look of fear on his face. I said, "Let's go and have a good time," and he said, "No." I said, "Everybody is fatter, bald, or older. Who cares?" And he said, "No." He works for a bank. I heard later that he had financial problems. . . . He really looked afraid to go. (Susan, student, twenty-fifth reunion, Garden High School)

By avoiding their reunions, Lisa, Joseph, Harvey's friend, and others thought that they could not only escape questions they did not want to answer, but also maintain their past identity among their former classmates. Since past identity is an integral part of present identity, the desire to maintain the former intact can cause people to refrain from exhibiting their present selves. By avoiding the reunion, people believe they can maintain some control over the way their former classmates perceived them.

There is risk, however, even in the strategy of avoidance. It is difficult to maintain a certain image when those who do attend reunions harbor a nagging suspicion that those who do not attend are in fact hiding something. Even if some do not attend their reunions because of a more-or-less genuine lack of interest or because of inconvenient scheduling, their former classmates are likely to suspect them of hiding something: "If you are a loser," said Greg (owner of a plumbing company, twentieth reunion, Garden High School) firmly, "you don't come to see people."

Moreover, the ability to limit information by being absent is undermined by the dense network of relations that typically characterize encounters between former classmates at reunions. People who are absent, especially if they were "class celebrities"—the class president, a star athlete, a popular girl or boy—are still part of the conversation. Consider the following example, related by a reunion organizer:

> People asked where so-and-so was and I knew and said, "I don't think she wanted to come because she could not afford it or she is not happy." And then we talked about another girl that we hadn't seen. Somebody else had been in touch with her and said that she was a lesbian and so she didn't want to come and be with the crowd. (Maryellen, school employee, twenty-fifth reunion, Central High School)

Not appearing at a reunion does not necessarily foreclose discussion. And the establishment of a situated identity does not depend on the presence of the person whose identity is in question: in describing identities after death—postmortem identity—D. R. Maines observed that "it is possible to have identities without bodies."[19] At reunions, people inquire about everyone they can think of. Thus, only those who have broken away from old friends altogether—or those no one was much interested in to begin with—are likely to be able to limit information effectively. If Lisa wanted to ensure that her past identity remained intact, she would have had to ensure that she was not discussed and, if she was discussed, that no one who knew the twists and turns of her life would be there to testify. But this is a virtual impossibility.

For this reason, attendance, accompanied by an active effort to control information, is typically a more successful technique of impression management than is avoiding the event altogether. Such a strategy is practiced when returnees attend but attempt to avoid revealing what they do not want others to know by controlling the conversation. Consider, for example, Randy (bartender, twentieth reunion, Garden High School), who is still waiting for a big breakthrough in his acting career, owned a restaurant and a bed-and-breakfast inn. "I had three or four million dollars worth of property," he declares, "but it got involved in all kinds of legal problems," to a point where he "had to back off, let it close down, let it be taken back actually." And thus, before his twentieth reunion he found himself with no property at all, taking temporary jobs to provide for his wife and newborn baby. One of the ways he chose to cope with the loss was by not giving people the opportunity to ask him crucial questions regarding his work and financial situation:

> I didn't want to be asked, "What are you doing?" or "How's it going?" I avoided that type of questioning and just asked, "How are you doing?" "Good to see you."

By not asking certain questions, people assume they will not have to answer the same questions addressed to them. But the attempt to control a conversation may very well fail. People may not be asked certain questions, but may still ask them of others. In Randy's case, for instance, though he tried to avoid such questions, there were people at the reunion who could not be put off.

HALF-TRUTHS

When there are matters that touch on identity and about which one is less than proud—jobs, economic status, etc.—one might misrepresent reality. In effect, one may lie in a way similar to what Goffman calls "passing" and what Zerubavel calls "fabrication."[20] And yet, although many of the returnees I spoke with suspected that people lied to them, only one actually admitted that she faked reality, and even she did not interpret her actions as lying. It may be suggested that my informants would be reluctant to reveal to me that they had lied and that this has skewed my data on the subject, but the ample accounts they gave of using half-truths—which differ from lies only in degree, not in essence—convince me otherwise, or at least convince me that bending the truth is much more common than outright lying.

Moreover, outright lies are dangerous. They can be exposed and the exposure can do more to discredit a situated identity than even the unadorned truth. Less dangerous, and more prevalent, is the half-truth— including exaggerations, omissions, misdirections—telling the truth about one's life, but not revealing the whole truth. At twenty-eight years old, Frank (administrator, tenth reunion, Central High School) was not happy with his current job and was embarrassed to tell his classmates that he lived in his mother-in-law's home. At his reunion, to cover what he saw and thought his classmates would see as flaws, he did not lie, but he did avoid "going into too many details." He gave a very general outline of his job and limited his description of his living situation to the name of the town, mentioning neither his exact position with his company nor that the house he lived in was not his own.

Similarly, Mario (garbage collector, Central High School) had been one of the most popular boys in his class. He played football and dated a lot. However, by the time of his twenty-fifth reunion, he had developed an alcohol problem which had caused him a great deal of trouble both in his personal life and professionally. At his reunion, he told no one of his problem, explaining that he lived upstairs from his father because he had just moved back to the area from Texas:

> I didn't tell them that I live in a pigsty. I said, "I live upstairs at my father's, trying to get my act together. I moved back from Texas." I think I used "moved back from Texas" as an excuse that I live upstairs at my father's. Nobody wants to be a failure.

Mario did not lie. What he reported was true, if only so far as it went. He was living with his father at the time of the reunion, and he had returned from Texas some time earlier. However, by no means did he elaborate on the reasons that brought him to live with his father; he kept linking his current living arrangements with his move back from out of state.

Telling half-truths poses less risk of exposure in front of classmates. It is not really lying—it is simply making reality appear more attractive.

The Limits of Impression Management

The threat of exposure is not, however, the most fundamental limit to the management of situated identity. Rather, that limit is located in the tension between different aspects of identity.

Even if returnees succeed in fostering the impression they wish to convey, they are left with the knowledge of their own efforts. Avoiding a reunion leaves the knowledge of an unwillingness to face former classmates. For those who lie, or simply stretch the truth, knowledge of the fabrication remains with them. Those who avoided discussing the specifics of their lives are well aware of what prompted them to do so. Randy, whom we met earlier, understood the reasons behind his "lack of interest" in other people. Summarizing the type of conversation he tried to lead at his reunion, he confessed, "I think I still wasn't comfortable with what I had just lost [i.e., his business] . . . so maybe I was blocking out what I wanted to know . . . because I didn't want the others to know what I did." After the reunion, he is left with himself. Similarly, the need to paint the picture of one's life in rosier colors and the urge to control information imply that something is wrong. Thus, controlling information might help returnees sustain an identity within the context of the reunion, an identity that is socially enacted. But it is not possible to escape the implications of that effort for an internally felt identity.

Discomfort with impression management is not limited to those who feel they have something to hide. Indeed, a general feature of reunions is a characteristically widespread skepticism. Although a few returnees believed the ability to deceive was limited by long familiarity, most did not share that faith. Many of the informants were certain that people did try to "fool" them. As one respondent put it, "I know everybody goes a little bit farther than what actually happened" (Leo, car dealer, tenth reunion, Main High School). "I'm sure that if they are not doing well, they are not going to tell anybody," affirmed Brian (technician, tenth reunion, Main High School). And another one added, "I knew everyone was pretty great in front and [I] felt that maybe behind all these great fronts some rough times had occurred" (Monica, student, tenth reunion). Even the "props"—those physical properties that may be used to set a scene, and that have a sort of face validity—are treated with skepticism: "There was this fellow," says Keith (artist, twentieth reunion, Central High School), "wearing a suit that must have cost $800 and . . . a very expensive watch. It might have been fake, all of it."

At times, the skepticism is based on clear-cut evidence. One respondent reported people at her reunion who

> bragged that they were successful but we found out later that most . . . were living in their parents' homes. They never really bought their own, they just kept the family home after the parents moved away. This one guy was bragging that he played tennis with the guy that does the news [on CBS]. We found out later that he didn't, he was lying. (Isabel, housewife, twentieth reunion, Garden High School)

A particularly dramatic example was provided by a reunion organizer who had access to the questionnaires sent to her by former classmates. Going over them, she found,

> Someone [originally wrote] that he works in the bag room, but he crossed that out and just wrote "TWA airlines." (Hope, housewife, twentieth reunion, Central High School)

Some of the returnees, she added, "could have lied about their occupations. How would you know? Well I wouldn't."

Skepticism is further reinforced by reunion-goers' own behavior. Many who attended discovered that their own responses fell somewhat short of what they understood to be the truth: "If they didn't look good," Irene (nurse, tenth reunion, Central High School) admits in the spirit of many other comments, "you lied and said they did." From their own behavior, those who attend reunions generalize. They become skeptical not only about others' accounts of their lives, but even of how others respond to them.

This skepticism creates technical problems for impression management. The mistrust which greets accounts makes it difficult for reunion-goers to convince their former classmates of the truth of even actual accomplishments. Knowing that returnees are not necessarily honest makes one recognize that the message one wants to convey may not have been correctly received, that the response may have been motivated more by courtesy than by honesty. But the consequences of skepticism go much further as the entire reunion begins to appear, to the returnees themselves, as an exercise in impression management. Although none of my respondents mentioned Goffman, many were surely alert to the possibility that the reunion should be read as a piece of dramaturgy and that there could be significant discrepancies between "fostered appearances and reality."[21] Faced with what they believed to be massive efforts at impression management, those who attend reunions begin to question the very significance of those impressions, regardless of their actual relation to a perceived truth. As Grace (secretary, twenty-fifth reunion, Central High School) put it, "The reunion wasn't really an opening-up situation." Eve was more expansive.

> [The reunion] is an external view, in school you knew more inti-
> mately what was going on in each other's lives. As for now, I have
> no idea. You see what they want you to see, you dress up, you are
> in party gear, but you haven't been intimately related with them
> like a next-door neighbor. (Beauty consultant, twentieth reunion,
> Central High School)

Implicit in the language of "fronts" and "opening-up" is an idea of personal identity that goes well beyond impressions. At times, this notion becomes explicit as reunion-goers admit that they are not sure who other people "really" were, or whether they "really" knew each other. In these circumstances, the sense of reality begins to implode. The implications of impression management for identity, in any sense, collapse under the weight of a massive self-consciousness.

Over and above a situation that one might survive by whatever technique one uses, is a personal identity that one must live with; an identity that transcends both time and place. Even if the situated identity is sustained—itself an uncertainty in light of the risks of disclosure and in the general skepticism that characterizes reunions—identities based on appearance do not go beyond the circumstances of the reunion itself if they are based either on matters felt to be superficial or on self-acknowledged deception. To be sure, the appearance may become the basis for an inner identity as broad, trans-situational self-concepts are built out of the responses of others. But this "looking-glass self"[22] requires that the actor have at least some conviction that the mirror into which he or she peers is honest and clear. If the actor knows that the mirror is distorted—whether by his or her own efforts, or by the general air of unreality that pervades reunions—it will provide no credible reflection. The identity built out of such a reflection, like the distorted images of a funhouse mirror, may provide momentary amusement, but little of even an illusion of the truth.

The Management of Personal Identity

Like the construction of appearance, maintaining an inner identity involves impression management. No less—or perhaps only slightly less—than the construction of appearances, it may involve deception. However, because an inner identity involves something internally felt rather than socially enacted, it cannot be constructed out of material the actor himself or herself believes to be untrue. Thus, while the construction of inner identities may involve deceptions, they are more likely to be self-deceptions than deceptions of others.

ADMISSIONS

From the point of view of situated identity, the admission—openly acknowledging flaws in one's identity—does have a virtue: it creates the impression, if not always the reality, of integrity. But it is not in the service of situated identity that reunion-goers are most likely to admit their failures, as in the service of personal identity. They are less interested in the impression of integrity than in their own belief in that integrity. The admission of failure is not easy; it may be a threat to the situated identity carefully constructed and built up over the years. Yet, to some returnees, the admission of failure appears the only way to avoid the internal conflict that would accompany an account that, even aside from any fear of discovery, the storyteller could not accept as the "real me."

Consider the following account related by a reunion organizer:

> Our class president was Richard Tylor. . . . Two weeks before the reunion, his business went bust and he was on the verge of personal bankruptcy. And he didn't want to go [to the reunion]. He said to me, "It is really hard for me to tell people that I'm doing badly." And I said, "Why in the world are you saying that, are you nuts?

... you still own your business, at least formally. Yes, it's bankrupt, but who the hell knows that and who the hell is going to ask? Just tell them what you do: you still do it ... it is not a lie ... nobody is asking for a loan and interested in seeing your financials; they just want to know what you do ... and I think you want to present yourself in an upbeat way. Maybe you are putting on a rosier face, but there is nothing wrong with that, because even if you go bankrupt tomorrow, that doesn't mean that two weeks from tomorrow you are not going to bounce back again, so what does one week mean? You should just ... go as Richard Tylor, the class president." [So what did he do at the reunion?] He just moped around, telling everybody about his personal problems. (Michael, lawyer, twentieth reunion)

Michael advised that Richard manage impressions by ignoring present events, treating the reunion as if it were taking place two weeks before it actually did. To be sure, he did not suggest that Richard actually lie, but rather that he should merely treat the events of his life selectively, abandoning what Michael called the "truth of the moment" in the name of what might be thought of, with some generosity, as a "higher truth." But Richard's strategy was different. Although I do not have his own account of the reunion, I do know that as a former class president, Richard had a past worth protecting. Nonetheless, he endangered the meanings of that past in the service of what appears to be his own felt sense of integrity. Richard, it seems, could not pretend that nothing had happened. By lying to his classmates he would have been lying to himself, something he did not like to do or did not have the energy to do. Hence Richard chose to tell the truth about himself; saying what he believed to be the truth about himself took priority over any impression he could foster among his classmates. As a consequence, former classmates might look down on him or, even worse, use the present in order to discredit Richard's past identity. On the other hand, they might appreciate his having told them what was really going on in his life.

In the case of Randy, whom we met earlier, we have more direct evidence of the process involved in admitting failure. Randy had suffered a serious business setback prior to his reunion. He hesitated about whether to tell his former classmates the truth and in some cases chose to avoid specific conversations. But he reported proudly, "I wound up telling the truth because I'm that kind of person" (Randy). As in Richard's case, the admission of failure may serve to create an impression of integrity. But for Randy and (I suspect) Richard, the impression of integrity made on others was far less important than the impression of integrity made on themselves.

DETACHMENT

Another technique commonly employed to protect inner identity is what might be called detachment—or, more specifically, an effort to detach one's "self" from the situation of the reunion. High school reunions are, among other things, a ritual enactment of specific cultural values, those that dominated the high school class as well as those that pervade former classmates' current lives. But some of those who attend reunions may never have thoroughly shared in those values; others may have drifted away. For them the issue is not a matter of admitting or concealing failure, but contesting what constitutes success and failure. For them, then, the central problem of the reunion is one of remaining true to the values they feel they have lived by, refusing to join in the management of impressions that contributed to an appearance of success they find empty. Moreover, by contesting these values, those who attend reunions detach themselves from those who, at least apparently, hold to these values. In a process similar to that analyzed by Sykes and Matza among deviant populations,[23] they neutralize the reunion as a source of identity. It is important to note that this detachment may be publicly enacted, but it is more clearly a matter of private conviction. One respondent, Jeffrey, neatly exemplified the dimensions of this process:

> I pretty much feel independent of my so-called position in life, because I don't put a lot of credence in that kind of thing. I don't care what somebody has achieved, I think that's a lot of bullshit. People are rich and full when they come into the world and I think they slowly get more and more messed up. So, I'm not big on achieving anything. . . . Who are these people? . . . [I am] like an old hippie kind of guy. . . . I'm not impressed by status. (Jeffrey, social worker, twenty-fifth reunion, Central High School)

Like many others who attend reunions, Jeffrey attempts, in an internal conversation, to discredit his former classmates as suitable partners in the establishment of his identity: "Who are these people?" To do this, Jeffrey questions their values, suggesting that "they slowly get more and more messed up," and proposing an alternative mode of evaluation from the point of view of "an old hippie kind of guy." Moreover, and perhaps more fundamentally, Jeffrey evokes a notion of selfhood quite different from that implicit in impression management. His identity, he argues, is "independent" of his "so-called position in life." Neither does his identity depend on achievement measured by a system he thinks is not praiseworthy: "That's a lot of bullshit."

A variant of this approach can be found in the accounts of a number of returnees who did not challenge the value system as a whole but only parts of it—parts that more often than not are determined by their own achievements.[24] And those achievements become the exclusive virtues by which they judge others. Consequently, all the people they meet throughout the event are perceived as imperfect, semideviant, or immature. Matthew, a twenty-eight-year-old teacher from a middle-class background, felt vulnerable in a room filled with doctors, lawyers, and business people because of his low income. Nonetheless, he insisted that his work was important, even if not well paid, and pointed to his successful marriage. Thus Matthew looks at his classmates through "marriage glasses":

> If a person is not married or has no serious relationship at twenty-eight or twenty-nine, . . . I would consider it a bit weird. . . Out of the norm. (Matthew, teacher, tenth reunion, Central High School)

Like other reunion-goers, Matthew found a way to cope with flaws in his own identity. For him, family life was the key to maturity and normality, and it is through that prism that he regards the reunion. This strategy reshapes reality to make whatever has happened in one's life the sole scale according to which others, as well as oneself, are judged. For example, those who sacrificed family life for the sake of career would look down on former classmates who had ended up raising five children while staying at home.

Another version of Jeffrey's and Matthew's responses to their reunions can be found among returnees who treated their former classmates' success with skepticism. By making light of others' achievements, by undermining former friends' present success stories, and by focusing on the darker side of other people's lives, one can cope with one's own failures. By recognizing that the grass is not necessarily greener somewhere else, one might be able to cope with the fact that one's own life story is not perfect without its imperfections threatening one's identity. Listen to Evelyn—whom we met earlier—and to Grace summarizing their reunion experience.

> In some ways [the reunion] takes away some of the pain. You think that everyone else is doing so much better, and then you see that even Andrea is not that happy. She was married, very, very smart,

[but] she went through a divorce. She was a hot-shot in high school. . . . She is a lawyer in a famous law firm, and she remarried, but she is not a happy person now. . . . I had this fantasy that she was doing great and I had gone wrong. . . . The reunion killed some of my fantasies. It brought me back to reality. I went there and I saw what people are doing. It is good to see that people are just people. (Evelyn)

I always think that the grass is greener somewhere else and then when you grow up you realize how phony that is, how everybody has a story and there are many things that they didn't want that happened. (Grace)

Minimizing other people's success stories does not run the same risks as other techniques. One is not exposed for what one is not. Nonetheless, anyone using this strategy might encounter success stories that are hard to dismiss. They might discover that their fantasies (or nightmares) have come true, at which point they might choose to use a variation of the same strategy: not minimizing other's success stories but emphasizing the costs inherent in achieving that success. In Garden High School, for example, one classmate became a physician and another became a lawyer. In the context of the predominantly lower-middle-class school reunion, both were the subject of a good deal of talk and could have constituted a problem. However, their less successful classmates did not feel that their own identities were threatened, pointing instead to the problems of professional life. "They have headaches. I leave work, I come home and relax" (Jimmy, fireman, twentieth reunion, Garden High School). Greg had the same type of reaction:

I wouldn't be happy being a doctor, I have a lot of friends that are doctors and I don't admire their lifestyle. I love what I do. I like the fact that I have the weekends off . . . that I'm not on twenty-four-hour-a-day call. (Greg)

I see a lot of these kids [his former classmates] and their values are very monetary. They have everything but love, so they have nothing. They are into drugs. (Barry, teacher, twenty-fifth reunion, Garden High School)

Neither Jimmy nor Greg nor Barry denied that their classmates had succeeded according to at least some criteria. However, they did question the value of such criteria, emphasizing the dark side of professional life as compared to their own ways of life.

The Limits of Personal Identity

Personal identity in contemporary America is often voluntary. People can, to a significant extent, select the ways in which they construct their understanding of themselves, the anchors by which they are held to their identity.[25] In some ways, they are free to choose specific roles and behaviors around which their identity can be worked out. Indeed, the ability of some returnees to reject the values of their classmates, to eschew the construction of an imposing situated identity in favor of the integrity of a personal one, is testimony to the degree of freedom in this regard.

But we should not imagine that this freedom is by any means complete. Even those who, like Jeffrey, place themselves above the moment are not able to ignore entirely the evaluative process that is an inevitable aspect of reunions. Jeffrey, even while disdaining the arts of impression management, is prepared to consider the possibility that he should judge himself as he imagines his former classmates judge him. Moreover, he is too aware that his entire ideology—his value system and his judgments of the people he met—is derived at least in part from his dissatisfaction with himself: "Maybe it's sour grapes on my part, you know what I mean? In other words, I have accomplished absolutely nothing. I feel so bad about myself, I really do." Thus, an insistence on a distinctive set of values as the basis of a personal identity is constantly threatened at reunions by the enactment of situated identity that is poorly aligned with the personal.

Moreover, no one—including those who present an alternative set of values—lives in a cultural vacuum. A person's mind, as Mead observed, is "taken from the community to which he belongs."[26] In light of this, then, it is not so surprising that Matthew acknowledged some doubts about his insistence on evaluating himself, and others, according to the standard of success in family life. He could not entirely remove the pain of confronting former classmates whose careers had been more successful. Sadly and bitterly Matthew comments on American society, of which he is an integral part:

> When you think about the doctors and the lawyers that make $200,000 a year, it makes you wonder. There is a bit of a pain there. You might fall into the trap of most Americans: most Americans equate money with success . . . but this is the kind of world we live in and I live in America, and we have to try [to achieve financial success].

The more one listens to Matthew, the more one hears his struggle to mask his problems with his own identity by seeking out only those who would confirm and reinforce his own choices. It is not easy to sustain a belief in one's personal identity independent of a situation.

Minimizing other people's success implies that personal identity does not depend directly or entirely on situated identity. But similarly, by acknowledging that one is not worse off than others, or emphasizing the disadvantages of other people's lives, one takes some of the sting away, but not all of it. It is patently obvious that Barry, Jimmy, and Greg wished they were doing something different. And it is telling to consider that one can be comforted by other people's failures or tragedies.

Still, these caveats notwithstanding, personal identity can be severed, at least in part, from situated identity. Richard, who chose to admit his business failure, might not have found much comfort "moping around" his reunion. He might well have felt embarrassment, even humiliation. But Richard put himself above a certain situation, sacrificing his situated identity in the name of a personal one. Making an admission is in effect a declaration of independence from social evaluation which, paradoxically, reflects back on one's situated identity as an enactment of integrity. At least Richard knows he is in touch with the "real me," even at the cost of admitting to others and to himself that life is full of surprises, some of which are undesirable. With this stance, at least we know where we stand. It should be noted, however, that by presenting ourselves as we "really are," our situated identity (and, dialectically, our personal identity too) might pay dearly. Thus even when personal identities are perceived as independent from their situated counterparts, that freedom is somewhat limited; at the very least, it comes at a great cost.

Like the maintenance of situated identity, the maintenance of personal identity requires impression management. The management of an inner identity is no more free of the threat of discovery than the management of appearance. However, the process of impression management and the threat of discovery are very different. In the case of situated identity, impression management is directed toward others. In the case of personal identity, impression management is directed toward oneself. In the case of situated identity, the danger of discovery is the danger of discovery by others. In the case of personal identity, the danger of discovery is that of self-discovery. To be sure, even in the management of personal identity, the other does not disappear altogether. Fellow returnees raise uncomfortable questions, either directly or by force of example. Even for matters internally felt, they provide something like a magic mirror by which one may look inward. Save in instances which I can only imagine are very rare indeed, are those who attend reunions able to maintain a personal identity entirely independent of the responses of others. As a result, the central problem in the management of personal identity within a public occasion such as a reunion becomes not impression management but the "neutralization" of others' judgments, real or imagined.

Integrity and Identity

Even those who practice deception often do so only when they claim, at least to themselves, that the deception represents a kind of truth. Isabel, a thirty-eight-year-old housewife from a working class neighborhood, wanted to paint her life story in brighter colors. She felt the need to present a situated identity different from the one she lived, particularly in terms of material success. And material success lends itself to representation through material artifacts, which are often viewed as an extension of oneself.[27] In Isabel's eyes, if she could not show material success, she would be considered a failure, a fate which she wanted to avoid. She describes her way of coping with the flaws in her identity:

> My diamond ring was stolen . . . and my husband said that in time he'd get me [another] one . . . but not in time for the reunion. I said, "I don't *even* have a diamond ring. . . . So (my friend) Linda said, "Let's go to the flea market, they sell zircons there." So we both went out . . . and we bought these humongous diamond rings, almost two karats, that cost $9.99.

The problem, of course, was that someone might expose the sham either by discovering the truth on their own or hearing it from Linda. Isabel was troubled by this possibility:

> [At the reunion] we went down to the bathroom and there [one of my former classmates] said, "Well, everybody must be doing really well because the diamonds on the fingers are killing me." It was embarrassing. Did they really know that my ring was a fake? . . . On the way home I told Linda, "While I was [in the bathroom] I thought that if you were to open your mouth and say it was a zircon I would have killed you."

Isabel feared that her fake diamond would be revealed, leaving her in a worse position than if she had worn no jewelry at all. She was afraid the friend who shared her secret would expose her. For Isabel the problem was solved because Linda not only convinced her to buy the ring, but also bought one for herself. However, such a solution is partial since there are people who know how to distinguish between false diamonds and real ones (as Isabel claims she can) and expose the show that Isabel and Linda had put together, making them look like frauds.

The important point, however, lies elsewhere. What appears as impression management—even a lie—should not be misconstrued. From the perspective of the participants themselves, it is not a deception. Rather, it constitutes an effort to select among different appearances and, often, to find that appearance that the reunion-goer believes is most closely aligned with what he or she "really" is. Describing the incident in the ladies room, Isabel insisted that, when her former classmate concluded that "everybody must be doing well," Isabel did not say anything. But she also insisted that she "wouldn't lie." For Isabel the zirconium ring is not a lie, because until she lost it, she had had a "real one . . . a perfect blue-white diamond." Thus, the zirconium ring, although a fake diamond, represented a real possession, one she had been deprived of not because of any putatively inner characteristic but because of what she conceived of as an accident of timing in its theft. In this sense, the fake represented the "higher truth" of the actual diamond. In wearing the zirconium ring, Isabel was not, at least not by her own construction, lying, but representing herself as she believed herself to be. So too, Michael, who suggested to Richard that he lie about his bankruptcy, invokes a notion of a higher truth. In Michael's opinion, "it was not a lie since formally he still owned his business." The "real" Richard was not bankrupt.

Even if people survive the show—which, of course, they do—they must survive themselves. And many seem to refuse to cheat themselves. Consider again Frank who, after trying to paint reality in rosier colors, admitted to me and to a few others that "I have not gotten far with my career. It is not as good as I would like it to be. In short, I'm not too happy with my career" (administrator, tenth reunion, Central High School). Beth confessed that she "wanted to be a doctor. I would have liked to be married, have many kids around the house, a big house with a backyard and a dog." With a smile she quietly added, "the dog is the only dream that I fulfilled" (Beth, optician, twentieth reunion, Central High School).

While some returnees were frank about disclosing the troubles and unhappiness they had faced since graduation, most did not, as Michael put it, "mope around," disclosing to the world what they perceive as the real truth about themselves. Still, it is obvious that people feel uncom-

fortable faking reality, telling half-truths, reshaping the world according to yardsticks that are not necessarily their own, minimizing other
people's success stories, controlling the conversation, or avoiding the entire encounter. Personal identities are not only brought into social situations; they exist independently of them. Even if returnees manage their
impressions and can maintain and sustain a specific situated identity,
their personal identities do not leave them in peace. More important,
however, is that people do not leave themselves in peace. My respondents
did not let themselves simply buy into the show they saw and enacted:
when the tension between situated identities and personal ones became
intolerable, they either sought legitimation for the use of management
techniques or later admitted that they had indeed resorted to what was
no more than a technique.

Between Inner Belief and Appearance

The management of personal identity is not "more innocent" than the
management of situated identity. The open admission, no less than the
deception, involves a strategic position of the self with regard to others, as
does the rejection, implicit or explicit, of a socially enacted value system
organized around material success. I do not mean to imply that personal
identity is somehow "real" in a way that situated identity is not. Like
situated identities, personal identities are accounts and no less vulnerable
to skepticism just because they are privately held rather than publicly
enacted. My claims are more modest. I mean simply to insist on the significance of personal identity for those who themselves attend reunions.
Moreover, I wish to revive the notion of personal identity—a notion
sometimes buried under the fascination with the metaphor of dramaturgy and the power of social situations. At the same time, I wish to
contrast personal identity with situated identity, exploring the mutual
dependency between them as well as the degree of freedom available to
each and the concomitant price tags they bear.

Those who attempt to manage the impression they make on others at
a reunion seldom know if their efforts are successful. Widespread skepticism undermines the perceived truth of virtually everything seen and
heard there. Appearances begin to seem, to the reunion-goers themselves, little more than polite fictions without relevance to identity. The
most one can say about impression management at reunions is that it
may work for the duration of the event. More importantly, impression
management fails to resolve internal conflicts.

Appearances generate identities by generating impressions, socially enacted and lodged in the responses of others. In contrast, personal identities, while mediated through particular responses, are internally held and felt. There is life after reunions and above specific social situations. As a result, while the management of situated identity allows for deception of various sorts, the management of personal identity depends far more heavily on the construction of one's own integrity.

Differences between personal identity and situated identity create the possibility of misalignment. Some may respond to this misalignment with indifference, maintaining an appearance and inward beliefs which bear little relationship to each other. However, my data suggest that this is not the typical response. Most returnees make efforts, often at great psychic cost, to align what they appear to be with who they believe themselves to be. But the process of alignment is not symmetrical. While it is fairly easy (conceptually, if not always in practice) to align appearance with internally felt beliefs, it is far more difficult to align internally felt beliefs with appearance.

In many instances, situated identity is a source of personal identity because we see ourselves reflected in the responses and reactions of others to us. But if we stray too far from who we "know" we are, appearance and impressions are severed from identity. We are no longer, in Goffman's phrase, "taken in by [our] own act."[28] Ironically, dramaturgical metaphors may provide their most powerful insights in precisely those situations where the participants in a social drama are least aware of their own efforts at impression management.

These conclusions differ from what is implicit in the long line of social criticism running from Riesman through Goffman to Bellah and his colleagues—all of whom confront us with claims that a single identity integrated across situations and over time is fast disappearing from American society. From such claims it appears that situations are not only independent from each other but that little personal identity persists across situations. I am skeptical of these claims. Although authenticity and integrity are themselves, in large part, socially and historically constructed concepts,[29] the reunion-goers' preoccupation with these concepts is nonetheless powerful.

Contemporary Americans not only assume continuity between their past and present and search for it where it is absent (see chapter 7), but they are also prepared to sacrifice what is publicly enacted and understood in favor of what is internally held and felt. To be more concrete, it is not enough to sustain an identity in a social setting if that situated identity cannot be connected to a personal identity. We may need to manage impressions at reunions (as well as in other social settings), but more than that we need to manage our own beliefs in ourselves once the show is over. The search to resolve the tension between what is publicly held and what is internally understood, together with the felt need for integrity, for an identity that extends beyond the situation and to nothing less than a life, calls the postmodernist claims of fragmentation into question.

Conclusion

Reunions and Beyond

$\mathcal{H}$ow do autobiographical occasions help us construct our identities? What are the resources they offer? How do they affect the outcome? How do we come to know who we were and who we are? These are the puzzles which occasioned this book. Class reunions were chosen as my research arena because they seem a perfect illustration of social and personal intersections between past and present, bringing together ghosts of the past and representatives of the present. Class reunions hold many promises. Now is the time to see whether any of these promises can be fulfilled. Can the past be relived? Can the present be informed? Can the puzzle of who we were and who we are be solved? Is the intersection of past and present a viable resource in the construction of identities?

Class reunions appear to be, first and foremost, parties—occasions for having fun. The hall is decorated; there is music in the background; returnees are well dressed; and smiles are everywhere. But after the reunion—after claims that "we had fun," and "I had a great time"— former classmates' accounts reveal a different reality. In effect, a paradox is exposed. One of the major arguments of this book is that the same social setting that provides resources for the construction of identity, is the very one which may threaten it.

But more than unfolding what is behind the public scenes of class reunions—themselves an integral part of American culture—the discourse enveloping reunions tells us something significant about autobiographical occasions and the culture within which they take place. The autobiographies recounted at reunions are typically texts of identity. They are efforts to say not only what one has done, but also who one is.

The accounts returnees give and the concerns they express take us beyond a specific social context and into the culture within which and through which ordinary Americans construct their identities and cope with the threats to these identities.

Although individuals can construct their identities in the privacy of their homes, identity construction is rarely a personal matter. Class reunions testify to the social dynamics of autobiographies and, thus, the dynamics of identity. The presence of an audience—especially when the audience is both a living witness to the past and a benchmark for the present—gives the dialogue between past and present its opportunity, its strength, its social character, and its drama. And yet that same audience also has the potential to threaten and undermine one's identity. The "right audience," the one that can inform the present with the past or validate changes, may be missing; it may hold different interpretations of the past, be detached from the play, or disregard the actor. Yet, although identity is bound up with social processes, it is still ultimately an individual possession. The question, then, is what resources are provided by autobiographical occasions to that possession.

Autobiographical occasions define the community in relation to which one's autobiography is told and one's identity is established. Class reunions not only define the community, but also invent it. By exploiting the past, even by their more passive existence as a particular kind of gathering, high school reunions provide returnees with a community toward which they can feel a sense of belonging and within which they can anchor their identities. Returnees leave their reunions feeling that they came from somewhere they belong. The community that is formed at reunions, however, is fragile, voluntary, selective, and limited; it is a one-night community. This may suggest that identities formed and presented there are also voluntary, selective, and fragile. And yet this type of community offers a sense of belonging without demanding much sacrifice, and thus it speaks so well to the American dilemma of individualism and collectivism.

A class that hardly existed as a unit in high school becomes a point of reference from which one can derive a broader perspective on life in general and one's own life in particular. And yet the perspective provided by reunions opens a Pandora's Box, an informal process of social control that presents former classmates with a hierarchy and a reminder of the norms according to which they evaluate and are evaluated. An invitation to a reunion initiates a process of self-reflection, provoking difficult questions regarding one's achievements and failures. What the self has become is assessed and what one should desire for oneself is recalled. High school reunions provide a site for an instant and condensed evaluation of every significant sphere of life: family, career, financial ability, and physical appearance. All this takes place in light of the past, its memories and expectations, and within a culture that believes in the need for progress. Moreover, those encounters occur with people who are exactly the same age and who grew up together. If age is such an important organizing principle in American culture and society, and if one of the best ways to gain perspective over one's life course is by looking at one's contemporaries,[1] then class reunions seem to provide a rare opportunity in modern American culture for "face-to-face interaction"[2] with an age-based peer group. Although it may only exist for an evening and only contain a limited number of one's peers, this group demands an account of one's life and becomes a reference group and a force through which the social order is confirmed and one's identity within that order is defined and assigned. Class reunions make us think about our life in terms that have been set by a group of which one is at best a partial member.

While the scope of the autobiography told at reunions is a wide one—in fact it covers the whole of one's life—the structure and the nature of the event limits to a significant degree the material available to the storytellers. The memory of a collective—a new dimension added by reunions—is shaped by the structure of the event and its constraints and, to a significant degree, by reunion organizers who exercise disproportionate power over the way the past is publicly enacted and perceived. The hope of touching one's personal past—of knowing who we were—presents many obstacles. The spatial context is missing and the time available for reminiscing is short. The voluntary character of reunions may leave returnees without potential resources of knowledge. Moreover, the agenda of the encounters is centered in the present more than in the past. The past that is finally reached is selective, unresolved, incomplete, and negotiated, and it depends on the crucial cooperation of the audience, the content of the memory, present circumstances, and the need to feel that we somehow can relate to it. The identity that may emerge out of such an occasion may very well resemble the past it encountered: selective, unresolved, incomplete, and negotiated.

Once the past is encountered, many wish to inform, confirm, or transform it with present information. This task, however, is no less problematic than others. The lack of time, the hectic nature of the event, and the usual superficiality of our public behavior all leave reunion-goers with knowledge that is at best partial, superficial, and sometimes even dubious.

More important, once the reunion is over, returnees can never be sure whether the knowledge they sought to convey has been received in the desired manner.

What then are the chances of using class reunions as a setting in which our present can either confirm the past or change it? The answer is, "it depends." It depends on the presence of specific people. It depends on the structure of the event. It depends on our faith that our messages have been received the way we wanted and that no one has suspected that we may have stretched the truth. But more important, it depends on whether what we attempt to convey threatens other people's sense of continuity, their past impressions and memories of past injustices. Although people attend their reunions looking for changes, they are actually struggling to ignore them, trying to make the past and present congruent. While invoking the notion of a "true self"—some inner essence which is independent of behavior and appearance—returnees are dealing with discontinuities. And thus, much as we dismiss other people's present, revise their past, claim that the changes are only external, or experience sadness because they did not carry out the dreams we had for them, so other people rewrite our own stories.

Moreover, reunions confront returnees with yet another threat, that between situated identities and personal identities, between what is publicly enacted and what is internally understood. If we are fortunate, there is no conflict between situated identities and biographical-personal identities. But we are rarely so fortunate, and the tension between the two facets of identity and the ways by which they are managed is displayed by the accounts given by the returnees. Those accounts reveal the complicated relationships between the two facets of identity. Reunions require skills of self-presentation, while at the same time testing individuals' capacity to present a socially desirable self without departing too greatly from their authentic sense of self. Put bluntly, as we do in any other social setting, we need to manage impressions at reunions, but because the ultimate audience at reunions is ourselves we also need to manage our belief in ourselves once the show is over.

People attend their reunions looking for their past, looking for a sense of belonging, looking for former friends they lost touch with, looking for themselves, looking for their identities. What they find is that the past is hard to encounter, they find social control aimed at themselves, and they find that their identities are threatened.

Finally, a personal observation: my original conception of my research site was of a primarily pleasant experience, one in which the predominant atmosphere of "a good time" and "fun" would prevail. Yet I end this book on a sad note. I found too many individuals who will never be sure "exactly" who they were and who have been made to realize that there are certain things they are never likely to become or to possess. I heard too many accounts revealing the struggle to create a sense of continuity and resolve the constant tension between the different facets of identities. In a sense, I met many people seeking to make sense out of their lives and still hoping that the next time they are called to account, everything will be different: the past will be able to inform the present; the present will be able to inform, confirm, or even change the past; both past and present will be aligned with each other; the entire crowd will be there as it used to be; the inevitable evaluation process will leave them satisfied; and they can still claim that they are who they were.

But reunions provide no more than partial answers to the formidable questions, 'Who were we?' and 'Who are we?' Nevertheless, although other autobiographical occasions in life proffer opportunities for the same questions to be asked, I doubt whether the puzzle can be answered any better than at class reunions. The same problems inherent in the resources offered by class reunions may be an integral part of other social settings in American culture, social settings which promise to provide answers to questions about our identity. But it is much easier to create high hopes than to fulfill them. The promise is hard to keep; I am skeptical that it ever can be.

Having considered the ethos of class reunions and the quality of the resources they provide, I would like to turn to the theoretical issues which are beyond this specific case study.

Beyond Reunions

This book examined the cultural resources and structural limits within which people construct and reconstruct their own identities. Such an examination has wide-ranging implications for at least five theoretical issues in sociology and current American culture: collective memory, community, social control, autobiographical occasions, and identity.

Collective memory, an issue central to the analysis of contemporary cultures, is currently garnering much attention from sociologists, anthropologists, and historians. One of the main debates within this field concerns the relationship of past to present and their respective power to shape our perceptions of the past.[3] This book neither altogether supports the constructionist views of the past shaped solely by present needs and circumstances, nor does it testify to the power of the past in shaping the present. In accordance with Schwartz's findings, my research suggests that the past is exploited by the present but "it cannot be literally constructed."[4]

On a different analytical level, this study departs from most works in the field of collective memory, which focus on the collective memory of nations, their heroes, wars, etc., and thus deal mainly with memory reached through *indirect* experience. Class reunions illustrate the way in which the memory of the collective is organized when the past is reached through the *direct* experience of the participants. It is worth noting, however, that the public enactment of collective memory at the group level does have similarities to its macrosocial (national) counterpart. It is selective with respect to who remembers and what is remembered, and those who organize it exercise disproportionate power over the way the past is publicly perceived while the voices of participants are ignored and neglected. A future research effort in this area may seek to address the power of agents of memory and the process of organizing public enactments of memories for crowds who were an integral part of that specific past. An important aspect of such a study would be to explore the implications of such enactments on the construction of personal memories.

The future and the quality of current communities within American culture have concerned many scholars.[5] This book witnesses a touching search for a community, a search for something in common among a group of people, for a place where we are known over time. Although as a form of community, class reunions are a telling comment on American culture, they also aptly correspond to the dilemmas of community and individualism within current American culture. The community offered by a class reunion demands very little and yet offers much: the sense of belonging. The search, it seems, is at least partially successful. Contemporary Americans may wish for more, but they are clearly willing to settle for what there is, and certainly would not relinquish the little they have.

Social control—an issue central to the analysis of contemporary social structures—has long been of interest in sociology. However, since the end of the 1960s, the concept of social control has been associated primarily with state-centered control, emphasizing coercive and formal measures aimed at deviant behavior. However, by focusing on formal and coercive forms of social control we may be overlooking other forms that are not sponsored by the state, and that operate on a micro-social level and are quite prevalent in different cultures. My work attempts to revive the anthropological approach to social control, something Stanley Cohen names the "second grid,"[6] and which identifies universal processes common to all social relations in modern cultures.[7] This tradition emphasizes "socialisation, conformity, internalisation of norms, value consensus,"[8] and so forth, thus stressing informal forms of social control. Such informal forms of social control were dominant in traditional societies and have been perceived to be absent from modern societies. Although difficult to decipher and not as powerful as their formal, state-centered counterparts, these forms remain with us and are still an integral part of our everyday life, and they certainly play a role when we construct our identities. The shape of modern society encourages, even requires, the invention of new forms of social control or a return to the traditional ones. It seems to me that future students in this field will have to focus on observing rituals and other cultural events within which and through which cultural values and the social order are recalled and reinforced.

A major theoretical issue of my study of class reunions concerns the efforts ordinary men and women in contemporary America make to construct their identities in autobiographical occasions. While we may avoid our class reunions, it is not easy to evade all the other encounters that demand similar narratives. Thus high school reunions are but one illustration of a much larger phenomenon. Professional conventions, family reunions, job interviews, first dates, psychotherapies, homecomings, and many other social encounters demand a similar account of one's identity.

While most discussions regarding autobiographies are centered around the relationship between narratives and identities, as well as about the narratives themselves, we lack a sociological analysis of the occasions that generate and affect the autobiography itself and thus the construction of identities.[9] In this book, I have attempted to illustrate autobiographies—and thus identities—as a social interactive enterprise which is structured, limited, and threatened by the very same social contexts that inspire their construction. I have emphasized some dimensions which were critical to the construction of identities within class reunions, such as the scope of the autobiography which is dictated by occasion, the effect of the structure of the occasions and the pressure to attend it on the narrative that is told, the type of the autobiographical other that awaits, and the focus of the occasion defining the social boundaries of the autobiography. A future research effort in this area may seek to study these dimensions in other occasions, and thus broaden our understanding of other occasions that may offer different resources and therefore result in different constructions of identity. Moreover, one may wish to address other dimensions that were not dealt with within the scope of this book. For instance, the notion of power relations within specific autobiographical occasions (such as psychotherapies and job interviews).

The question is, what has the study of class reunions taught us about the construction of identities in contemporary America? What have we learned about American culture? My findings raise questions about current claims regarding the disappearance from American society of a single and coherent life story across situations and over time. Such postmodernist claims imply not only that situations are independent from each other, but also that situated identity has assumed an import beyond that of biographical-personal identity. Although the different facets of identity have a life of their own, contemporary Americans find it difficult to completely separate them and have trouble living with the tension between what is publicly held and what is internally felt. I mean neither to imply that the management of biographical-personal identity is what might be thought of as "more honest" than the management of situated identity, nor to suggest that biographical-personal identity is "real" in a way that situated identities are not. Both are accounts which are equally open to skepticism. But this work seeks to revive the notion of biographical-personal identity—a notion that was buried under the fascination with Goffman's dramaturgy and the power of social settings—while contrasting it with its situated counterpart, exploring the mutual dependency between the two facets of identity as well as the degree of freedom available to each and the concomitant price-tags they bear.

Moreover, continuity of one's own identity and that of others is something people attempt to construct under almost all circumstances. Discontinuities are usually explained away. Because high school reunions bring past and present together so vividly, they offer an excellent opportunity to study the tolerance for change. It was my finding that reuniongoers went to extraordinary lengths to maintain a seamless coherence between past and present. Such struggle to construct a world where almost everything makes sense and is consistent and coherent says something about American culture, in which change may be a respected topic of discussion but is ignored when identity is involved. The postmodernist claims of fragmentation of the self are called into question by the quest to resolve the tension between what is publicly held and internally understood, and the impressive struggle to maintain a sense of continuity, of an identity that extends beyond a particular situation to nothing less than a life.

The self has not disappeared from the lives of ordinary Americans; the need to construct and to account for the self in various social contexts persists. As an example of such settings, high school reunions present us with individuals who are still profoundly concerned about their shortcomings in occupational achievement, material success, physical appearance, marriage, and parenthood, variations on the very same criteria by which identity was based fifty years earlier. Identity, it seems, remains anchored in the institutional structure. The identity we present to others must meet the classical social standards while we try not to stray too far from our biographical-personal identity and from the construction of a continuous life story. In an age that is defined by academics as postmodernist, ordinary Americans still believe in the American dream and in a coherent and integrated inner self beyond situations and over time.

Appendix

When I was sixteen, I interrupted my schooling in Israel, where I grew up, to spend six months in the United States. As part of an international exchange program, I spent two months at a summer camp and four months in the John F. Kennedy High School in Merrick, New York. Ten years later, I returned to the United States to go to graduate school which I attended for five years. The research for this book was done during that time. The writing, however, began in New York City and ended in Jerusalem.

Writing about autobiographical occasions makes one reflective and sensitive to the point where a simple question such as, "When did you begin working on the book?" is hard to answer. Yet, it seems to me that the book began, in effect, with my attending a reunion. In the spring of 1988, my mother's friend, who was worried about my being so far away from home, invited me to attend a reunion of former graduates of a prestigious Israeli high school. The reunion was held in the basement of a synagogue in New York City. Although I should have felt "at home" at that reunion—after all, all of the participants were Israelis speaking Hebrew, eating Israeli food, singing songs that I knew by heart, holding a memorial service for the Israeli soldiers who died in the wars, and arguing about the conflict in the Middle East—I felt much more "at home" when observing the American reunions I studied later on. Nonetheless, this social gathering, in which Israeli graduates from different cohorts currently living in different parts of the United States and Canada made the trip to New York on a rainy Sunday in order to get together, was critical in forming some of the ideas I followed through on later, especially those dealing with the search for a community and the construction of a memory of a collective.

This book is about high school reunions. But it is also an effort to theorize about how individuals construct their identities within autobiographical occasions, and how those occasions affect the narratives told. Although this book is not just a report of empirical research, it is based firmly in such research. I collected data in a number of ways, and used this data in developing concepts and illustrating my arguments, as well as drawing my conclusions. What follows is an account of what I did, how I did it, and why I did it. In short, I explain how I know what I claim to know, as well as the limitations of this study.

I knew class reunions constituted a prime research arena for studying autobiographical occasions, their effect on the narratives told, and the issues for identity they raise. The first decision I made concerned the type of class reunion I was interested in. I wanted to study public school reunions: nothing private, nothing exclusive, nothing selective. I was interested in "neighborhood" schools. I never thought, though, that gaining access to class reunions would present a major obstacle; it proved to be a lot more difficult than I had imagined.

In the spring of 1989 I sent letters to twenty randomly selected public high school principals in the area of my study. In the letter (followed up by a phone call) I asked them to connect me with the organizing committees of the reunions. Only two of the twenty high schools provided me with any information. The meager responses I elicited taught me that the highly institutionalized fundraising that is associated with reunions in American universities does not exist in high schools. The initiation to organize such an event is left to former classmates and, in many cases nowadays, to professional companies. More often than not, public high schools are neither involved in nor knowledgeable about their graduates' reunions. To my dismay, neither of the two schools that did respond was suitable as a research site.[1] I had to find new avenues.

Through a company that arranged reunions[2]—a company that in effect controlled major parts of the reunion market in the area of my study—I was able to spend the summer of 1989 partying every weekend. At that point I wanted to observe as many reunions as possible, to get a broad sense of the phenomenon. All in all, that summer I observed ten class reunions of ten different schools celebrating different anniversaries. I took notes and I held short conversations with a few people at each reunion, but I did not include what I saw and heard as part of my data set. Still, the time I spent at those reunions was seminal for preliminary impressions and thoughts, as well as for framing the concerns I was interested in.

In February 1990, my research plan was ready. I had defined the cohorts and type of schools I wanted to study, I knew I wanted to observe the organizational process, and I had prepared questionnaires for both returnees and nonreturnees. But the reunion company did not permit me to join their meetings with the organizing committees, at which they basically tried to convince the committees to hire their services. And there was no other way for me to get in touch with those committees. Moreover, just when I was about to receive the mailing lists from the company and send out the questionnaires before the reunions, the president of the commercial company changed her mind. She feared that her customers' trust would be jeopardized and that the company might be sued for disclosing information without the consent of the people involved. More than anything else, I believe, the company got tired of my project, and the whole plan of attending reunions and interviewing attendees and nonattendees began to unravel.

Left with no sources of data, in January 1990 I circulated flyers in my department asking for help, specifically for information about people who were organizing their reunions or who were planning to attend.[3] Through those personal contacts I was able to gain access to a twentieth class reunion in a lower middle class neighborhood, which I later named Garden. The reunion took place in March 1990 in a catering hall in Garden. I was also allowed to hand out questionnaires to the attendees.[4]

Although I was thrilled about this opportunity to begin my research, I still felt I needed more, and thus again called the company and met with the vice president. The meeting was a success: we worked out our differences. I could attend any reunion I wanted and could distribute questionnaires to attendees at the end of the events. I was still denied access to the mailing lists, but we worked out a way by which I could send my questionnaires to those who chose not to attend. It was not ideal, but it was adequate and, more important, it was the best I could get. I probably could not have conducted the research without the company's help, and I remain grateful.

Originally I had wanted to systematically observe four class reunions: two ten-year reunions (with returnees in their late twenties) and two twenty-year reunions (with returnees in their late thirties). I considered it important to be able to control the time span and to interview people at different points in their lives.[5] While many of those who graduated in 1980 (who were about twenty-eight years old at the time of their tenth reunion) are still somewhat unsettled, most of those who graduated in 1970 (who were about thirty-eight years old at the time of their twentieth reunion) are already established in their careers, own their homes, and have families. Although the different cohorts I studied experienced "the same historical events (war, migration, prosperity) at different ages, resulting in different life trajectories,"[6] it nonetheless seems to me that the process which individuals experience before, during, and after their reunions is the same regardless of their ages. The content may be somewhat different—those who experienced the '60s as young adults frequently referred to this period, while the younger generation, who were children at the time, did not—but the form is the same. In addition to different cohorts, I wanted to study two different schools: a middle-class high school and a lower-middle class high school. I wanted to be able to control the socioeconomic background as much as possible. Again, what I discovered is that when it comes to the construction of identities, the content may be somewhat different, but the dreams and the form are the same. The same problems inherent in an encounter with the past await returnees no matter what their ages and no matter what their socioeconomic background.

Although I did not plan to study more than four reunions, one of the schools had its twenty-fifth reunion that same summer and I could not resist the temptation of studying another cohort from the same school. Ultimately, however, the difference between those graduates who were thirty-eight and those who were forty-three years old seems insignificant. In both cases we are dealing with people who are more or less settled, who have established their careers and families.

In the end, I observed five class reunions which were held between March and October of 1990. In order to maintain the privacy of the individuals I interviewed, I have named these schools Central, Garden, and Main. I observed the reunion of the class of 1965 at Central High School, the class of 1970 at Central and Garden High Schools, and the class of 1980 at Main and Central High Schools on the occasion of their twenty-fifth, twentieth, and tenth reunions.

Each of the school classes included over three hundred graduates. Main and Garden High Schools are located in lower middle class neighborhoods—whose demographics are similar[7]—where, ten and twenty years after graduation, many former classmates are municipal employees and technicians, with only a smattering of professionals. Central High School is in a middle-class neighborhood where many of the graduates are now professionals, including a considerable number of doctors, lawyers, and executives.[8] Although now there are many African-Americans living in the Garden and Main neighborhoods, and a few living in the Central neighborhood, there were few African-American families in any of these areas during the period when the graduates I studied were in high school. So the reunions I attended were almost entirely white. Of my 94 interviewees, two were African-Americans (who attended the Main tenth reunion) and one was Chinese (who attended the Central twenty-fifth reunion). All three areas are on the East Coast of the United States within traveling distance of a major city that serves as financial and commercial center and where many of the graduates work and some of them live. In the text, I have used pseudonyms for the individuals who people my narrative, but I have maintained accuracy about their genders, ages, and occupations.[9]

On Method

In all of the reunions I studied I followed the same research procedure. I had two goals during the reunions: observing the event and getting people to be interviewed. Hence, I kept extensive notes, paying attention to formal events and carrying on informal conversations with the returnees. At the same time I presented myself and my research project. An integral part of convincing people to become subjects of a study was, in my opinion, the way I presented myself. They had to open their homes, their offices, and more important, their hearts to a complete stranger. Thus I went to the reunions wearing a black business suit, a white blouse, and black high heels, an outfit adopted by very few returnees. It was apparent, therefore, that I was not part of the party, since most women did not wear business suits. At the same time I wanted to convey the message of respect for the event and for the people.

I arrived at the reunions about a half-hour before the event was scheduled to begin, and most often found myself helping the organizers to make last-minute preparations while taking note of the setting of the hall, any special decorations, and so on. The first hour of the event I spent on ticket collection; it helped the organizers and, more important, I felt I could not force myself on people who were meeting friends they hadn't seen in years. I felt I had to give people time to get over the first excitement of seeing all those old-new faces. During that time I observed the hugging, the kissing, and the sense of surprise among the returnees. At no point during the reunion did I try to interrupt ongoing conversations. After all, it was a private party and I wanted to diminish any intrusive presence, not magnify it. Moreover, the event is short and hence rarely can a researcher spend time with or follow returnees to get a "perspective in action."[10] I did not eavesdrop on other people's conversations, a procedure I consider unethical as well as impractical given the crowded circumstances of a reunion. I did have some short conversations, initiated by former graduates or their bored spouses who were interested in what I was doing at their party. They usually presumed I was a journalist covering the event for the local paper. On all of these occasions I told them who I was and what I was doing. The usual reaction was a huge smile—which I interpreted as another sign of a widespread perception that too much money was being spent on strange topics that academia chooses to study. No one, however, objected to my presence.

As I did not want to attract too much attention, I wrote most of my notes in the bathroom. Since I rarely trust my memory on such occasions, I found myself running to the bathroom after practically every conversation I had or after a few intriguing observations.

Good timing is always important, especially when one needs a favor, and I needed one. Thus, about ninety minutes after the official beginning of the evening, I began to approach people, explaining my project. Here, again, I encountered smiles, even some broad laughter, as well as genuine curiosity and interest. I asked the returnees if they would be willing to be interviewed, emphasizing that the interview would be short and would not take place during the reunion. A few asked me directly what I intended to ask them about. On all such occasions, I told them that I was interested in their high school memories and their experiences at their reunions.

Roughly 90 percent of those I approached agreed and gave me their home or business telephone numbers. Those who refused either did not want to be bothered or didn't have time. Some refused because their spouses were not keen about the idea. A few were willing to be interviewed over the phone but not in person. Since I insisted on face-to-face interviews, I never talked with those who agreed only to speak to me on the phone. My cohort was also limited to people who lived within traveling distance of the towns where the reunions were held, because interviewing people who lived at a distance was not practical.

After every ten personal encounters, I took a few minutes' break so that I would sound fresh and enthusiastic about the study to the subsequent subjects, and to myself; during the breaks I would also take notes on events at the reunion, such as awards ceremonies. At midnight, I stopped asking people for interviews. By then, I felt that it was too late to discuss business. But by that time, I typically had a list of about 60 phone numbers, all located within an hour-and-a-half's drive from where

I lived. I stayed until the last guest left the affair so that I could complete my notes about developments at the reunion and distribute my questionnaires to returnees as they left. In addition, at three of the five reunions I observed, reunion yearbooks were handed out at the end of the evening and I certainly did not want to miss such documents.

I used mail questionnaires to get in touch with the people who did not attend their reunion. Despite the inherent problems of using such a method (e.g., the low response rate, the need to devise a questionnaire whose length would not deter people), it was my only option to communicate with those graduates. I was interested in the nonreturnees for two reasons: (a) although I never thought that the differences between those who attend and those who do not attend was a major concern (for a detailed discussion see chapter 1), there were still a great many of them, too many to overlook; (b) the commercial company was very interested in understanding why people do or do not attend. Coming up with some answers—about which I am not sure they were happy—was the only way I could repay them for the help they gave me.

Although some returnees buy their tickets at the door, most buy their tickets well in advance. Thus, a week before each event, the commercial company had compiled a mailing list of those who had decided not to attend. As we agreed, a week before the reunion I brought the commercial company 100 questionnaires and stamped envelopes. The secretary put address labels on the envelopes without my seeing them. We made sure that the questionnaires were randomly sent, but only to people who lived within easy traveling distance from the location of the reunion. (At the time, sending questionnaires to people living 3,000 miles away made little sense, since I was afraid that the end result would be biased towards the distance factor. Later, however, I learned that distance was not a factor.) The only reunion for which I could not pursue this procedure regarding the nonreturnees was Garden's, where the organizers handled all communication with their former classmates by phone. Thus there were no addresses available, and they would not give me the phone lists without first calling the people involved (a gesture I was in no position to request). When I met the organizers they were both overworked with organizing their reunion and there was no way I could ask them to make more phone calls. All in all I sent out 400 questionnaires to those who did not attend (for Central's three reunions and Main's one reunion).

Sending questionnaires to people who did not return to their reunions forced me to use the same method for the returnees; otherwise I could not compare the two groups. Thus, at the end of each of the five reunions

I studied, I planned to hand out 100 questionnaires and stamped envelopes. At Garden's twentieth reunion I was successful, partially because I was accompanied by a colleague who helped with the distribution. At Central's twentieth and tenth reunions, which I attended alone, I was able to distribute 90 questionnaires. At Main's tenth reunion, I managed to distribute 100 questionnaires. At Central's twenty-fifth reunion I handed out only 65 questionnaires, since the turn-out at that reunion was rather small. All in all I distributed 445 questionnaires. I distributed the questionnaires at the end of the event, literally at the door, to minimize the chances of participants' losing them. The evening is exciting enough without holding onto some papers. No one ever refused to accept the questionnaires. On the contrary, people seemed eager to take them. Perhaps at first glance the questionnaires looked like another souvenir from an unforgettable night.

Both types of questionnaires consisted of questions that had to do with the following issues: demographics (sex, marital status, number of children, occupation), memories from high school, relationships with former classmates, reasons for coming (or for not coming) to the reunion, and an optional section where one could provide phone numbers for an interview. None of the questions on either type of questionnaire were open-ended. The questionnaires for attendees also included a section on the preparation process for the reunion (e.g., buying a new outfit), as well as a section on those topics they were most interested in learning about with regard to their former classmates' lives (e.g., occupation, marital status, reminiscing).

The response rate for returnees was 45 percent, while the response rate for those who did not attend was 29 percent, a difference accounted for by common sense: one cannot expect those who did not show any interest in their reunions in the first place to be eager to fill out a questionnaire about the reunion sent to them by a stranger. This costly effort made up a sample of 200 questionnaires of those who attended and 115 of those who did not attend. Later, all the questionnaires were coded and analyzed; the results are the focus of chapter 1.

About two weeks after the reunion, I had already received most of the responses to the mail questionnaires and I was able to compile a list of people who had expressed interest in being interviewed (both from the questionnaires and from conversations at the event itself). Other than making sure I had more or less the same number of men and women drawn in roughly equal proportion from each of the five reunions I observed, I selected the people I was to telephone randomly.

The next step was to make the calls and to try to set times for the interviews. I always called office numbers after 10 A.M. in order to give people a chance to arrive at work, get their coffee, and recover from the morning rush. I called home numbers between 8 P.M. and 9 P.M. Any earlier and I would intrude on the hectic preparations for dinner, baths for the kids, and the like. Any later and some of my interviewees were unwinding from their work day and less likely to be responsive. Weekends were always bad. Since I felt that my potential informants were doing me a big favor without getting anything in return, I was always very cautious.

The overwhelming majority of the people I called tried to set a time to be interviewed. However, a few regretted having given me their phone numbers and refused to be interviewed or wanted to be interviewed over the phone. A few were willing to be interviewed but could not find the time. Roughly 95 percent of the phone calls ended in interviews.

All the interviews with returnees and nonreturnees were conducted between May 1990 and 15 December 1990. I suspected that after mid-December people would have a hard time finding time for an interview that had nothing to do with their Christmas shopping.

Being a foreigner in the United States turned out to be an advantage during the interviews. I often found myself unable to follow many of the terms used by my informants. My response was to ask questions that would have looked suspicious had they come from somebody who was part of the American culture. It took time but slowly I started to understand the code of the answers and the world behind expressions such as "nerd," "bookworms," "happy-go-lucky," "honor student," and "jocks." I learned that when people described themselves as "very shy" they meant that they were considered "nerds." There was a whole new language out there that I had to unpack in order to understand the significance of what I was told.

Although I entered the interview with a schedule, the interview was open-ended and I often departed from the original plan. This form enabled me to let the informants express themselves freely and to bring their own meanings and categories into the interview. I wanted to hear them talking. When I listened to and transcribed the interviews later, I regretted that I had not asked more questions and that I had not departed from my original plan more often than I did.[11]

Originally, I had hoped to interview as many people who did not attend their reunions as those who did. But the reality was that most of the people who were kind enough to send back their questionnaires were not willing to be interviewed. Even with those who gave their phone numbers, it was often impossible to set a time. I ended up conducting only 11 interviews with people who did not attend their high school reunions. Although I have referred to these interviews at various points in this book, they were, in my opinion, the least successful part of the research.

I conducted 71 interviews with people who attended one of the five reunions I studied. Except for Main's tenth reunion, where the organizers could not be reached, I made sure I interviewed at least one person who was part of the organizing committee, crucial for the discussion of the public enactment of the past (chapter 5). As mentioned, the policy of the commercial company precluded my attending the meetings preceding the events, so I had to rely on accounts provided by the organizers after the event. I also conducted ten additional interviews with people who attended or organized other reunions, the principal of Central High School, whom I met at all three of Central's reunions, and the vice president of a commercial company which had been organizing class reunions in the area of my study for the past ten years. The total of 94 interviews—which were transcribed in full and content-analyzed—are the primary source of data out of which my analysis emerges. I taped 92 interviews and took extensive notes during the remaining two, once because my tape recorder was not functioning properly, and once because the interview was conducted at a workplace where taping was prohibited under all circumstances.

The interviews lasted an average of 75 to 90 minutes. Two interviews took ten minutes each, and one interview took two and a half hours. About one-third of the interviews took place during office hours or on lunch breaks. If my informants were high up in the hierarchy of the company for which they worked, the interview took place in the office and during office hours (while the secretary held the calls and served coffee). If my informants were the secretaries, the interview always took place during lunch time and almost always away from their desks, in the corner of the building or on a bench outside it.

About two-thirds of the interviews took place at people's homes, which meant that in many cases there were all kinds of interruptions. Sometimes it was a spouse who wanted to listen (and in some cases to be heard), other times it was parents who were around monitoring the event, or children who wanted attention. There is no doubt in my mind that there is a difference between interviews in which a person is alone and one during which a spouse or a child walks around. It does not mean that those interviews were meaningless or not as sincere, but at times I felt that my informants were uncomfortable because of another's presence. Trying to blend into the atmosphere, I found myself entertaining children, playing with dogs, patting cats, folding laundry, and unpacking groceries. I held two interviews in my apartment. In a few cases the interviews took place in public places—restaurants, pubs, coffee shops, public libraries, and once even a laundromat. Although my informants were free from company, the combination of background noise and a less-than-professional tape did not help much later in deciphering what had been said.

I made it a habit not to confirm the appointments I made with people. At the same time, though, I gave all my informants my home phone number in case they needed to change the time. Only one informant did so. Not confirming appointments is risky, but also avoids providing the interviewees with an opportunity to back out. Only twice did prospective interviewees forget about the interview and a new interview had to be scheduled.

Naturally, some interviews were better than others; some people are much more talkative and articulate than others. What I found—although this is irrelevant to my study—was that in general I enjoyed talking to older interviewees: with a few exceptions, the older the informants were, the more they had to say, the better they expressed themselves, and the longer their answers to my questions were.

On some days I was a better interviewer and a better listener than on other days. Some questions elicited quick, unhesitating responses. Some questions had to be repeated. Some were never answered. Some were thought of too late to be asked. After the interviews, when I began listening to the tapes and reading the transcripts, I was surprised to find myself often impressed with interviews which I barely remembered, and less enthusiastic about interviews I had originally thought were very good.

Although I chose my informants randomly, in order not to generate bias, I did conduct some "informant interviewing." Informant interviewing presumes that "some interviews are more important than others because the respondent knows more, has better insight, or is more willing to share what he or she knows with the interviewer."[12] The organizers of their class reunions are prime examples for this category. An additional category of importance is "key people," former graduates who either held a key role within the group in the past (e.g., the one voted "most likely to succeed") or in the present (e.g., the person who became the success story of the class). I believe that there are certain people whose voices need to be heard in order to get a better insight of the phenomenon studied.

Data such as the mail questionnaires, the lists of locations of former graduates, and the class yearbooks can be quantified and in many ways pose fewer problems regarding techniques of analysis. Most interview material—my primary source of data—is more problematic. Following Zussman,[13] I regrouped the interview material around substantive themes, first at the level of a chapter, then at the level of a chapter sub-heading. Thus, for example, to the file whose theme was "encountering the past" I assigned all relevant accounts of such encounters, any mention of reminiscing, and anything else that I came across during the interviews that was related to this theme. Most often, I ended up with tens of pages, sometimes even more than a hundred, of accounts surrounding a particular issue. Before writing any sections I ran a computer search for relevant words, terms, or phrases. Thus, before writing on the meaning of success, I ran a word search for "success." Before writing the chapter on continuity of the self, I ran a word search for "change," "didn't change," and "the same." In addition, before writing any chapter, I read all the interviews over and over again. In many ways, I let the data tell me the story.

Throughout the writing process, I found myself quoting certain people more often than others. Those people are either key informants in the sense that they have special knowledge of or insight into the phenomenon studied, or key cases in the sense that they show some process or problem with special clarity.

For the purpose of analyzing past resources as a potential explanation of the difference between those who attended and those who did not attend, I statistically analyzed two yearbooks: Central High School's class of 1980 (which attended its tenth reunion the year of my study) and Central High School's class of 1970 (which attended its twentieth reunion the year of my study), counting a total of 1,415 graduates. I counted the number of extracurricular activities for each classmate.

Toward the end of my study, my relationship with the commercial company took a more positive turn and they were willing to help me with what they considered strange academic interests and wishes. I was given lists of those who attended and those who did not attend, with the names of the states where they lived at the time of their reunions (the exact addresses were erased in advance). Thus I was able to analyze statistically the distance factor and see whether it had an impact on attendance. Since Garden High School could not provide me with similar information, I matched Main High School and its twentieth reunion (an explanation of this procedure can be found in note b to table 3 in chapter 1).

On Generalization

I did not set out to complete an ethnography of class reunions, nor to capture the total life of this cultural event. Like Geertz's anthropologists who "don't study villages . . . [but] they study *in* villages,"[14] I approached Garden, Central, Main, and their respective reunions as strategic sites which would allow me to listen to people account for their lives. I was interested in how social contexts help us construct our identities, specifically how we come to know who we were and who we are. I chose class reunions as my research arena because they seem to be a perfect illustration of an autobiographical occasion for social and personal intersections between past and present. Class reunions provide a good illustration since they are public, ritualized, very condensed, and time-bounded events; that is exactly what makes reunions among the best places to see how issues I was concerned about are articulated and enacted. Those issues, however, are not limited to such vantage points. How successful my strategy was for these purposes depends on the answer to one question: How generalizable are my findings?

The question of generalization is itself composed of a number of different questions, each appropriate to a different level of research. On one level, I have various samples of individuals—returnees, nonreturnees, 28-year-olds, 38-year-olds, middle-class people, lower middle class people. At another level I have a sample of only five reunions, four of which were handled by the same commercial company. At the first level, the appropriate question is how well my various samples represent the relevant populations of people within each class. At the second level, the appropriate question is both how well the five reunions represent reunions more generally, and how well class reunions represent American culture more generally.

In the instances of my mail questionnaires, along with the analysis of the distance factor and, to some degree, the analysis of yearbooks (discussed in chapter 1), I tend to claim that my findings are generalizable in a statistical sense.

However, there are forms of research that constitute a hard case for statistical analysis. Although my informants were chosen randomly, they were all people who met me first at their reunions and agreed to be interviewed, which would indicate an interest in what I did. Although the overwhelming majority of people I approached systematically at class reunions agreed to be interviewed, a few refused. Moreover, I (except in one case) never interviewed people who lived too far away from where I conducted the research. More important, although I arrived at the interviews with a schedule, the interviews consisted of open-ended questions which enabled my informants to depart from my original questions, something I encouraged. Further, few people express themselves in precisely the same manner, something which makes the use of statistical tools and terms difficult. Thus, although on certain matters I quantified the interviews (mainly to myself), in order to be sure about the patterns that emerged (and the patterns did emerge), I prefer to use such phrases as "most," "many," "few," and "rarely" to get the message across, and more important to allow myself to display a range of responses, techniques, accounts, excuses, and so forth, the substance from which real life (social science included) is made. In many ways (to borrow again a phrase from Geertz) this study is "marked less by a perfection of consensus than by a refinement of debate." [15] I do feel that to a great degree my "sample" of returnees is representative of the class and its reunion. I would not claim, however, that my "sample" of nonreturnees (as far as interviews are concerned) is representative even of the relevant population at the reunions.

Since gaining access to class reunions that are organized privately was almost impossible, I had no choice but to use the reunion company as my major link to the events, which may create problems in generalizing from the data collected. After all, most of the reunions I observed were outcomes of the same concept. Therefore, for another perspective I conducted ten formal interviews and had many more informal conversations with people who attended different class reunions. Each of these interviewees went to a different high school in a different year. In addition, I collected descriptions of reunions from books and newspaper clippings. This step reassured me that studying reunions mainly through a company does not detract from learning what reunions are all about. Although there are variations, most reunions have the same shape and form. Moreover, in many ways what matters are the problems inherent when one's personal and social past encounters one's personal and social present. And those problems are similar whether the reunion is organized by a company or solely by class members. In effect, from later observations I made in Israel (which focused on the organizational process of reunions), it seems that the questions regarding one's life go far beyond specific events and specific countries.

The high schools whose reunions I studied were "shopping mall high schools," [16] and in that sense they were typical of most American high schools. Moreover, they were located in the suburbs, where most of my informants still live. Although those who live in the suburbs "are disproportionately drawn from the ranks of the affluent and powerful, more Americans live there than anywhere else."[17] As a result of social trends, "it is likely that in the very near future the majority of Americans will live in the suburbs."[18] In addition, the reunions I attended did not include special effects, extraordinary efforts, or national celebrities, their very innocuousness making them interesting and generalizable. The people I later interviewed were housewives busy with everyday chores, firemen and policemen worrying about their coming retirement, teachers frustrated about their salaries, secretaries and technicians trying to make ends meet, and lawyers and other professionals who were proud of their achievements. Certainly I did not even come close to meeting representatives of every type of the American way of life, but I did encounter many of its middle-class and lower middle class variants. If Main, Garden, and Central do not represent all of contemporary America at a moment of reflection, they do represent a wide range of it.

A similar consideration with regard to generalizability of data applies to the relationships between class reunions and the more general issues regarding the construction of identities. Class reunions are an integral part of American culture. But more important, the oral texts of identity occasioned by an individual's class reunion are not limited to the vantage points of that event. The accounts returnees gave and the concerns they expressed take us beyond a specific social context and into the larger culture within which and through which ordinary Americans construct their identities and cope with the threats to those identities. Thus, high school reunions are but one illustration of a much larger phenomenon.

Notes

INTRODUCTION

1. See Georg Simmel, *Conflict and the Web of Group Affiliations* (Glencoe, Ill.: The Free Press, 1955).

2. *The Random House College Dictionary* (New York: Random House, 1973), 91.

3. Ralph H. Turner, "The Self-Conception in Social Interaction," in *The Self in Social Interaction*, ed. Chad Gordon and Kenneth Gergen (New York: John Wiley and Sons, 1968), 94.

4. Robert Zussman, "Autobiographical Occasions," *Contemporary Sociology* 25, no. 2 (1996): 143.

5. See C. Wright Mills, "Situated Actions and Vocabularies of Motives," *American Sociological Review* 5, no. 6 (1940): 904–13; Marvin B. Scott and Stanford M. Lyman, "Accounts," *American Sociological Review* 33, no. 1 (1968): 46–62; John P. Hewitt and Randall Stokes, "Disclaimers," *American Sociological Review* 40, no. 1 (1975): 1–11; Randall Stokes and John P. Hewitt, "Aligning Actions," *American Sociological Review* 41 (1976): 838–49.

6. See Hayden White, "The Value of Narrativity in the Representation of Reality," in W. J. T. Mitchell, ed., *On Narrative* (Chicago: University of Chicago Press, 1981).

7. See, for example, Stanley Cohen, *Visions of Social Control* (Cambridge: Polity Press, 1985).

8. See David Lowenthal, *The Past Is a Foreign Country* (Cambridge: Cambridge University Press, 1985).

9. See Steven Spitzer, "Social Amnesia and Social Control," paper presented at the workshop, Controlling Social Life, Florence, Italy, 1989; Jon Hendricks and Calvin B. Peters, "The Time of Our Life," *American Behavioral Scientist* 29, no. 6 (1986): 662–78; Mildred M. Seltzer and Lillian E. Troll, "Expected Life History: A Model in Nonlinear Time," *American Behavioral Scientist* 29, no. 6 (1986):

746–64; Barry Schwartz, "The Social Context of Commemoration: A Study in Collective Memory," *Social Forces* 61, no. 2 (1982): 374–402; Maurice Halbwachs, *The Collective Memory* (New York: Harper and Row, 1980); and Frederick Bartlett, *Remembering* (Cambridge: University Press, 1950).

10. See Edward Shils, *Tradition* (Chicago: University of Chicago Press, 1981).

11. Howard Schuman and Jacqueline Scott, "Generations and Collective Memory," *American Sociological Review* 54, no. 3 (1989): 362.

12. See for example, Schwartz, "Commemoration" (above, n. 9).

13. John P. Hewitt, *Self and Society* (Boston: Allyn and Bacon, 1991), 123.

14. Ibid.

15. See Kenneth J. Gergen, *The Saturated Self* (New York: Basic Books, 1991), and, on the concept of "fragmentation," Anthony Giddens, *Modernity and Self-Identity* (Stanford, California: Stanford University Press, 1991).

16. See William James, *The Principles of Psychology* (New York: Dover, 1890); Dennis H. Wrong, *Skeptical Sociology* (New York: Columbia University Press, 1976); Shils, *Tradition*; Andrew J. Weigert, J. Smith Teitge, and Dennis W. Teitge, *Society and Identity* (Cambridge: Cambridge University Press, 1986); David Carr, *Time, Narrative and History* (Bloomington: Indiana University Press, 1986); John P. Hewitt, *Dilemmas of the American Self* (Philadelphia: Temple University Press, 1989); and Giddens, *Modernity*.

17. Hewitt, *Self and Society*, 123.

18. See Giddens, *Modernity*, and Carr, *Time*.

19. Giddens, *Modernity*, 54.

20. Hewitt, *Dilemmas*, 166–67.

21. Ibid., 172.

22. Ibid., 179.

23. Ralph Turner, "Self-Conception," 94.

CHAPTER ONE

1. When reunions offer both a dinner and a picnic, the informal picnic is not perceived as prestigious and fewer people attend.

2. See Jack Sparacino, "The State of the Reunion: Who Goes and Why?" *Psychology Today* 14 (1980): 78–79.

3. Douglas H. Lamb and Glenn D. Reeder, "Reliving Golden Days," *Psychology Today* 20 (1986): 22.

4. See note 9 to the introduction. See also Lowenthal, *Past*.

5. Lamb and Reeder, "Reliving Golden Days," 22. See also Sparacino, *State of the Reunion*.

6. For purposes of quantitative analysis, I defined "not married" as either single, divorced, separated, or widowed.

7. In fact, my findings indicate that, among the people who attended their reunions, fewer like parties in general than those who did not attend.

8. Andrea Fontana, "Introduction: Existential Sociology and the Self," in *The Existential Self in Society*, ed. Joseph A. Kotarba and Andrea Fontana, 3–17 (Chicago: University of Chicago Press, 1984).

9. Hewitt, *Dilemmas*, 178–79.

CHAPTER TWO

1. Michael Moffatt, *Coming of Age in New Jersey: College and American Culture* (New Brunswick: Rutgers University Press, 1989), 72.

2. Herbert J. Gans, "Symbolic Ethnicity: The Future of Ethnic Groups and Cultures in America," in *Ethnic and Racial Studies* 2, no. 1 (1979): 16.

3. See, for example, Robert N. Bellah et al., *Habits of the Heart* (New York: Harper and Row, 1985), and Harve Varenne, *Americans Together* (New York: Teachers College Press, 1977).

4. Mary C. Waters, *Ethnic Options* (Berkeley: University of California Press, 1990), 150.

5. Tamar Katriel, *Communication and Culture in Contemporary Israel* (Albany, N.Y.: State University of New York Press, 1991), 13.

6. See Arthur G. Powell, Eleanor Farrar, and David K. Cohen, *The Shopping Mall High School* (Boston: Houghton Mifflin, 1985). The phrase, "shopping mall high school," aptly describes all the schools whose reunions I studied.

7. The size of the classes I studied may have a bearing on this; each class numbered several hundred. It seems to me, however, that whether the class consisted of one hundred people or four hundred, it is the structure of the class that is the crucial factor. The experience of other countries suggests that a high school experience of a stable group of students moving together from one year to the next, with teachers coming into the same classroom rather than the students dispersing into different locations, can encourage the formation of a collectivity, if not of an entire class, at least of a group that transcends the individual or a specific clique.

8. For further discussion of high school cliques, see Ralph W. Larkin, *Suburban Youth in Cultural Crisis* (Oxford: Oxford University Press, 1979).

9. Informants whose schools are not mentioned did not attend Garden, Central, or Main. See the appendix for a detailed explanation.

10. Fred Davis, *Yearning for Yesterday* (New York: The Free Press, 1979), 6.

11. See Hewitt, *Dilemmas.*

12. Miriam S. Moss and Sidney Z. Moss, "Reunion Between Elderly Parents and Their Distant Children," *American Behavioral Scientist* 31, no. 6 (1988): 667.

13. Halbwachs, *The Collective Memory,* 130.

14. Waters, *Ethnic Options,* 92.

15. A similar approach to a community can be found in Moshe Shokeid's study of Israeli emigrants in New York, *Children of Circumstances* (Ithaca: Cornell University Press, 1988), where their "one-night stand" ethnicity (see p. 99) is explained more in terms of problematic identity and less in terms of obligations and commitments. See also Hewitt, *Dilemmas,* and Andrew J. Weigert, *Mixed Emotions* (Albany: State University of New York Press, 1991).

16. Gans, "Symbolic Ethnicity," 12.

CHAPTER THREE

1. Jane Ammeson, "From Supermom to Superanchor, Paula Zahn Makes High Ratings," *Midway Magazine,* October (1990): 23.

2. Tamotsu Shibutani, "Reference Groups as Perspectives," *American Journal of Sociology* 60 (1955): 562–69.

3. Michel Foucault, *Discipline and Punish: The Birth of the Prison* (New York: Vintage Books, 1979), 184.

4. See Eviatar Zerubavel, "Personal Information and Social Life," *Symbolic Interaction* 5, no. 1 (1982): 97–109.

5. See Larkin, *Suburban Youth.*

6. Emile Durkheim, *The Elementary Forms of Religious Life* (Glencoe, Ill.: The Free Press, 1915), 475.

7. See Stanley Cohen, *Visions of Social Control* (Cambridge: Polity Press, 1985).

8. See, for example, Erich Goode, *Sociology* (Englewood Cliffs, N.J.: Prentice Hall, 1988); Ian Robertson, *Sociology* (New York: Worth, 1987); Donald Light, Jr., and Suzanne Keller, *Sociology* (New York: Alfred A. Knopf, 1979).

9. Foucault, *Discipline and Punish;* see also idem, *The History of Sexuality* (New York: Vintage Books, 1990).

10. Steven Spitzer, "Security and Control in Capitalist Societies," in *Transcarceration: Essays in the Sociology of Social Control,* ed. John Lowman, Robert J. Menzies, and T. S. Palys (Aldershot: Gower, 1987), 55.

11. See, for example, Robert E. Park's discussion of gossip as a form of social control, *On Social Control and Collective Behavior* (Chicago: Phoenix Books, 1967). See also Allan V. Horwitz, *The Logic of Social Control* (New York: Plenum, 1990).

12. See Emile Durkheim, *The Rules of Sociological Method* (Glencoe, Ill.: The Free Press, 1964).

13. See Michel Foucault, *The Foucault Reader,* ed. Paul Rabinow (New York: Pantheon, 1984).

14. Michel Foucault, "Technologies of the Self," in *Technologies of the Self,* ed. Luther H. Martin, Huck Gutman, and Patrick H. Hutton (Amherst, Mass.: University of Massachusetts Press, 1988), 16–49; Nicholas Rose, *Governing the Soul: The Shaping of the Private Self* (London: Routledge, 1990).

15. Hewitt, *Dilemmas,* 84.

16. See Erving Goffman, *The Presentation of the Self in Everyday Life* (Garden City, N.Y.: Doubleday, 1959).

17. See Diane Barthel, *Putting on Appearance* (Philadelphia: Temple University Press, 1988).

18. See Andrew J. Weigert, *Mixed Emotions* (Albany: State University of New York Press, 1991).

19. For further discussion of the relationship between different discourses and the creation of a "truth," see Foucault, *Discipline and Punish.*

20. Shils, *Tradition,* 326.

21. See Howard P. Chudacoff, *How Old Are You?* (Princeton, N.J.: Princeton University Press, 1989).

22. Ibid., 186.

23. See David Riesman, *The Lonely Crowd* (New Haven: Yale University Press, 1969).

24. See Bellah et al., *Habits of the Heart.*

25. In his book, *The Image* (New York: Atheneum, 1987), Daniel J. Boorstin defines "pseudo-event" as "a happening that possesses the following characteristics: (1) It is not spontaneous, but comes about because someone has planned

it. . . . (2) It is planted primarily (not always exclusively) for the immediate purpose of being reported or reproduced. . . . (3) Its relation to the underlying reality of the situation is ambiguous. . . . (4) Usually it is intended to be a self-fulfilling prophecy" (pp. 11–12).

26. Joshua Meyrowitz, *No Sense of Place* (New York: Oxford University Press, 1985), vii.

27. Eric Hobsbawm, "Introduction: Inventing Traditions," in Eric Hobsbawm and Terence Ranger, *The Invention of Tradition* (Cambridge: Cambridge University Press, 1989), 1.

28. See Riesman, *The Lonely Crowd.*

29. See Durkheim, *Religious Life.*

30. Foucault, *History of Sexuality*, 60.

CHAPTER FOUR

1. See Elizabeth Tonkin, *Narrating Our Pasts* (Cambridge: Cambridge University Press, 1992).

2. Erving Goffman, *Stigma* (New York: Simon and Schuster, 1963), 66–72.

3. See Charles Taylor, *The Ethics of Authenticity* (Cambridge, Mass.: Harvard University Press, 1992).

4. Peter L. Berger and Hansfried Kellner, "Marriage and the Construction of Reality: An Exercise in the Microsociology of Knowledge," in *Social Reality*, ed. Harvey A. Farberman and Erich Goode (Englewood Cliffs, N.J.: Prentice Hall, 1964), 72.

5. Charles H. Cooley, "The Social Self: On the Meanings of 'I'" in *The Self in Social Interaction*, ed. Chad Gordon and Kenneth Gergen (New York: John Wiley and Sons, 1968), 90.

6. See Weigert, Teitge, and Teitge, *Society and Identity.*

7. Hewitt, *Dilemmas*, 182.

8. Goffman, *Presentation of Self.* For discussion of the dramaturgical perspective see also Dennis Brissett and Charles Edgley, eds., *Life as Theater* (New York: Aldine de Gruyter, 1990).

9. I observed this meeting as part of a study that was done in Israel, in 1993.

10. James, *Principles of Psychology*, 293–94.

11. See Goffman, *Presentation of Self.*

12. This finding is based on the estimation of a professional company which had organized hundreds of class reunions in the eight years it was involved in this field.

13. Attending reunions without one's spouse raises suspicions. Former classmates tend to wonder whether there are marital problems or if there is some reason to be embarrassed to show their spouses. People who did not come with spouses tended to regard those who did as people who lack confidence and maturity.

14. See *The Sociology of Georg Simmel*, ed. Kurt H. Wolff (Glencoe, Ill.: The Free Press, 1964).

15. Goffman, *Relations in Public* (New York: Harper and Row, 1971), 19.

16. For discussion of the notion of making general assumptions on the basis of fragmented information, see Eviatar Zerubavel, "Personal Information and Social Life," *Symbolic Interaction* 25, no. 2 (1982): 143–48.

17. A divorced or separated couple from the same class presents a complicated problem. Although nothing approaching reliable data is available, my observations as well as accounts I heard in the interviews suggest that the informal rule in these cases is for only one former partner to attend, in order to avoid undesirable encounters. "If I had known," said Daniel, "that Leila [his ex-wife] was going to be there, I probably wouldn't have come. It wasn't worth it" (college professor, twentieth reunion). An ex-spouse's plans regarding the event are often revealed through social networks.

18. By *performance team* I mean "any set of individuals who cooperate in staging a single routine" (Goffman, *Presentation of Self*), 79.

19. Ibid., 82.

20. Ibid., 79.

21. Ibid.

22. Lowenthal, *Past*, xxv.

CHAPTER FIVE

1. Shils, *Tradition*, 50.

2. Frederick Bartlett, *Remembering* (Cambridge: Cambridge University Press, 1950).

3. See note 9 to the introduction.

4. For further discussion of these two theoretical approaches, see Schwartz, "Social Change and Collective Memory: The Democratization of George Washington," *American Sociological Review* 56, no. 2 (1991): 221–36.

5. See Maurice Halbwachs, *On Collective Memory*, ed. Lewis A. Coser (Chicago: University of Chicago Press, 1992).

6. See Michael Schudson, "The Present in the Past versus the Past in the Present," *Communication* 11 (1989): 105–13.

7. Schwartz, "Commemoration," 396.

8. Schuman and Scott, "Generations and Collective Memory," 362.

9. See Maurice Halbwachs, *The Collective Memory* (New York: Harper and Row, 1980).

10. Ibid. See also Halbwachs, *On Collective Memory*.

11. See, for example, Barry Schwartz, "Social Change and Collective Memory: The Democratization of George Washington," *American Sociological Review 56, no. 2* (1991): 221–36.

12. See, for example, Diane Barthel, "Nostalgia for American's Village Past: Staged Symbolic Communities," *International Journal of Politics, Culture, and Society 4, no. 1,* (1990): 79–93.

13. See, for example, Nachman Ben-Yehuda's work on the role Masada mythical narrative played in Israeli society and culture, *The Masada Myth* (Madison: University of Wisconsin Press, 1995).

14. See Robin Wagner-Pacifici and Barry Schwartz, "The Vietnam Veterans Memorial: Commemorating a Difficult Past," *American Journal of Sociology 97,* no. 2, (1991): 376–420.

15. The term "moral entrepreneurs" comes from the field of deviance and is mainly associated with Howard S. Becker's book, *Outsiders* (Glencoe, Ill.: The Free Press, 1963). Within this context, moral entrepreneurs are social reformers—moral crusaders—who initiate a new rule or set of rules. The use of this

notion, however, has been expanded to other fields such as cultural initiations and enterprises (see Wagner-Pacifici and Schwartz, "Vietnam").

16. According to the National Association of Reunion Planners (1990), whereas in 1981 "all reunions were organized by volunteers," roughly a decade later there were "several hundred reunion planners with businesses of various sizes all over the country."

17. Don Handelman, *Models and Mirrors* (Cambridge: Cambridge University Press, 1990), 17.

18. Ibid.

19. Key informants may be also called informant interviewees, meaning that there are "some interviews [that] are more important than others because the respondent knows more, has better insight, or is more willing to share what he or she knows with the interviewer" (Zussman, *Intensive Care: Medical Ethics and the Medical Profession* [Chicago: University of Chicago Press, 1992], 243). The organizers of the reunions I studied definitely fit the first two criteria.

20. Hence, major parts of the first section of this chapter are based on in-depth interviews with the key members of the organizing committees of four out of the five reunions studied (the organizers of the tenth class reunion of Main High School were inaccessible); the owner of a commercial company whose sole business is organizing reunions and which effectively controls the bulk of the reunion business in the area of my study; and four other people who organized their reunions which were not part of my formal study.

21. Intellectual development is one of the three major functions of high school. The other two are social and political activities (see Larkin, *Suburban Youth*).

22. Sherry B. Ortner, "On Key Symbols," *American Anthropologist* 75 (1973): 1338–46.

23. Schudson, "Present in the Past," 106 (emphasis added); see also Schwartz, "Commemoration."

24. See Ortner, "On Key Symbols."

25. Some class reunions are less formal, consisting of a picnic. However, although nothing approaching reliable data is available, it seems that most class reunions are formal events and not informal ones.

26. Alan Radley, "Artefacts, Memory and the Sense of the Past," in *Collective Remembering,* ed. David Middleton and Derek Edwards (London: Sage, 1990), 52. See also Eviatar Zerubavel, "Social Memories: Steps to a Sociology of the Past," *Qualitative Sociology* 19, no. 3 (1996): 283–99.

27. This conclusion is based on the observations of an ongoing study of high school reunions in Israel.

28. See Halbwachs, *On Collective Memory* and *The Collective Memory.*

29. Schwartz, "Commemoration."

CHAPTER SIX

1. Hewitt, *Self and Society,* 123.

2. See Halbwachs, *The Collective Memory* and *On Collective Memory.*

3. Lowenthal, *Past,* 49.

4. Mark Freeman, *Rewriting the Self* (London: Routledge, 1993), 29.

5. Alfred Schutz, "The Homecomer," *American Journal of Sociology* 50, no. 5 (1945): 369–74.

6. That is how the question was phrased in the mailed questionnaires. The returnees could, however, mark more than one option.

7. Memories often spill over into other past times in people's lives (e.g., junior high school); the theoretical issues involved are the same, even if the content is different.

8. For a detailed discussion of the role of spouses at reunions see chapter 4.

9. Halbwachs, *The Collective Memory*, 51.

10. Berger, *Invitation to Sociology* (Garden City, N.Y.: Anchor Books, 1963), 57.

11. See Weigert, Teitge, and Teitge, *Society and Identity.*

12. Hewitt, *Dilemmas,* 158.

13. Lionel Trilling defines sincerity as "a congruence between avowal and actual feeling" in his *Sincerity and Authenticity* (Cambridge: Harvard University Press, 1972), 2.

14. This sentence or a version of it has appeared on many invitations I have seen.

15. Eight-and-one-half percent reported that they were not sure about their attendance at future class reunions, while only 12.5 percent stated that they did not intend to go to future reunions.

CHAPTER SEVEN

1. William James, *Psychology: The Briefer Course* (New York: Henry Holt and Co., 1910).

2. Erik H. Erikson, "Identity and the Life Cycle," *Psychological Issues* 1, no. 1 (1959): 23.

3. See Giddens, *Modernity;* Gergen, *The Saturated Self.*

4. Hewitt, *Self and Society,* 123.

5. Roy F. Baumeister, *Identity* (New York: Oxford University Press, 1986), 15.

6. See Giddens, *Modernity,* and Carr, *Time.*

7. Dan P. McAdams, *The Stories We Live By* (New York: William Morrow and Company, 1993), 76.

8. The notion of a "true self" is used here as a folk concept—a set of beliefs that are implicit if not explicit among the people who attended their reunions— and not as an empirical or scientific notion (on the self as an empirical notion, see for example Ralph Turner, "The Real Self: From Institution to Impulse," *American Journal of Sociology* 81, no. 5 [1976]: 989–1016). The contents of the "true self" or "inner self are essentially contents of meanings" (Baumeister, *Identity,* 164); see also Jack D. Douglas, "The Emergence, Security, and Growth of the Sense of Self," in *The Existential Self in Society,* ed. Joseph A. Kotarba and Andrea Fontana, 69–99 (Chicago: University of Chicago Press, 1984).

9. We usually think of the past as over and unalterable—and indeed it is. But the meaning or significance of the past is open to negotiation.

10. See Schudson, "Present in the Past."

11. Viktor Gecas, "The Self Concept," *Annual Review of Sociology* 8 (1982): 24.

12. On the importance of such an exercise, see Norman Denzin, "Interpretive Biography," *Qualitative Research* 17 (Newbury Park: Sage, 1990).

13. See Stokes and Hewitt, "Aligning Actions."

14. In effect, it seems to be pure construction. On the notion of constructionism, see for example Erich Goode and Nachman Ben-Yehuda, *Moral Panics* (Oxford: Blackwell, 1994).

15. It is important to note that this section is based on only a few examples, partly because each class has only a few celebrities. Moreover, as we saw in chapter 1, not having the "right" present resources does not encourage attendance at class reunions. Thus, we will find fewer people attending reunions whose current life is not "in order," or who can be defined as "failures."

16. See Hewitt and Stokes, "Disclaimers."

17. See Schudson, "The Present in the Past."

18. Baumeister, *Identity*, 130.

19. It is a difficult question to answer, whether this inability to ignore what they perceive as present change has to do with failures that are too obvious to overlook, or with "poetic justice." It is my feeling that we are talking more about the latter. Returnees were willing to cling to mere shreds of information (or even none at all) regarding other returnees' present in order to maintain a sense of continuity. Still, one would expect them to go through the same motions with their former class celebrities, and yet they do not.

20. Gergen, *The Saturated Self*, 138.

CHAPTER EIGHT

1. On the issue of alignment and misalignment of aspects of identity, see Stokes and Hewitt, "Aligning Actions."

2. See Goffman's *Stigma* and *Presentation*. See also, Brissett and Edgley, *Life as Theater*.

3. Arlie R. Hochschild, *The Managed Heart* (Berkeley: University of California Press, 1983), 47. See also Weigert, *Mixed Emotions*.

4. See George Herbert Mead, *Mind, Self, and Society* (Chicago: University of Chicago Press, 1962), and Cooley, "Social Self."

5. See Riesman, *The Lonely Crowd*, Christopher Lasch, *The Culture of Narcissism* (New York: Norton, 1979); Gergen, *The Saturated Self*; Bellah et al., *Habits*; and Goffman, *Presentation*. See also Efrat Tseelon, "Is the Presented Self Sincere?: Goffman, Impression Management, and the Postmodern Self," *Theory, Culture, and Society* 9 (1992): 115–28.

6. See Weigert, *Mixed Emotions*.

7. Weigert, Teitge, and Teitge, *Society and Identity*, 1.

8. See David A. Snow and Leon Anderson, "Identity Work Among the Homeless: The Verbal Construction and Avowal of Personal Identities," *American Journal of Sociology* 92, no. 6 (1987): 1336–71; Weigert, Teitge, and Teitge, *Society and Identity*; and Wrong, *Skeptical Sociology*.

9. For a detailed discussion of the philosophical roots and main premises of this perspective, see, for example, Hewitt, *Self and Society*, and Sheldon Stryker, *Symbolic Interactionism* (Menlo Park, Calif.: Benjamin/Cummings, 1980).

10. See Mead, *Mind*, and Gregory P. Stone, "Appearance and the Self: A

Slightly Revised Version," in *Social Psychology through Symbolic Interaction,* ed. Gregory P. Stone and Harvey A. Farberman (New York: Wiley, 1981).

11. See Hewitt's *Self and Society* and *Dilemmas.*

12. See Hewitt, *Dilemmas;* George J. McCall and J. L. Simmons, *Identities and Interactions* (New York: The Free Press, 1978); and Snow and Anderson, "Identity Work."

13. Ibid., 179.

14. Hewitt, *Dilemmas,* 166–67.

15. Turner, "Self-Conception," 94.

16. Wrong, *Skeptical Sociology,* 86.

17. Snow and Anderson, "Identity Work," 1347.

18. Goffman states that we are all engaged in "stigma management," since everyone is stigmatized in one way or another throughout his or her life. "The normal and the stigmatized are not persons but rather perspectives" (*Stigma,* 138). Reunion-goers' stories and dilemmas, however, resonate more closely with the patterns described in Goffman's *Presentation* than the ones in *Stigma.* Most returnees are not people who deviate from an official norm, but rather people whose "deficiency" concerns unfulfilled dreams or an unsatisfactory present. Thus, high school reunions provide us with a rich source of material for understanding the way in which not-so-spoiled or potentially spoiled identities are managed, as reunion-goers come to grips with what they have done with their lives and how their identities are forged.

19. D. R. Maines, quoted by Weigert, Teitge, and Teitge, *Society and Identity,* 111.

20. See Goffman, *Stigma;* Zerubavel, "Personal Information and Social Life," *Symbolic Interaction* 5, no. 1 (1982): 97–109.

21. Goffman, *Presentation,* 59.

22. See Cooley, "The Social Self."

23. See Gresham M. Sykes and David Matza, "Techniques of Neutralization: A Theory of Delinquency," *American Sociological Review* 22, no. 6 (1959): 664–70.

24. This approach is similar to one way of coping with ambivalence, where "individuals try to resolve ambivalence by eliminating one set of contradictory norms, either socially by giving up membership in one group or epistemically by ceasing to believe in one set of norms" (Weigert, *Mixed Emotions,* 131).

25. See Bellah et al., *Habits,* and Waters, *Ethnic Options.*

26. Mead, *Mind,* 270.

27. See Simmel, *The Philosophy of Money* (London: Routledge and Kegan Paul, 1979).

28. *Presentation,* 19.

29. See Taylor, *Ethics of Authenticity;* Trilling, *Sincerity and Authenticity.*

CONCLUSION

1. On the notion of age as an organizing principle in American culture see Chudacoff, *How Old?* On the notion of the importance of one's contemporaries in gaining a perspective over one's life course, see Riesman, *The Lonely Crowd.*

2. Goffman, *Interaction Ritual* (New York: Pantheon Books, 1967).

3. For a detailed discussion see Schwartz, "Commemoration." See also, idem, "Introduction: The Expanding Past," *Qualitative Sociology* 19, no. 3 (1996): 275–99, and Shaunna L. Scott, "Dead Work: The Construction and Reconstruction of the Harlan Miners Memorial," *Qualitative Sociology* 19, no. 3 (1996): 365–93.

4. Schwartz, "Commemoration," 396.

5. See for example Bellah et al., *Habits,* and Varenne, *Americans Together.*

6. See Stanley Cohen, "The Critical Discourse on 'Social Control': Notes on the Concept as a Hammer," *International Journal of the Sociology of Law* 17 (1989): 347–57.

7. On similar issues see M. P. Baumgartner, *The Moral Order of a Suburb* (New York: Oxford University Press, 1988).

8. Cohen, "Social Control and the Politics of Reconstruction," in David Nelken, ed., *The Futures of Criminology* (London: Sage, 1994), 64.

9. Zussman, "Autobiographical Occasions," 143–48.

APPENDIX

1. The form which the first reunion took was so unique that I thought it would not serve the study, and I was denied access to the other reunion by the organizer, who told me that it was "a private matter and we don't want a stranger there."

2. In the spring of 1989 I contacted the company and met with the vice president, the first meeting in an eighteen-month relationship. At the outset, the major problem I faced was that of trust, or, more accurately, mistrust. The reunion organizing market is very competitive and the company suspected that my story about doing research was a cover-up, my true motive being industrial espionage. Although I had a letter from the university verifying my identity and my intentions, it took more than that. My frequent disadvantage as a foreigner in the United States became my salvation at that particular moment. A combination of my spouse's diplomatic license plates and my own heavy accent helped reassure the company that I was indeed the person who I claimed to be.

3. Two people in my department contacted me. The daughter of one woman had her tenth reunion coming up in June, 1990, and she gave me the phone number of the reunion organizer. The other response was from a woman whose sister's twentieth reunion was set for March, 1990; once again I was able to obtain the organizer's phone number, as well as a personal introduction that could smooth the process.

I met with both organizers. The organizer of the tenth reunion was very casual about my presence at their reunion and about providing me with the mailing lists. In the end, I did not continue to study this specific reunion. The second appointment was with the committee organizing its twentieth reunion in a lower-middle-class neighborhood, which I later named Garden. The committee consisted of a couple; he had been the class president and she had been a cheerleader who won the title of "class flirt." Although the meeting was pleasant and they were very supportive of my project, it took three more meetings at their home to work out the details.

4. In return, a colleague and I helped with ticket collection at the beginning of the event.

5. Although it may be interesting and important to study other cohorts as

well (thirtieth, fortieth, and fiftieth reunions), this study was limited to three cohorts. Nevertheless, my interest in older cohorts is not merely idle curiosity. One thing often missing when one studies relatively young people is the issue of mortality. Although each cohort had lost some of its members (to car accidents, the Vietnam War, drugs, and other tragedies), losing former friends to cancer and heart attacks is more frightening, and also more forcefully raises concerns relative to one's own mortality. I do not underestimate the grief felt at learning that former friends have died in war or from drug abuse, but knowing that a former friend passed away from something that can actually happen to us "around the corner," as one of my informants said, is much more frightening. I still regret that I did not study the older cohorts as well.

6. David H. Demo, "The Self-Concept Over Time: Research Issues and Directions," *Annual Review of Sociology* 18 (1992): 303–26.

7. The similarity between the two towns enabled me to match the two schools and their class reunions.

8. At that point I decided not to pursue the tenth reunion, whose organizer I met through personal connections. Not only did I have enough reunions for my study, but this specific group was more upper-middle-class and I preferred to study Central's tenth reunion.

9. In an earlier draft of this book, I tried to change my informants' occupations. But changing identities jeopardized what I thought was important, and threatened to misrepresent reality.

10. Snow and Anderson, "Identity Work," 1343.

11. It seems that at the end of every research project—mine, of course, included—there is a feeling that there is only this last question, the ultimate one, that one should have asked but did not. My only comfort—as partial as it is—is that behind this "ultimate question" there is always another one and another one.

12. See Zussman, *Intensive Care*, 243.

13. Ibid.

14. Clifford Geertz, *The Interpretation of Cultures* (New York: Basic Books, 1973), 22.

15. Ibid., 29.

16. Powell, Ferrar, and Cohen, *Shopping Mall High School*.

17. Baumgartner, *Moral Order*, 6.

18. Ibid.

References

Alexander, Norman C., and Pat Lauderdale. "Situated Identities and Social Influence." *Sociometry* 40, no. 3 (1977): 225–33.

Ammeson, Jane. "From Supermom to Superanchor, Paula Zahn Makes High Ratings." *Midway Magazine* (October, 1990): 23–27.

Barthel, Diane. "Nostalgia for America's Village Past: Staged Symbolic Communities." *International Journal of Politics, Culture, and Society* 4, no. 1: 79–93.

Barthel, Diane. "The American Commune and the American Mythology." *Qualitative Sociology* 12, no. 3 (1989): 241–60.

———. "Attitudes Toward History: The Preservation Movement in America." *Humanity and Society* 13, no. 2 (1989): 195–212.

———. *Putting on Appearance.* Philadelphia: Temple University Press, 1988.

Bartlett, Frederick. *Remembering.* Cambridge: Cambridge University Press, 1950 [1932].

Baumeister, Roy F. *Identity.* New York: Oxford University Press, 1986.

Baumgartner, M. P. *The Moral Order of a Suburb.* New York: Oxford University Press, 1988.

Bellah, Robert N., Richard Madsen, William M. Sullivan, Ann Swidler, and Steven M. Tipton. *Habits of the Heart.* New York: Harper and Row, 1985.

Becker, Howard S. 1963. *Outsiders.* New York: The Free Press, 1985.

Ben-Yehuda, Nachman. *The Masada Myth.* Madison, W.I.: University of Wisconsin Press, 1995.

Berger, Bennett M., ed. *Authors of Their Own Lives.* Berkeley: University of California Press, 1990.

Berger, Peter L., and Thomas Luckman. *The Social Construction of Reality.* Garden City, N.Y.: Anchor Books, 1966.

Berger, Peter L., and Hansfried Kellner. "Marriage and the Construction of Reality: An Exercise in the Microsociology of Knowledge." In *Social Reality,* ed. Harvey A. Farberman and Erich Goode, 70–86. Englewood Cliffs, N.J.: Prentice Hall, 1973.

Berger, Peter L. *Invitation to Sociology: A Human Perspective*. Garden City, N.Y.: Anchor Books, 1963.

Boorstin, Daniel J. *The Image*. New York: Atheneum, 1987 [1961].

Brissett, Dennis, and Charles Edgley. *Life as Theater*. New York: Aldine de Gruyter, 1990.

Carr, David. *Time, Narrative, and History*. Bloomington: Indiana University Press, 1986.

Chudacoff, Howard P. *How Old Are You?* Princeton, N.J.: Princeton University Press, 1989.

Cohen, Stanley. "Social Control and the Politics of Reconstruction." In *The Future of Criminology*, ed. David Nelken, 63–88. London: Sage, 1994.

———. "The Critical Discourse on 'Social Control': Notes on the Concept as a Hammer." *International Journal of the Sociology of Law* 17 (1989): 347–57.

———. "Thinking About Social Control." Paper given at a workshop on Controlling Social Life. The European University Institute, Florence, Italy, May–June, 1989.

———. *Visions of Social Control*. Cambridge: Polity Press, 1985.

Cooley, Charles H. "The Social Self: On the Meanings of "I." In *The Self in Social Interaction*, ed. Chad Gordon and Kenneth Gergen, 87–91. New York: John Wiley and Sons, 1968 [1902].

Davis, Fred. *Yearning for Yesterday*. New York: The Free Press, 1979.

Demo, David H. "The Self-Concept Over Time: Research Issues and Directions." *Annual Review of Sociology* 18 (1992): 303–26.

Denzin, Norman. "Interpretive Biography." *Qualitative Research* 17. Newbury Park: Sage, 1990.

Douglas, Jack D. "The Emergence, Security, and Growth of the Sense of Self." In *The Existential Self in Society*, ed. Joseph A. Kotarba and Andrea Fontana, 69–99. Chicago: University of Chicago Press, 1984.

Durkheim, Emile. *The Rules of Sociological Method*. Glencoe, Ill.: The Free Press, 1964 [1938].

———. *The Elementary Forms of Religious Life*. Glencoe, Ill.: The Free Press, 1915.

Erikson, Erik H. "Identity and the Life Cycle." *Psychological Issues* 1, no. 1: 19–171.

Fontana, Andrea. "Introduction: Existential Sociology and the Self." In *The Existential Self in Society*, ed. Joseph A. Kotarba and Andrea Fontana, 3–17. Chicago: University of Chicago Press, 1984.

Foucault, Michel. *The History of Sexuality*. New York: Vintage Books, 1990.

———. *The History of Sexuality: The Use of Pleasure*. New York: Vintage Books, 1990.

———. "Technologies of the Self." In *Technologies of the Self*, ed. Luther H. Martin, Huck Gutman, and Patrick H. Hutton, 16–49. Amherst, Mass.: University of Massachusetts Press, 1988.

———. *The Foucault Reader*. Edited by Paul Rabinow. New York: Pantheon Books, 1984.

———. *Discipline and Punish: The Birth of The Prison*. New York: Vintage Books, 1979.

Freeman, Mark. *Rewriting the Self*. London: Routledge, 1993.

Gans, Herbert J. "Symbolic Ethnicity: The Future of Ethnic Groups and Cultures in America." *Ethnic and Racial Studies* 2, no. 1 (1979): 1–20.

Gecas, Viktor. "The Self Concept." *Annual Review of Sociology* 8 (1982): 1–23.

Geertz, Clifford. *The Interpretation of Cultures: Selected Essays.* New York: Basic Books, 1973.

Gergen, Kenneth J. *The Saturated Self.* New York: Basic Books, 1991.

Giddens, Anthony. *Modernity and Self-Identity.* Stanford, Calif.: Stanford University Press, 1991.

Goffman, Erving. *Relations in Public.* New York: Harper and Row, 1971.

———. *Interaction Ritual.* New York: Pantheon Books, 1967.

———. *Stigma: Notes of the Management of Spoiled Identity.* New York: Simon and Schuster, 1963.

———. *The Presentation of Self in Everyday Life.* Garden City, N.Y.: Doubleday, 1959.

Goode, Erich. *Sociology.* Englewood Cliffs, N.J.: Prentice Hall, 1988.

Goode, Erich, and Nachman Ben-Yehuda. *Moral Panics.* Oxford: Blackwell, 1994.

Gould, Robert E. "Measuring Masculinity by the Size of a Paycheck." In *Feminist Frameworks,* ed. Alison M. Jaggar and Paula S. Rothenberg, 47–50. New York: McGraw-Hill, 1984.

Halbwachs, Maurice. *On Collective Memory.* Chicago: University of Chicago Press, 1992.

———. *The Collective Memory.* New York: Harper and Row, 1980 [1950].

Handelman, Don. *Models and Mirrors.* Cambridge: Cambridge University Press, 1990.

Hendricks, Jon, and Calvin B. Peters. "The Times of Our Life." *American Behavioral Scientist* 29, no. 6 (1986): 662–78.

Hewitt, John P. *Self and Society.* Boston: Allyn and Bacon, 1991 [1976].

———. *Dilemmas of the American Self.* Philadelphia: Temple University Press, 1989.

Hewitt, John P., and Randall Stokes. "Disclaimers." *American Sociological Review* 40, no. 1 (1975): 1–11.

Hobsbawm, Eric. "Introduction: Inventing Traditions." In *The Invention of Tradition,* ed. Eric Hobsbawm and Terence Ranger, 1–14. Cambridge: Cambridge University Press, 1989 [1983].

Hochschild, Arlie R. *The Managed Heart.* Berkeley: University of California Press, 1983.

Horwitz, Allan V. *The Logic of Social Control.* New York: Plenum Press, 1990.

Humphrey, Lin T., and Theodore C. Humphrey. "The High School Reunion: A Traditional Festival?" *Journal of Popular Culture* 19 (1985): 99–106.

Ingleby, David. "Mental Health and Social Order." In *Social Control and the State,* ed. Stanley Cohen and Andrew Scull, 141–88. Oxford: Blackwell, 1983.

James, William. *Psychology: The Briefer Course.* New York: Henry Holt and Co., 1910.

———. *The Principles of Psychology.* New York: Dover, 1890.

Kanter, Rosabeth Moss. *Men and Women of the Corporation.* New York: Basic Books, 1977.

Katriel, Tamar. *Communication and Culture in Contemporary Israel.* Albany, N.Y.: State University of New York Press, 1991.

Larkin, Ralph W. *Suburban Youth in Cultural Crisis.* Oxford: Oxford University Press, 1979.

Lasch, Christopher. *The Culture of Narcissism.* New York: Norton, 1979.

Lamb, Douglas H., and Glenn D. Reeder. "Reliving Golden Days." *Psychology Today* 20, no. 6 (1986): 22–30.

Light, Donald Jr., and Suzanne Keller. *Sociology.* New York: Alfred A. Knopf, 1979.

Lowenthal, David. *The Past is a Foreign Country.* Cambridge: Cambridge University Press, 1985.

Lyman, Stanford M. "Foreword." In *The Existential Self in Society,* ed. Joseph A. Kotarba and Andrea Fontana, vii–xii. Chicago: University of Chicago Press, 1984.

Mannheim, Karl. *Essays on the Sociology of Knowledge.* New York: Oxford Press, 1952.

McAdams, Dan P. *The Stories We Live By.* New York: William Morrow and Company, 1993.

McCall, George J., and J. L. Simmons. *Identities and Interactions.* New York: The Free Press, 1978.

Mead, George Herbert. *Mind, Self, and Society.* Chicago: University of Chicago Press, 1962 [1934].

Meyrowitz, Joshua. *No Sense of Place.* New York: Oxford University Press, 1985.

Mills, C. Wright. "Situated Actions and Vocabularies of Motive." *American Sociological Review* 5, no. 6 (1940): 904–13.

Moffatt, Michael. *Coming of Age in New Jersey: College and American Culture.* New Brunswick: Rutgers University Press, 1989.

Moss, Miriam S., and Sidney Z. Moss. "Reunion Between Elderly Parents and Their Distant Children." *American Behavioral Scientist* 31, no. 6 (1988): 654–68.

National Association of Reunion Planners. *Fact Sheet,* 1990.

Ortner, Sherry B. "On Key Symbols." *American Anthropologist* 75 (1973): 1338–46.

Park, Robert E. *On Social Control and Collective Behavior.* Chicago: Phoenix Books, 1967.

Powell, Arthur G., Eleanor Farrar, and David K. Cohen. *The Shopping Mall High School.* Boston: Houghton Mifflin, 1985.

Radley, Alan. "Artefacts, Memory, and the Sense of the Past." In *Collective Remembering,* ed. David Middleton and Derek Edwards, 46–59. London: Sage Publications, 1990.

Riesman, David. *The Lonely Crowd.* New Haven: Yale University Press, 1969 [1961].

Rose, Nicholas. *Governing the Soul: The Shaping of the Private Self.* London: Routledge, 1990.

Robertson, Ian. *Sociology.* New York: Worth Publishers, 1987.

Schudson, Michael. "The Present in the Past Versus the Past in the Present." *Communication* 11 (1989): 105–113.

Schuman, Howard, and Jacqueline Scott. "Generations and Collective Memories." *American Sociological Review* 54, no. 3 (1989): 259–381.

Schuetz, Alfred. "The Homecomer." *American Journal of Sociology* L, no. 5 (1945): 369–76.

Schwartz, Barry. "Introduction: The Expanding Past." *Qualitative Sociology* 19, no. 3 (1996): 275–82.

———. "Social Change and Collective Memory: The Democratization of George Washington." *American Sociological Review* 56, no. 2 (1991): 221–36.

———. "The Social Context of Commemoration: A Study in Collective Memory." *Social Forces* 61, no. 2 (1982): 374–402.

Scott, Marvin B., and Stanford M. Lyman. "Accounts." *American Sociological Review* 33, no. 1 (1968): 46–62.

Scott, Shaunna L. "Dead Work: The Construction and Reconstruction of the Harlen Miners Memorial." *Qualitative Sociology* 19, no. 3 (1996): 365–93.

Seltzer, Mildred M. "Reunions: Windows to the Past and Future." *American Behavioral Scientist* 31, no. 6 (1988): 644–53.

Seltzer, Mildred M., and Lillian E. Troll. "Expected Life History: A Model in Nonlinear Time." *American Behavioral Scientist* 29, no. 6 (1986): 746–64.

Shibutani, Tamotsu. "Reference Groups as Perspectives." *American Journal of Sociology* 60 (1955): 562–69.

Shils, Edward. *Tradition.* Chicago: University of Chicago Press, 1981.

Shokeid, Moshe. *Children of Circumstances.* Ithaca: Cornell University Press, 1988.

Simmel, Georg. *The Philosophy of Money.* London: Routledge and Kegan Paul, 1978.

———. *The Sociology of Georg Simmel.* Edited by Kurt H. Wolff. Glencoe, Ill.: The Free Press, 1964.

———. *Conflict and the Web of Group Affiliations.* Glencoe, Ill.: The Free Press, 1955.

Snow, David A., and Leon Anderson. "Identity Work Among the Homeless: The Verbal Construction and Avowal of Personal Identities." *American Journal of Sociology* 92, no. 6 (1987): 1336–71.

Sparacino, Jack. "The State of the Reunion: Who Goes and Why?" *Psychology Today* 14 (1980): 78–79.

Spitzer, Steven. "Social Amnesia and Social Control." Paper presented at a workshop on Controlling Social Life, The European University Institute, Florence, Italy, May–June 1989.

———. "Security and Control in Capitalist Societies." In *Transcarceration: Essays in the Sociology of Social Control,* ed. John Lowman, Robert J. Menzies, and T. S. Palys, 43–58. Aldershot: Gower, 1987.

———. "Crime Control in Capitalist Society." In *Social Control and the State,* ed. Stanley Cohen and Andrew Scull, 312–33. Oxford: Blackwell, 1983.

Stokes, Randall, and John P. Hewitt. "Aligning Actions." *American Sociological Review* 41 (1976): 838–49.

Stone, Gregory P. "Appearance and the Self: A Slightly Revised Version." In *Social Psychology through Symbolic Interaction,* ed. Gregory P. Stone and Harvey A. Faberman. New York: Wiley, 1981.

Stryker, Sheldon. *Symbolic Interactionism.* Menlo Park, California: Benjamin/Cummings, 1980.

Sykes, Gresham M., and David Matza. "Techniques of Neutralization: A Theory of Delinquency." *American Sociological Review* 22, no., 6 (1959): 664–70.

Taylor, Charles. *The Ethics of Authenticity*. Cambridge: Harvard University Press, 1992.

The Random House College Dictionary. New York: Random House, 1973.

Tonkin, Elizabeth. *Narrating Our Pasts*. Cambridge: Cambridge University Press, 1992.

Trilling, Lionel. *Sincerity and Authenticity*. Cambridge: Harvard University Press, 1972.

Tseelon, Efrat. "Is the Presented Self Sincere? Goffman, Impression Management, and the Postmodern Self." *Theory, Culture, and Society* 9 (1992): 115–28.

Turner, Ralph H. "The Real Self: From Institution to Impulse." *American Journal of Sociology* 81, no. 5 (1976): 989–1016.

———. "The Self-Conception in Social Interaction." In *The Self in Social Interaction*, ed. Chad Gordon and Kenneth Gergen, 93–106. New York: John Wiley and Sons, 1968.

Varenne, Harve. *Americans Together*. New York: Teachers College Press, 1977.

Wagner-Pacifici, Robin, and Barry Schwartz. "The Vietnam Veteran Memorial: Commemorating a Difficult Past." *American Journal of Sociology* 97, no. 2 (1991): 376–420.

Waters, Mary C. *Ethnic Options*. Berkeley: University of California Press, 1990.

Weigert, Andrew J. *Mixed Emotions*. Albany: State University of New York Press, 1991.

Weigert, Andrew J., J. Smith Teitge, and Dennis W. Teitge. *Society and Identity*. Cambridge: Cambridge University Press, 1986.

White, Hayden. "The Value of Narrativity in the Representation of Reality." In *On Narrative*, ed. W. J. T. Mitchell, 1–23. Chicago: University of Chicago Press, 1981.

Wrong, Dennis H. *Skeptical Sociology*. New York: Columbia University Press, 1976.

Young, James E. *The Texture of Memory*. New Haven: Yale University Press, 1993.

Zerubavel, Eviatar. "Social Memories: Steps to a Sociology of the Past." *Qualitative Sociology* 19, no. 3 (1996): 283–99.

———. "Personal Information and Social Life." *Symbolic Interaction* 5, no. 1 (1982): 97–109.

Zussman, Robert. "Autobiographical Occasions." *Contemporary Sociology* 25, no. 2 (1996): 143–48.

———. *Intensive Care: Medical Ethics and the Medical Profession*. Chicago: University of Chicago Press, 1992.

Index